Y0-BSM-674

Directors in **Action**

Directors in
Action

Selections from **ACTION**

The Official Magazine of
THE DIRECTORS GUILD OF AMERICA

Edited by Bob Thomas
Introduction by Frank Capra

THE BOBBS MERRILL COMPANY, INC.
INDIANAPOLIS • NEW YORK

ISBN 0-672-51714-0 Hardcover
ISBN 0-672-51715-9 Paperback
Library of Congress Catalog Card Number 72-80807
Designed by Martin Moskof
Manufactured in the United States of America

First printing

Contents

1761775

Introduction

The question is sometimes asked, "Who, or what, is the Directors Guild of America?" In fact, "What in heck is a *guild?*" some want to know.

A guild is an association formed among persons whose interests or pursuits are the same or similar, for the purpose of mutual protection, assistance, and advantage.

Protective guilds originated far back in history. In ancient Rome they were called *corpora* and *collegia*. With the development of commerce in the eleventh century, traders formed *merchant guilds* to protect their rights and goods in cities and on the road. In some towns they built *guildhalls,* places of assembly.

Those merchant guilds, which sold the goods, became so rich and powerful that the artisans who made the goods—weavers, bakers, shoemakers, etc.—had to form *craft guilds* to protect themselves against the merchants. Which is precisely the raison d'être of the Directors Guild of America (DGA): to protect the creative and economic interests of directors in radio, television, and film.

Our DGA was born in the halcyon days of radio in the early 1930s, when radio directors organized themselves into the Radio Directors Guild and sought and achieved working contracts with the radio networks.

In Hollywood, the same necessity to protect craft interests rose among the talent groups. Writers, actors, and directors organized into guilds. The embryo Screen Directors Guild developed officially on January 15, 1936, when it held its first general meeting in Los Angeles with 29 film directors present. These charter members adopted bylaws and articles of incorporation, and elected the guild's first officers. They were: King Vidor, president; Lewis Milestone, first vice-president; Frank Tuttle, second vice-president; William K. Howard, secretary; John Ford, treasurer.

Board members were: Frank Borzage, Clarence Brown, John Cromwell, Howard Hawks, Wesley Ruggles, Rouben Mamoulian, William Wellman, Gregory La Cava, Edward Sutherland, and Bruce Humberstone.

By the end of 1936, SDG (Screen Directors Guild) had 93 members. The following year, assistant directors were brought into the guild. By 1938, SDG represented 95 percent of Hollywood's directors and assistants, but they were still only a guild in name.

As might be expected, the producing companies fought hard, long and bitterly against recognizing SDG as the bargaining agent for film directors and their assistants. But they were finally "persuaded." The first SDG working agreement became effective on March 13, 1939. The agreement established the film director's creative function and his right to screen credit, as well as wages and working conditions for assistant directors. In 1944, salary minimums were finally extended to directors.

For several years, the Radio Directors Guild (audio) and the Screen Directors Guild (visual) went their respective ways (airwaves and screen), unaware that they were on an electronic collision course. For out of audio-airwaves and visual-film a lusty child was born with both capacities. They named it television. The offspring soon outgrew its astonished parents. Radio and film both claimed the child as theirs—including its directors. But since most of television's new directors had come from radio, they quickly joined with radio brethren to form a new hybrid: Radio and Television Directors Guild (RTDG).

Hollywood's Screen Directors Guild remained aloof, yet it secretly worried over what beggarly threat this new "boob tube" folderol would pose to its aristocratic private preserves. In 1950 film directors managed to salvage a so-so contract with the networks that concerned itself with television film. But all of us knew that a jurisdictional war between the television guild and the screen guild was inevitable. It awaited a spark. The spark flared in the shape of a strip of wide film impregnated not with photochemicals but with electronic ions: audio-visual magnetic tape.

Hollywood's screen guild (SDG) exclaimed: "Tape is a mere extrapolation of film. Therefore, tape is *our* thing!" . . . "No!" countered New York's RTDG. "Tape is electronic! It's *our* bag!"

The year 1958 was important in guild history. That was when I, then president of the Screen Directors, invited Mike Kane, president of the Radio and Television Directors, to discuss a merger. In 1960 the two competing organizations combined to form the Directors Guild of America. In 1965 the new DGA was joined by the Screen Directors International Guild, which comprised directors of documentaries, commercials, and educational and government films. And so, almost all of what you see today in theaters, schools, or clubs, or hear on radio, or view on television, has been directed by members of the all-encompassing Directors Guild of America.

And if any wags are tempted to snicker, "Oh, isn't that cozy! All you dear directors lumped together in just one li'l ol' guild," we directors will be tempted to lump you with those who bug us with thát other "funny" irritant: "Who, and what, in heaven's name, is a director?"

Well, since the word "director" has as many curious uses as the word "relevant," allow us to restrict the question to "Who, and what, is a *film* director?"

Well, for openers, take D. W. Griffith—the creator of a film art which creates directors. Griffith (the first and perhaps the greatest of all filmmakers) is the only person living or dead who can be pointed to as the creator of an art form—*any* art form.

"But how would I spot a director—say, in a social gathering?"

By elimination. Actors are actors, always "on," easy to pick out—unless you're the type who can't spot a rainbow, or Milton Berle's cigar. Writers talk well—and loud and long; they use words like "id," "libido," "meaningful." But if you see an uninterested guy who seems to be someplace else—watch him! You're getting warm. And if his face is worried, his hair gray, and he rocks on his heels; if he stares vacantly out of windows, says little, and says it with all the fascination of a mediocre quartet playing "Kamennoy Ostrov" at a tea social—ask him if he's a film director. You may be shaking hands with Ford, King, Jewison, Fellini, Chukhrai, Truffaut, or Kurosawa.

And now that you've met a film director, please don't ask him what he *does*.

That will only stimulate a series of dangling non sequiturs that will send you off babbling to yourself. But if the director is an ex-actor, an ex-writer like Huston, Wilder, Seaton, or Bogdanovich, or a Middle European who flaunts white gloves and rhetoric at the drop of a monocle, he might tell you that all directors have a common pursuit: to tell a yarn with film. To which you might open your eyes wide and retort, "That explains everything! Just as all Presidents have a common pursuit: to live in the White House."

But wait. Let us assume Mr. Director has a story and a finished script. Now all he has to do is translate that script into film, right? Wrong. Scripts are only the basic guidelines to what eventually is viewed on the screen. Casting, acting, staging, photography, music, sound effects, and film editing are but a few of the artistic and scientific components of the overall authorship of a film. Only the director has the creative ability, and—more importantly—the *opportunity,* to meld all the components into a film that is stamped with his own style, pace, and thrust.

Artistically, filmmaking involves the gamut of classic arts: literature, drama, music, the dance, painting, architecture, costuming—you name it. Technically, it involves engineering, electronics, photochemistry, logistics, blue screen, sodium screen—that's enough.

Would you believe the dollar's involvement, too? You can't. But take our word for it, it is huge, chancy, unpredictable. When the shooting and shouting are over— and the one to twenty million dollars have all been spent—the director ends up with ten cans of film and the most suspenseful question of his life: "Do I pop champagne or cut my throat?" Only the biggest jury in the world can give the answer—the audiences. And it's ten to one their verdict will be "Thumbs down!" One can get better odds on a crooked wheel.

Feeling sorry for film directors? No? Read on.

There are nitty-gritty hazards during photography that drive film directors up a sound stage's padded walls. Time, for instance. A four-million-dollar budget and a ten-week shooting schedule mean a cost of 133 dollars per minute. Just a quick trip to the john will cost you over a thousand bucks. Or bad weather on location can kill you—even put gray in your hairpiece. And "star sickness," better known as "the sulks," has its own bizarre status as a disruptive influence. The cure: bonuses, a new car, or firing a patsy or two.

These hangups all directors have in common. They are not resolved by rare talent but by rare patience. And if you haven't got a truck-and-trailerload of patience, that is one answer to "What has a director got that I haven't got?"

"All right, all right! A director has loads of trouble and bigger loads of patience. But doesn't he do anything besides *moan?* Has he no special *talents?*"

Yes, he does! And now we will reveal, for the first time on any stage, the director's jealously guarded arcanum of filmmaking: the dark, esoteric mystery the nine Muses first revealed to D. W. Griffith, then to directors all over the world as they grew in wisdom and favor. To illustrate the importance the Muses attached to this rare gift, one need only recall that they held nine special psychomancies—four at the Castalian Spring on Mount Parnassus and five more at the sacred fountains of Hippocrene—before they conjured up the perfect abracadabra for the aesthetic guidance of the film director. This then is our hitherto undisclosed craft secret, as revealed to us by the Muses.

A film tale is fashioned out of some 500 to 1,000 discrete bits—pieces we call scenes. As our tale unfolds it grows in virtue or skulduggery bit by bit, scene by scene. Now, if the bits were photographed one after another in chronological order, keeping this "growth" factor growing naturally from scene to scene would be no Herculean feat.

But film scenes are *not* photographed in a 1, 2, 3, 4 . . . 1,000 sequence. No, sir. They are shot in a hodgepodge order to conform to a shooting schedule which is laid out to conform with the lowest possible budget.

A shooting schedule may call for starting with scenes 51-2-3, then leapfrogging to scenes 230 . . . 239, then backtracking to Scene 97, etc., until all 1,000 bits have been photographed. Two examples will clear up *why* we can't shoot scenes in a sensible chronological order:

1. If a picture begins and ends in Hong Kong, transporting a shooting company *twice* to Hong Kong would—to paraphrase a Goldwynism—be "like pouring good money up the drain." So we shoot Hong Kong's beginning and end scenes in one trip.

2. A 25,000-dollar-per-week actor may be in 50 scenes scattered throughout the whole script. Shooting chronologically would take ten weeks, at a salary cost of 250,000 dollars to finish with that actor. Compressing all his scenes into one week's shooting will save nine weeks of Mr. Actor's salary—a saving of 225,000 dollars. Got it? Good.

But now—what happens to the "growth" factor if Scene 100 is shot today, and Scene 101 is shot six weeks later in another city—or even in another country?

Aha! That is the magic of the Muses. That is what much-loved and oft-misquoted good Samuel G. might call the "mucus" of film directing. The director has been given the precious gift of keeping that growth factor *in his head!* And not only for scenes 100-101, but for all *other* scenes not photographed in sequential order.

And here comes a statement you may never understand—or swallow: The film director, by virtue of a special talent and the very nature of his job, is the only member of the screen's hierarchy peculiarly fitted to carry that growth factor in his head.

"But is this—this—growth factor so all-fired important in filmmaking?" Yes, sir! When a director is on his schtick, here is what happens when the 1,000 bits shot in shooting-schedule order are strung together in chronological sequence: The finished film tale will give audiences the illusion it had been photographed from beginning to end in one *continuous session.* Catch on? No? Hm-m-m. You must be Ross Hunter's second cousin.

Anyway, please don't judge this book by its cover—or its introduction. Compressed in this book is "the best of *Action.*" What is *Action?* Well, in 1966, the Directors Guild, like every other institution from U.S. Steel to the Fairfax PTA, got the itch to publish a house organ to beat its own tomtoms. Being directors, they had a brilliant inspiration—they called it *Action!* David Zeitlin, of *Life* magazine, was its first editor. But since 1968, *Action's* tub-thumper has been Bob Thomas, the Hollywood correspondent and biographer. When Bob Thomas temporarily ran out of Hollywood bios to graph, he collected the cream of *Action's* articles and assembled them into this splendid anthology of goodies about directors, their styles, and their films. You will find the book much more interesting than its introduction.

FRANK CAPRA

Directors in **Action**

I.
Orson Welles and *Citizen Kane*

In 1939 RKO Radio Pictures signed a contract with a twenty-four-year-old actor-director from radio and the theater, Orson Welles. The contract called for Welles' services as actor, writer, director and producer, and the film world questioned the studio's wisdom in making such a deal. A trade paper editorialist sniffed: "RKO is going to rue its contract and I would be willing to wager something that Welles will not complete a picture."

On June 24, 1940, Welles began filming *Citizen Kane*. He had hand-picked a cast, many of them members of the Mercury Theater, and he chose a crew with equal care. Filming was completed on October 23, 1940, after 82 shooting days. Some 276,505 feet of film had been exposed. The production had cost 686,000 dollars, of which Welles received 100,000 dollars.

Although Welles had completed the film, it is likely that RKO did come to rue its contract. Before the film even opened it was under attack — Louis B. Mayer tried to buy the negative and remove *Citizen Kane* from circulation in order to avoid offense to William Randolph Hearst. Initially theaters refused to show it. In spite of almost unanimously enthusiastic reviews, the movie didn't find its audience until many years later.

Today, of course, *Kane* is an acknowledged masterpiece. Yet it continues to excite almost as much controversy as it did over 30 years ago. Perhaps no other American film has been so attacked, defended, praised and analyzed as *Citizen Kane*.

At the time of its release, Welles described the film as "the story of a search by a man named Thompson, the editor of a news digest, for the meaning of Kane's dying words. His researches take him to five people who know Kane well—people who liked him or loved him or hated his guts. They tell five different stories, each biased, so that the truth about Kane, like the truth about any man, can only be calculated by the sum of everything that has been said about him."

To celebrate this celebrated film, ACTION followed the pattern of Thompson and interviewed survivors of *Citizen Kane* for their opinions and memories of the film and its maker. Critic and historian Arthur Knight added an up-to-date view of the classic.

CITIZEN KANE

Cast

Charles Foster Kane	Orson Welles
Jedediah Leland	Joseph Cotten
Susan Alexander	Dorothy Comingore
Bernstein	Everett Sloane
Emily Norton	Ruth Warrick
James W. Gettys	Ray Collins
Walter P. Thatcher	George Coulouris
Kane's Mother	Agnes Moorehead
Carter	Erskine Sanford
Thompson	William Alland
Raymond	Paul Stewart
Matiste	Fortunio Bonanova
Headwaiter	Gus Schilling
Rawlston	Philip Van Zandt
Miss Anderson	Georgia Backus
Kane's Father	Harry Shannon
Kane III	Sonny Bupp
Kane, age 8	Buddy Swan

Producer-Director	Orson Welles
Original Screenplay	Herman J. Mankiewicz, Orson Welles
Photography	Gregg Toland
Music, Composer and Conductor	Bernard Herrmann
Special Effects	Vernon L. Walker
Art Director	Van Nest Polglase
Associate	Perry Ferguson
Editing	Robert Wise
Recording	Bailey Fesler, James G. Stewart
Costumes	Edward Stevenson
Assistant Director	Eddie Donahoe

Citizen Kane Remembered

John Houseman

Orson and I had worked together in the Mercury Theater, but then we came to a parting. I couldn't control him any more, and it simply wasn't fun. He had gone off to Hollywood to develop some properties for RKO: *Heart of Darkness* and *Smiler with a Knife*. For one reason or another, they didn't pan out.

One day Orson was in New York, and he invited me to have lunch at 21. He asked me: "Would you work with Herman Mankiewicz on a script he's developing for me?" I knew how erratic Herman could be, but Orson said that Herman had broken his leg and it was a good time to get some work out of him.

Orson described the story: it was to be a multifaceted tale about—let's face it— Hearst, or at least some legendary publisher. I was intrigued, and I agreed to come out and work two or three weeks with Herman.

Herman and I, plus a nurse to care for his broken leg, went off to Victorville and started work on the script. By the end of 12 weeks we had produced a 200-page script. It was Herman's, really; I merely edited his work.

My work was finished, and Orson took over and visualized the script. He added a great deal of material himself, and later he and Herman had a dreadful row over the screen credit. As far as I could judge, the co-billing was correct. The *Citizen Kane* script was the product of both of them.

Richard Wilson

I had been the original stage manager with Mercury Theater, and Bill Alland and I came out to Hollywood with Orson when he made the RKO deal. How we came out is a story in itself. Orson had this idea of doing *Five Kings*, based on the Shakespeare chronicles and to be played in two evenings. We opened in Boston at 7:30 P.M. and the play was still going at 1:30 A.M. It got rave reviews, but we ran out of money. To raise new funds, Orson decided to play the old George Arliss vehicle, *The Green Goddess,* in vaudeville. The idea was to lay the groundwork with a film depicting an air crash in the Himalayas, then condense the play to 15 minutes.

It was a disaster. When we appeared in Pittsburgh, the film ran backwards, and everything was a shambles. Orson shocked the theater management by suggesting to the customers that they demand their money back. There seemed to be no other course than to take one of the many film offers that Orson had received. RKO offered the best one.

Heart of Darkness, from the Joseph Conrad novel, had been one of Orson's favorite Mercury Theater broadcasts (as had *The Magnificent Ambersons*). He worked on a script, but RKO turned it down. Then he attempted *Smiler with a Knife,* which was about a furtive figure in the public eye. When RKO turned down *Smiler, Citizen Kane* was born.

Again it was a story of a public figure who had a profound effect on the population. Orson was from Chicago, and I believe he was as much influenced by Samuel Insull and Colonel Robert McCormick as he was by the figure of Hearst.

Actually Orson had known a previous motion-picture experience. He had unearthed an old play by William Gillette called *Too Much Johnson.* To begin the first act, he filmed a 20-minute segment in which Edgar Barrier chased Joseph Cotten all over New York. Then there were 10-minute films that introduced the second and third acts. So he had already completed a 40-minute picture.

Orson had already shot long tests for *Heart of Darkness*—the tests could actually have been inserted into the finished picture. He used in *Citizen Kane* many of the people he had brought out for *Heart of Darkness*—Everett Sloane, George Coulouris, the burlesque comic Gus Schilling and others.

I left at the beginning of the summer to conduct a season of summer theater, but when I returned *Citizen Kane* was still shooting. I even acted in the picture, playing one of the reporters in the press conference. One of my fellow reporters was a bit actor named Alan Ladd.

One day the entire RKO front office, led by Sid Rogell, came down to the set to see what was going on. Orson suspended the shooting and we played baseball in the street until the studio brass had departed. Then Orson resumed production, his creative integrity intact.

None of us knew what a furor the picture was going to raise. But then, we didn't expect anything special from the Martian broadcast.

William Alland

I remember sitting in a production meeting with Orson and a few others before the start of *Citizen Kane*. The time had arrived to select a cameraman, and Orson said, "If I could only get Gregg Toland—that's the man I want." Orson had never even met Gregg, but he had admired Gregg's work.

Someone at the meeting spoke up: "There's no chance of getting Toland. He's under contract to Sam Goldwyn."

"I know that," said Orson. "But I'd still like to have him photograph the picture."

Just then the telephone rang, and Orson answered it. A voice on the other end of the line said: "This is Gregg Toland. I understand you're making a picture at RKO. I'd like to work with you on it."

Thus began one of the most successful artistic relationships I've ever seen. Orson and Gregg respected each other, and they got along beautifully. No matter what Orson wanted, Gregg would try to get it for him. Gregg had a tremendous responsibility, because Orson was in almost every scene. But Gregg kept an eye on everything.

I played the reporter and the voice of the *March of Time,* but I also walked through Orson's scenes for him. I wasn't the stand-in; there was a stand-in for lighting purposes. When the scene had been lighted and Orson rehearsed his part, I studied his choreography and repeated it as Orson watched from behind the camera.

Then I had the responsibility of watching Orson during the scene and approving or rejecting the take. I didn't pass artistic judgment; I merely checked to see if Orson was getting what he wanted. After each scene, he would glance at me. If I smiled, the take was okay. If I remained poker-faced, he'd shoot it again.

There was one scene which stands out above all others in my memory; that was the one in which Orson broke up the roomful of furniture in a rage. You must realize that Orson never liked himself as an actor. He had the idea that he should have been feeling more, that he intellectualized too much and never achieved the emotion of losing himself in a part.

When he came to the furniture-breaking scene, he set up four cameras, because he obviously couldn't do the scene many times. He did the scene just twice, and each time he threw himself into the action with a fervor I had never seen in him. It was absolutely electric; you felt as if you were in the presence of a man coming apart. Orson staggered out of the set with his hands bleeding and his face flushed. He almost swooned, yet he was exultant. "I really felt it," he exclaimed. "I really felt it!"

Strangely, that scene didn't have the same power when it appeared on the screen. It might have been how it was cut, or because there hadn't been close-in shots to depict his rage. The scene in the picture was only a mild reflection of what I had witnessed on that movie stage.

Ralph Hoge

I worked with Gregg Toland for 20 years, and when he went on *Citizen Kane*, I continued with him as head grip. So I was close to the filming and I recognized the contribution made by Gregg. Orson would rehearse a scene as he would do it for the stage. Then Gregg would explain to him why it could not be done for the screen in the same way. Gregg was careful to take Orson aside and explain these things in private. Orson was easily convinced on matters he was unfamiliar with—but not in public; you couldn't convince him of anything in front of other people.

Perry Ferguson, the art director, deserved a lot of credit for the success of *Citizen Kane*. It was he who devised important scenes merely by using a hunk of cornice, a fireplace in the background and a foreground chair. By using such props and Gregg's depth-of-focus lens, Orson could create the illusion of a huge set. Obviously we couldn't afford to duplicate the grandeur of San Simeon. So it was done by suggestion. The suggestion was very effective. Some of those who saw that sequence will swear that they remember a side wall. There was none.

The same was true of the opera-house scene. It was Gregg's idea to shoot from backstage, showing the lights in the theater, but not the audience. There are still people who are convinced they saw the audience in the opera house. They never did.

The shooting of *Citizen Kane* was slow at the start because we had to prove certain new techniques. But then the picture moved along. There was a great feeling about *Citizen Kane*. It was Orson's first picture, as it was for many of those connected with the picture, and everyone was eager to succeed. Everyone was trying to make a good picture. But we didn't realize how good it would be.

Paul Stewart

The telephone rang and I heard the unmistakable voice of Orson Welles, speaking from California. "I want you to come out and do a part for me in my picture," he said. "Have you got an agent?"

"Yes," I said. "But what's the part?"

"Never mind. Just come out."

Well, when Orson said he had a part for you, you went. So I left New York to play my first role in a picture at 500 dollars a week, three weeks' guarantee. I was on *Citizen Kane* 11 weeks. For the first three or four weeks, I didn't work at all.

Naturally I stood around the set watching. And I was amazed at the way Orson worked. In those days we had an 8:00 o'clock call on the set—Orson had to report at 5:00 A.M. when he was wearing the old-man makeup.

The first hour on the set nothing happened. Orson gave Gregg Toland the setup, then everyone became anecdotal. We just sat around telling stories about radio, the theater, etc. After a while Orson began to rehearse. He had a man who walked through his scenes for him, and we rehearsed with this fellow while Orson directed. Then he stepped in and shot the scene with himself in it. Sometimes we didn't get a shot until 3:00 in the afternoon. Of course, lighting was very difficult because of the depth of focus. Eastman Kodak had developed its fastest film for Gregg, but it was still not what we have today.

It wasn't uncommon for Orson to shoot 84, 93, 55 takes of one scene. During the Senate hearings with George Coulouris, Orson did more than a hundred takes. One day he shot a hundred takes and exposed 10,000 feet—without a single print!

I'll never forget the day Orson shot the burning of the sled. One of the stages at the Selznick studio had been made into the warehouse with a working furnace. The scene had to be just right because the audience had to see the sled go in and the word "Rosebud" consumed in flames. When the ninth take had been shot, the doors of the stage flew open and in marched the Culver City Fire Department in full fire-fighting regalia. The furnace had grown so hot that the flue had caught fire.

Orson was delighted with the commotion.

After the fire had been extinguished, one of the firemen asked me, "What's going on here?"

"Mr. Welles is making a picture here," I said.

Orson's *War of the Worlds* scare was still a vivid memory, and the fireman nodded and murmured, "It figures."

My first shot was a close-up in which Orson wanted a special smoke effect from my cigarette. I was rigged with tube that went under my clothes and down my finger to the cigarette, but somehow the contraption wouldn't exude smoke.

"I want long cigarettes—the Russian kind!" Orson ordered. Everyone waited while the prop man fetched some Russian cigarettes.

Just before the scene Orson Welles warned me: "Your head is going to fill the screen at the Radio City Music Hall"—at that time *Citizen Kane* was booked for the Music Hall. Then he said in his gruff manner, "Turn 'em." But just before I started, he added quietly in his warm voice, "Good luck."

I blew the first take. It was 30, 40 takes before I completed a shot that Orson liked—and I had only one line. That was almost 30 years ago, but even today I have people repeat it to me, including young students. The line was: "Rosebud .... I'll tell you about Rosebud ...."

Agnes Moorehead

That was a most memorable period for all of us. It was my first motion picture, as it was for Orson and nearly everyone else in the cast. He trained us for films at the same time he was training himself. All of us were learning.

Orson believed in good acting, and he realized that rehearsals were needed to get the most from his actors. That was something new in Hollywood; nobody seemed interested in bringing in a group to rehearse before scenes were shot. But Orson knew it was necessary, and we rehearsed every sequence before it was shot. Sometimes we did a whole scene on records. No, that wasn't because we were trained in radio. Many of us had known long experience on the stage. I had done many plays, and Orson himself had appeared on Broadway with Katharine Cornell and had acted with the Abbey Players. Then, of course, the Mercury Theater had presented some distinguished plays on Broadway, as well as having programs on radio.

It was exciting to work with Orson. There was no one quite like him to create excitement. While we were making *Citizen Kane,* we felt that excitement, though I must admit we didn't realize the hullabaloo that the picture was going to bring.

Joseph Cotten

I happened to be in *Citizen Kane* purely by chance. I had been playing in *The Philadelphia Story* in New York when we closed for the summer so Katharine Hepburn could make a picture. That summer I came out to Hollywood myself to do a radio show, and that's when I ran into Orson. I was with him a great deal during the preparation of *Citizen Kane,* and it was quite a unique introduction to films for me. Orson and Herman Mankiewicz sat beside Herman's swimming pool and discussed the script. At night I went to Orson's tiny office on the RKO lot and saw the production sketches. Orson had a visual artist sketch all the scenes, and the sketches were changed from day to day as the script changed.

We shot all night for two or three nights to finish up my part so I could rejoin the road tour of *The Philadelphia Story.* One night I was faced with playing a drunk scene, the one in which I wrote a bad review of Kane's wife. I thought about how to play it. The thing you don't do when faced with a drunk scene is to get drunk. But how do you avoid all the stock clichés of a drunk? Orson and I came to the conclusion that fatigue would be akin to the kind of numbness that too much drinking can bring. So we started shooting after dinner, having completed a full day's work that day. I had nothing to drink, but by three o'clock in the morning I was drunk. I felt so heavy-footed and tired that I didn't have to act drunk at all. I was so tired that I did a tongue-trip. I had the line, "I'd like to try my hand at dramatic criticism," but the words came out: "crammatic crimetism." The line remained in the picture.

We were still shooting when morning came. I remember that the eight o'clock whistle blew and the sound man cracked, "That's an interference we don't generally have on a picture."

After Orson called an end to shooting, the prop man brought on a silver tray with drinks. The big stage door was open and we saw the sunshine outside. Someone suggested, "Why don't we go outside and have our drink?"

There we were—Orson, Aggie Moorehead, Everett Sloane, Paul Stewart, myself and others—sitting around in the morning sun and having drinks. I'll never forget actors from other pictures walking down the street and seeing us. I can just imagine what they were saying: "Those actors from New York! Imagine them sitting around in the morning drinking Scotch and sodas off a silver tray!" They didn't know that we had been working for 24 hours straight.

Some people have a faculty for self-destruction, and I suppose that is developed in Orson to a high degree. He never has a conventional thought; that's what keeps him alive. He has a constant fear of conformity, and I suppose he felt if he accepted one grain of discipline, it would destroy his genius. I think it was Einstein who said that there are several hundred wavelengths and we have only discovered seven. Well, I believe there are several wavelengths for people, too. Orson's just happened to be different.

James G. Stewart

I was in charge of the dubbing department at RKO when Orson came on the lot to do *Heart of Darkness*. His idea was for the camera to portray Joseph Conrad as the storyteller, with himself, Orson, doing the narration. He thought the camera should be handheld, and he made extensive tests with a shoulder-mounted support—the first I had ever seen.

Heart of Darkness didn't work out, nor did *Smiler with a Knife*. Then came *Citizen Kane*.

Orson's demands on the picture were almost impossible, but you tried to satisfy him. He was enormously stimulating to work with because he never saw anything in conventional terms. He simply wasn't interested in conventionality, and yet he wasn't different just to be different. He wanted to do things in the best, most dramatic way. He tried to draw out of you the best possible work, and he acted more as a critic than a director.

Orson discovered he could rely on me for anything. For instance, the Madison Square Garden scene. That was shot on a bare sound stage with no audience and no sound tricks, except that Orson adapted the manner of speaking in a reverberant room, waiting for the echoes to die. He gave the track to me and said, "Make it sound like Madison Square Garden."

This was in the days before magnetic recording, and I had to reprint eight or ten dialogue tracks on film to get the right sound. Orson never liked to look at anything until it was completed, so I finished the recording and played it for him.

"You're a bigger ham than I am," he commented after hearing it. "Who's going to look at me with that sound coming at them? It's great, but give me about half as much."

He was right. In my enthusiasm I had overdone the effect, and I toned it down considerably.

10

Citizen Kane provided many memorable moments. I was there the night the picture was run for Louella Parsons. She walked out before it was over, but her chauffeur stayed to the end.

Robert Wise

One of the remarkable things about *Citizen Kane* is the way that Orson sneaked the project onto RKO. He told the studio that he was merely shooting tests. But five or six of the sequences ended up in the picture. The projection-room scene was one. Also the shot through the skylight onto Dorothy Comingore. After Orson had been shooting for a while, the RKO bosses finally became aware of what he was doing. Then they said, "Okay, go ahead."

I came to the picture when he was in the latter stages of shooting; Orson had been working with an older editor and the situation wasn't satisfactory. During the cutting Orson became very much involved, of course. He sat in the cutting room and made cuts or asked for changes. But he didn't hang over my shoulder at all times.

I worked six months on the picture, and during some of the time I was putting in an 18-hour day. An unusual thing happened when *Citizen Kane* was put together. The heads of the production companies were so concerned about the reaction from Hearst that they asked to see a print of the picture. If they considered it too dangerous, they would shelve it.

So I was assigned to take the print to New York—it was my first trip there. One night in the projection room of the Radio City Music Hall I ran the film for the company heads and their lawyers. They decided that the picture didn't have to be shelved, but certain changes had to be made to make it less indelicate. They were mostly line changes, and several of the actors had to be brought in to loop the dialogue. I was on the phone almost every night to my assistant in Hollywood, Mark Robson, to confer about the cutting. Finally, after six weeks of diddling, we got *Citizen Kane* in shape for release.

Mark Robson

Citizen Kane was a remarkable experience for all of us connected with it, especially for the close-up view of the peculiar genius that was Orson Welles. Orson the Magnificent! You could well call him that, because he was a magnificent director —probably the greatest that we have had in the last 30 years. He was *avant-garde,* an innovator, an experimenter; he was theatrical, but in the great sense. He saw the world through cynical, melodramatic eyes.

He was also a magnificent failure. The interesting thing about Orson was that he seemed to run to disaster. His ultimate failure was his success. He never prepared himself for it. He didn't really want success; he seemed to need failure. I don't think he ever really understood how good he was. He thought he was a fraud, and it amazed him when other people thought differently.

Many things happened on *Kane* that seemed to indicate his courting of disaster. He had a huge set of Xanadu built on Stage 9 at RKO and then he didn't know what to do with it. He feigned sickness and stayed home until he figured out how to use the set. What he finally decided was brilliant. Meanwhile the entire cast and crew remained idle.

Again in the middle of production he left everyone sitting while he went off on a lecture tour. That seemed typical of his need for failure.

Europeans adore Welles because they think he was rejected by America. Even the young people in this country revere him because they believe he was rejected by the Establishment. I don't think it was that at all. Orson was typical of those in this country who achieve so much so fast so young. By forty he had disappeared from the American scene. He was a loser—but only because he hadn't prepared himself to win.

Citizen Kane Revisited

Arthur Knight

When in 1952 the British film magazine *Sight and Sound* published the results of an international poll to discover "the ten best films of all time," Orson Welles' *Citizen Kane* fell just short of the magic number, tying with Jean Renoir's *La Grande Illusion* and John Ford's *The Grapes of Wrath* for the eleventh position. In a similar poll ten years later sent to substantially the same group of film critics and historians, *Citizen Kane* was the clear-cut victor—"the best film of all time," if one were to read such listings literally.

What the perspective of an intervening decade had clarified was the fact that *Kane* was indeed a seminal film, or, as *Time* magazine put it, a "watershed" film. When it first appeared in 1941, most critics busied themselves with pointing out similarities to previous pictures by earlier directors. Welles' technique was described as "eclectic," and the whole thing regarded as a spectacular, precocious stunt. (Welles, incredibly enough, was only twenty-five when he made it.) As had been the case with *The Cabinet of Dr. Caligari* a mere 20 years earlier, the more serious critics wrote it off as a kind of dead end for movies, a one-time happening that had no broader implications for the medium.

Although 20/20 hindsight now makes it apparent that *Kane* was at least ten years ahead of its time, and possibly more, it is no accident that the charge of eclecticism was leveled against Welles when the picture was released. In preparation for his film, he spent literally hundreds of hours in projection rooms—first in New York's Museum of Modern Art, later on the RKO lot—running off pictures from the past. (John Ford was his particular favorite.) He put himself through the same rigorous course of viewing and reviewing that the French auteur directors found so valuable at their Cinémathèque in Paris, or that film students in our colleges and universities are being exposed to today. Welles seemed to sense that just as the abstract expressionist must first master the basics of composition and perspective, or a serial composer learns harmony and counterpoint before practicing the more advanced forms of his art, so should the filmmaker be acquainted with all that had gone before—if only to avoid repeating mistakes.

What too many critics overlooked at the time was that, in addition to those techniques and devices that Welles' acquisitive eye picked up during some six months of intensive screenings, he also brought to the medium an unprecedented awareness of the potency of sound. Throughout the 1930s the infant talkies were still learning how to talk. By the time that Welles entered upon the Hollywood scene, at the very end of 1939, the photographed play had become pretty much a thing of the past. Dialogue had grown more naturalistic, acting more intimate; the camera had regained much of its former mobility. But the sound track, with notably few exceptions, merely reproduced dialogue, natural sounds and music (generally of the "Mickey Mouse" genre). Welles proceeded to change all this.

What is often forgotten about Welles is that his extraordinary career in the 1930s embraced not only some of the most exciting theater of the decade—his all-Negro *Macbeth* in a Haitian setting, his modern-dress *Julius Caesar*, his production of Marc Blitzstein's jazz opera *The Cradle Will Rock*—but also highly intensive work in radio. Both of these involved a highly creative use of sound. No one who ever saw his *Macbeth* will forget the rhythmic pounding of jungle drums as an underscoring of the mounting tragedy. No one who ever heard his famous *War of the Worlds* on radio will

Welles (extreme right) directing Dorothy Comingore (extreme left).

forget the adroit cut-aways from a dreary dance band in a New York hotel to the terse announcements of inexplicable foreign objects near Princeton, New Jersey. Long before he came to films, Welles had mastered the added dimension that sound can bring to visuals.

Citizen Kane is virtually a sound man's manual of areas for his special exploration. The film begins with a long series of lap dissolves as the camera moves closer and closer to the one lighted window in Xanadu, Kane's fortress-like Florida estate. To cement the images together, Bernard Herrmann (Welles' composer from his CBS radio days) threaded a series of chords on mounting figures in the strings—a perfect aural counterpoint to the camera's slow rise from the barred gates to the distant light. Herrmann's music is used effectively to establish period (as in the Gay Nineties "Oh, Mr. Kane!" number); but more often Welles borrowed from radio the technique of introducing music in the middle of a scene, then allowing it subtly to change the mood in anticipation of the scene that follows. These musical bridges, unique at the time, have since became standard technique for all film composers.

But if Welles inspired a new direction for film music, he was even more original in his manipulations of the sound track. His radio training, for example, made him particularly aware of the timbres of voices—their hollow, reverberating sound in a cavernous room (such as the Thatcher Memorial Library), the tinny, filtered sound of a voice-over commentator ("News—on the March!"), the echoes of an empty stairwell ("I'm going to send you to Sing-Sing, Gettys! To Sing-Sing"). Indeed, the entire newsreel sequence that follows the death of Kane (except when edited out for most television presentations) demonstrates Welles' special awareness of the qualities of sound; it is as if, in addition to tracing Kane's career through the simulated newsreel clips, he was also tracing the advances in sound-recording techniques. Another, more

14

Welles as Kane in the opera sequence.

Rehearsing the "Oh, Mr. Kane" number.   How it appeared on the screen.

familiar radio device, one that he was to use far more extensively in the subsequent *Magnificent Ambersons,* is the sound montage—a quick series of flashes revealing the thoughts or reactions of several people or an entire group in words and images. The brilliant breakfast sequence, in which the gradual deterioration of a marriage is compressed into less than two minutes of dialogue tied together by swish pans, is perhaps the most notable example of this technique in *Kane.*

Genuine creativity, however, lies less in noting the similarities between two media than in observing their differences, and in turning these to an advantage. In both radio and the theater, for example, it is quite impossible to have two or more conversations going on simultaneously. One must see or hear (or both) the sources of the words in order to identify readily each of the speakers. Indeed, one of the theater's more unpardonable sins is stepping on another's lines. And yet in normal conversation, as Welles clearly understood, we do precisely that most of the time. One seldom waits until a friend has completed a statement before making a response. One never waits until a room is utterly quiet before offering an observation. Voices mount over voices to create tapestries of sound. With uncanny insight, Welles realized that not only can the camera isolate out each of the speakers in a Babel of conversation, but also that the rerecording panel provides complete control over each channel of voices. Thus, he could mix, blend and balance the dialogue tracks in a completely naturalistic way and still not lose those words or sentences that he considered particularly significant. Such sequences as the party given to celebrate the victory of *The Inquirer* over *The Chronicle* or, late in the film, the lawn fete at Xanadu provide multiple illustrations of this technique.

Equally adroit and original was Welles' use of dialogue to motivate a cut. Typical is his bridging of several years as banker Thatcher dictates a Christmas letter to the youthful Kane, ending it with "A merry Christmas . . ." Then, as the voice continues with ". . . and a happy new year," a jump cut brings us face to face with an older, angrier Thatcher who has lost all taste for his willful, wayward protégé. Overlapping dialogues (accompanying lingering lap dissolves) frequently lead into the various flashback sequences of the film, while sudden stabs of sound—such as the harsh screech of a white cockatoo—vividly punctuate other transitions. Perceptively, the British critic Dilys Powell wrote of *Citizen Kane* in 1941 as the work "of one who controls and is not controlled by his medium." Many of the sound techniques that Welles introduced in this virtuoso first effort still await further exploration by filmmakers today.

More obvious, perhaps, are the visual innovations of the picture. Contrary to studio practice at the time, Welles felt that all his sets should have ceilings. This not only affected the sound quality, giving it a greater range of camera angles to shoot from—particularly the low-angle shots he favored because they emphasized the bulk (and the stature) of his hero. While this created lighting problems for his cinematographer, the late, great Gregg Toland, it also encouraged Toland to experiment with new film stocks and, especially, with new lenses. It seems odd today, but during the 1930s the standard photography—even for such realistic films as *I Am a Fugitive from a Chain Gang*—called for soft focus and diffused lighting. Toland's wide-angle lenses created a revolution. Not only did the new focal lengths lend depth to sets that were relatively modest, but they kept everything, whether near or far, in needle-sharp focus.

Welles augmented this effect by his extraordinary utilization of split-screen processing in such sequences as Boss Gettys grimly surveying Kane from what seems to be the very top of an enormous convention hall, or when Kane in a large close-up types out his review of his mistress's disastrous operatic debut while a drunken Jed Leland—who should have been writing it—weaves his way down the entire length of the deserted newspaper office.

Looking back on *Citizen Kane* from the vantage point of more than a quarter of a century, it is astonishing how fresh and original it still appears. The crispness of its black and white photography, the rightness of its performances, the intricate interlocking of its multifaceted story have lost none of their fascination. What time has revealed, however, is the very special way that innovative techniques work their way into the fabric of filmmaking in general. Unfortunately, Welles himself was to have shockingly few opportunities to direct again after Kane was completed—and never with the freedom or autonomy he enjoyed during its production. But the men who worked with him and were encouraged by him to expand their horizons—men like his co-producer (and co-writer) John Houseman, men like Toland and Herrmann, men like Robert Wise and Mark Robson, who were his editors, not to mention the superb acting company that formed the nucleus of his Mercury Theater—they moved on to make films for other directors and other studios. But because their paths had crossed Welles', because they had worked on *Citizen Kane*, their entire approach to the medium was profoundly changed. And gradually, less by imitation than by inspiration, *Citizen Kane* has altered the look not only of American films, but of films the world over.

—1969

II.
Directors at Work

The director has come full circle in the history of the American film. In the dawning years, such directors as D. W. Griffith and Mack Sennett had the freedom to exercise their gifted imaginations. The 1920s introduced bigness, and by the advent of sound the major studios commanded the movie market. Studio heads such as Jack L. Warner, Harry Cohn and Louis B. Mayer ruled the industry with iron-handed control, employing large numbers of staff directors.

In 1933 MGM listed these directors under contract: Harry Beaumont, Charles Brabin, Clarence Brown, Tod Browning, Frank Capra (on loan from Columbia), Jack Conway, John Emerson, Jacques Feyder, George Fitzmaurice, Victor Fleming, John Ford, Sidney Franklin, Edmund Goulding, Howard Hawks, George Hill, Robert Z. Leonard, Ray McCarey, Elliott Nugent, Harry Pollard, Charles Reisner, Edward Sedgwick, Edgar Selwyn, W. S. Van Dyke, Sam Wood.

Many directors rankled under the dictates of the studio bosses, who often switched directors in midproduction and denied directors the right to edit their own films. One who rebelled was Frank Capra. He wrote in his autobiography, *The Name Above the Title:* "That simple notion of 'one man, one film' . . . became a fixation with me, an article of faith. . . . I walked away from shows I could not control completely from conception to delivery."

With the decline of the big studio, directors once again assumed preeminence in the making of films. ACTION has surveyed the state of the film director in this final third of the twentieth century. This section, "Directors at Work," demonstrates the wide diversity of their theories and methods.

Stanley Kubrick opens the section with a discussion of the intense response, pro and con, to *2001: A Space Odyssey*, a film Kubrick believes illustrates the growing appreciation of film as a visual medium. Kubrick and Alfred Hitchcock, whose own long career has been based on the belief that motion pictures should move, both touch on the difference between film and theater, the role of the screenplay and the relationship between the audience and their films.

Like Hitchcock, Roger Corman built his reputation in genre films, earning the title "King of the Grade B's" from a series of inexpensive horror and science-fiction movies.

Both directors, experts at manipulating the unconscious fears of the audience, discuss how they achieve their effects.

Don Siegel, who, like Corman, attracted the admiration of cultists abroad before achieving critical recognition in his own country, describes the progress of his career from working in the film library at Warner Brothers to directing a body of low-budget, profitable genre movies. Siegel is now beginning to do more personal films with bigger budgets, moving into the kind of position that three of his fellow directors—John Frankenheimer, John Schlesinger and Robert Altman—have enjoyed for most of their careers.

Compared to Corman and Siegel, these directors exercise a considerable amount of directorial freedom. Yet in spite of their autonomy, all three, in discussing their approaches and working methods, stress the collaborative nature of filmmaking, the importance of group participation. Frankenheimer works closely with his writer, cameraman, art director and assistant director before shooting even starts. Schlesinger prefers to have the entire movie company attend the screening of the rushes. Altman brings a small group of production people with him from picture to picture. Each of them acknowledges the complementary need for preparation on the one hand and flexibility on the other.

Flexibility—or the ability to take advantage of the spontaneous occurrence—is a virtue that George Stevens and Richard Lester cultivated in their years working in the short-film form—Stevens making two-reel comedies, Lester, television commercials. Both men talk about how their particular apprenticeship affected their feature-film-making.

A different kind of apprenticeship was served by Gordon Parks, who for many years took still photographs for *Life* and other magazines. Parks describes how he made the transition from still to motion pictures—a move that coincided with the film industry's recognition that it needed blacks to delineate the black experience.

Finally Mel Brooks, who shares Parks' belief that a film's primary purpose is to entertain, reveals how he puts together his unique brand of cinematic comedy.

Stanley Kubrick

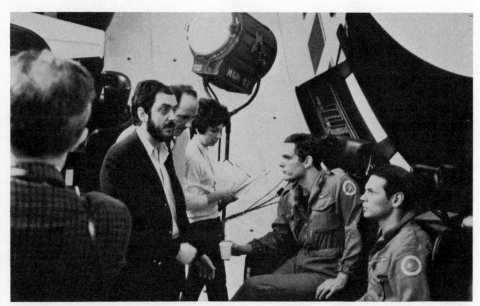

Kubrick (left) on the set of *2001* with actors Keir Dullea and Gary Lockwood.

Maurice Rapf

Stanley Kubrick was a magazine photographer before he became a director in 1953 with Fear and Desire. *He first drew critical attention with his low-budget* The Killing *in 1957. Since then his meager but notable output consists of six films:* Paths of Glory, Spartacus, Lolita, Dr. Strangelove, 2001: A Space Odyssey *and* A Clockwork Orange. *Of these probably none received so inauspicious a critical reception as* 2001 *and, perversely, none has equalled its huge grosses at the box-office.*

Why this gap between critical and commercial reaction? Kubrick conceded that the all-important first preview in New York was a disaster. He also admitted that it was the first time he himself had seen the film in the presence of an audience. Aware of the unfavorable reaction, he made 30 cuts in the composite print, shortening the film by 19 minutes within a week after its opening.

Could a few excisions (actually a 12 percent cut in total length) turn what the critics had called "a monumental bore" or, at best, "a glorious failure" into what many, seeing the film after the cut, were to regard as one of the most visually stimulating movies of all time? As one who admired the shortened version, Maurice Rapf, then a critic for Life *magazine, sought out Kubrick for an explanation of the changes. What follows are excerpts from Kubrick's comments on this and other questions of film technique.*

From the day it opened *2001: A Space Odyssey* got great reaction from the paying audience. All the theater managers say the only adjective they can use is "phenomenal," because of the numbers of people who buy tickets a second, third and fourth time to see the film. The managers report that after each show people come up and want to know where they can buy tickets again. So this poor reaction on that first [preview] screening I attribute to the audience and to the originality of the film. The film departs about as much from the convention of the theater and the three-act play as is possible; not many films have departed further than that, certainly not big films. I don't know why there was this concentration of nonreceptive people, but there was.

First of all, the audience that is seeing the film now is reported as being 80 percent thirty-five or under, down to five years old. I would say the audience must have been 90 percent from thirty-five to sixty at that screening. So the preview audience and the paying audience have been two ends of the moviegoing scale.

Secondly, the lukewarm New York reaction has not been the case anywhere else, for some strange reason. I haven't had time to look through this, but in Chicago we got three rave reviews out of four. In Boston we got all rave reviews, including critics whom you wouldn't expect to like it, such as Marjorie Adams, who said the film is like adding a new dimension to life. It's gotten virtually unanimous rave reviews out of New York. I don't know the reason for the New York reaction. The audience, with the exception of a few mumblers that go out, has reacted more intensely, more favorably than to any other picture that the managers can remember.

I myself usually get ten or 12 letters about a picture over a period of the whole life of the film. I've been getting about two letters a day since the film opened. Two or three have been cranky letters, asking for their money back; the rest are from people saying, "This film has changed my life," and "I've seen the film six times," and things like that. So all indices of the film would indicate that for some strange reason chemistry that night was bad and also very unrepresentative of anything that's happened since then.

I tightened the picture all the way through. I had started thinking about doing it right from the first screening because even though the total reaction of that screening was not representative or good, I could still see places that, as I watched it with an audience, I thought were just going on a bit. It's probably the hardest thing to determine, as to how much weight to give. I just felt as I looked at it and looked at it that I could see places all the way through the film where I would tighten up, and I took out 19 minutes. The picture had been originally two hours and 41 minutes long.

A number of very perceptive people, and a lot of just ordinary people, saw the long version and flipped over that. I don't believe that the change made a crucial difference. I think it just tightened up, and some marginal people who might have gotten restless won't get restless. But the people that dug the film dug it in its original length, and the people that hated it hate it at the present length.

Special effects were the reason the film was late, the reason that it was so close to the wire. I spent a year and a half, June 1966 practically up to the beginning of March 1967, running through the 205 special-effects shots. The last ones were arriving in California as they were doing the negative printing. You can't finish this picture without the special effects; they're integrated in almost every sequence so the thing never really got put together except a sequence at a time to look at it, or a reel at a time.

All of the money spent on the film shows on the screen. In most films you have a bunch of guys talking to each other and you make use of about three or four sets and that's about it. There really isn't a lot to look at, and everybody is waiting for the big action sequence. I remember as a child being frustrated by one war picture after another where John Payne and Randolph Scott would talk and talk and you'd be waiting for the big attack. It would finally come at the end of the film for two minutes with some process shots and a lot of cheated action. Forgetting all the other things that a film is, there is always—to me anyway—a disappointment in not really seeing anything up on the screen that is beautiful or interesting to look at. Largely it's just a matter of photographing a lot of people talking to each other on sets that are

more or less interesting with actors that are better or worse. Essentially films are confined to being elaborated three-act stage plays. They have had a great problem breaking out of that form.

In *Space Odyssey* the mood hitting you is the visual imagery. The people who didn't respond, I now, for want of coming up with a better explanation, categorize as "verbally oriented people." Every child that sees the film—and I've spoken to 20 or 30 kids—knows that Doctor Floyd goes to the moon. You say, "Well, how do you know?" and they say, "Well, we saw the moon." Whereas a number of people, including critics, thought he went to the planet Clavius. Why they think there's a planet Clavius I'll never know. But they hear him asked, "Where are you going?" and he says, "I'm going to Clavius." Now, I knew at that time that most people wouldn't realize that Clavius was a crater on the moon, but it seemed to me a realistic way of talking about the moon. He wouldn't say, "I'm going to the moon to the crater Clavius." With many people—BOOM—that one word registers in their head and they don't look at 15 shots of the moon; they don't see that he's going to the moon.

Communicating visually and through music gets past the verbal pigeonhole concepts that people are stuck with. You know, words have a highly subjective and very limited meaning, and they immediately limit the possible emotional and subconscious designating effect of a work of art. Movies have tied themselves into that because the crucial things that generally come out of a film are still word-delivered. There's emotion backing them up, you've got the actors generating feeling, etc. It's basically word communication.

"The Blue Danube" is a magnificent piece of music for the beautiful, graceful motion of the space station. To me it just seemed like a perfect representation of what was going on. Also it helped to get away from the idea that space would be eerie and strange. Space travel will become very ordinary very soon, and it will be particularly significant for its beauty. It seemed to me "The Blue Danube" was a magnificent piece of music to use, particularly since I had decided to use existing music and not original music.

The screenplay is the most uncommunicative form of writing ever devised. It's hard to convey mood and it's hard to convey imagery. You can convey dialogue, but if you stick to the conventions of a screenplay, the description has to be very brief and telegraphic. You can't create a mood or anything like that, so the screenplay that was written was about a 40,000-word prose piece by Arthur B. Clarke and me. That was the basis of the deal and the budget, etc. Then a screenplay was made from that by me and Arthur, and then Arthur afterwards wrote the novel based on the screenplay.

I've always said the two people who are worthy of film study are Charlie Chaplin and Orson Welles as representing the two most diverse approaches to filmmaking. Charlie Chaplin must have had the crudest, simplest lack of interest in cinematics. Just get the image on the screen; it's the content of the shot that matters. Welles is probably, at his best, the most baroque kind of stylist in the conventional film-telling style. I think perhaps Eisenstein might be a better example because where Chaplin had all content and no style, to me Eisenstein has all style and no content. *Alexander Nevsky* stylistically is possibly one of the most beautiful movies ever made; its content to me is a moronic story, moronically told, full of lies. It's the most dishonest kind of a film. And I would have thought that perhaps a study of Chaplin's greatest films and *Alexander Nevsky* would be worthwhile, because somewhere within that you'd see how two completely diverse approaches can make a fascinating film.

People now realize how easy it is to make a film. Everybody knows that you use

a camera and everybody knows that you use a tape recorder, and it's now getting to the point where a filmmaker almost has the same freedom a novelist has when he buys himself some paper. I haven't seen all the underground films; I've been away for three years. If they haven't already, there's no doubt that at some point someone's going to do something on a level that's going to be shattering. First of all, they all need a little more experience. It's getting to the point now for a few thousand dollars you can make a film, and a hell of a lot of people can lay their hands on a few thousand dollars if they want it badly enough.

—1969

North by Northwest.

Alfred Hitchcock

Bob Thomas

*Alfred Hitchcock, who like Kubrick believes in the primacy of the
visual in film, has been putting his principles into practice for nearly 50 years,
ever since his first film,* The Pleasure Garden, *in 1925. He chatted about this and
a variety of other topics in an interview in his Universal City office.*

Beginnings

I'm American-trained. My first work was at the Paramount Studio in London—
then it was Famous Players-Lasky. All of the personnel at the studio were American,
and as soon as you entered the studio doors you were in an American atmosphere. I
started out as a designer of titles working with Mordant Hall, who was a critic later
for *The New York Times,* and for Tom Geraghty, who had been a writer for Douglas
Fairbanks.

Later I worked for UFA in Berlin. The man I was working with spoke no English
and looked a little bit like Harpo Marx. We were both designing titles and we com-
municated by means of drawings. But finally I was forced to learn the language and
that came in handy, because my first directing job was in Munich and I had to direct
some of the actors in German.

First Direction

My first picture was called *The Pleasure Garden* and it was filmed in Munich. But
I also had locations to shoot in Italy and that was quite an experience. You know
how film companies now go on location with 90 people and loads of equipment?
Well, when I left the Munich station at 20 minutes to eight on Saturday evening I
was accompanied only by the actor, whose name was Miles Mander, the cameraman,
a newsreel man who was to shoot film on shipboard, and a camera. No lighting, no
reflectors, nothing else at all, except the film—10,000 feet of it. After I got on the
train the cameraman told me not to declare the camera or the 10,000 feet of film as
we crossed the border into Austria. The studio wanted to save money on the customs.
"Where is the camera hidden?" I asked. "Under your bed," he told me. When we
crossed the border the customs officials did not discover the camera, but they found
the film stock in the baggage car and confiscated it. I arrived in Genoa on a Monday
morning without any film and on Tuesday noon I had to shoot the departure of an
ocean liner from the port. So I sent the cameraman to Milan to buy some film stock.
I spent more time doing the accounts than I did directing the picture. Most of my
evenings were spent translating marks into lire via pounds. I happened to flash the
10,000 lire which I had for expense money and that night it was stolen from my hotel
room. I had to borrow money from the cameramen and actor to meet expenses, and
they weren't very nice about that. During one of the scenes a native girl was supposed
to wade out into the sea with the idea of drowning herself, then the leading man was
to go into the water in an attempt to rescue her, only to hold her head under the
water and drown her. When I set up for the scene I noticed the cameraman, the leading actor and the native girl were in conference. The leading man told me, "She can't
go into the water." I asked him, "You mean she's refusing to do her part?" Then the

two cameramen had to explain to me about menstruation. I was twenty-five years old and I had never heard of it; I had had Jesuit education, and such matters weren't part of it. I hadn't really wanted to be a director; I was content to go on writing scripts and being an art director. But I finished *The Pleasure Garden* and it turned out well. At least *The London Daily Express* termed me "a young man with a master mind."

The Visual Medium

A film like *Guess Who's Coming to Dinner?* could well have been done as a play. It is a series of duologues—between the man and his wife, between the father and the colored man, between the colored man and his father, etc. The result can be very interesting and entertaining as has been proved. I don't decry dialogue, but I feel that the technique is not necessarily cinematic. I did a dialogue film, *Dial M for Murder*, which was taken from a successful play. I could have phoned that one in. But *Rear Window* is a pure motion picture, even though the man never moves from one position. You can't tell the story in the theater and you can't tell it as succinctly in a novel. What the man sees is everything. The oral part comes when he says to someone, "I saw something over there." But the person he's talking to doesn't see it. Later the person does see it and that solves the whole plot. The cinema is a succession of images put together like a sentence. Together they create a story. Chaplin did this brilliantly in a picture called *The Pilgrim*. He had first a scene of prison gates with a guard posting a picture of an escaped criminal, Chaplin. The next scene shows a long, lanky man coming out of a river after a swim to discover that his clothes are gone. The next scene is in a railroad depot where Chaplin is dressed in a parson's clothes which are much too big for him. Here in three brief scenes Chaplin told you everything you needed to know: The tramp has escaped from jail and he has stolen a preacher's clothes. I commended him on this one time, and he didn't realize what he had done. That kind of technique is rarely practiced today, but it is really not too difficult. All you have to do is apply your mind to it.

Films vs. Theater

Since talk came in, the films have been invaded by a lot of things that belong to the theater. Dissolves and fade-outs are theater techniques—curtains. Nowadays we use more of the quick cuts, and that is probably good. But techniques that apply in one case do not necessarily apply in another. Take the hand-held camera. This fellow who directed the Beatles did a fine job with the hand-held camera in catching the mood and jumpiness of the Beatles. But when he applies the technique to a Broadway show such as *A Funny Thing Happened on the Way to the Forum*, it does not work. The reason is that comedians need more time to do their techniques. People like Phil Silvers need to set up their pieces of business.

Writing

One of my biggest problems is writing and that is why I can't make films more often. No matter how much I try to indoctrinate a writer with my mode of operation, many of them say, "I only see it this way." Well, they are writers and creative people, but they don't necessarily take the audience into account. I do find that the bigger the writer, the easier he is to work with. I've had great luck working with men such as Ben Hecht, Thornton Wilder and Robert Sherwood. It's the lesser ones who are the problems. Many of them are writing for their reputation, not for the film. But, of course, I need writers. I am a visual man, but unfortunately I also must have delineation of character and dialogue. The plot I can depict, but I must have convincing characters and good dialogue.

Silent-Film Directing

It was much easier. There were no nuances of dialogue to be concerned with, and the acting was much more elemental. The whole atmosphere was relaxed. We always had a three-piece orchestra on the set—violin, cello and piano—to provide the proper mood when a mother was bending over a cot to look at her dying baby.

Murder

One of my problems with writers is that when you tell them it is going to be a murder story, they start thinking in low-key terms. That is not my method. I think murder should be done on a lovely summer's day by a babbling brook. The liveliest fellow at a party might well be a psychopathic killer. Take real-life murders, like the district attorney's wife or Doctor Finch's wife. The events leading up to the actual violent act might well be light and even humorous. Murderers often have to be delightful people; otherwise they wouldn't attract their victims. They often are after sex or money, and they need to use their wiles to get it. But it is hard to get writers to understand that. The average writer writes on the nose, whereas a suspense story should be written contrapuntally. In real life, murderers do not go around with black mustaches or with their faces in green light.

Backgrounds

I make it a rule if I am going to use a theater, I will integrate it into the plot, not just use it as a background. For instance, in *Torn Curtain* I made the ballerina the catalyst for the story. I always try to use the background in the story. For instance, *North by Northwest*. I put Cary Grant into an auction, and the question was, "How will he get out of there?" The solution was for him to bid at the auction. In the same picture I wanted to use the face of Abraham Lincoln on Mount Rushmore for a definite purpose. I wanted Grant to slide down Lincoln's nose, hide in a nostril and be flushed out by a sneezing fit. In that way I would have been using everything for a payoff. But the authorities would not let me use Lincoln's face, and Grant had to slide down between the faces. If I had made *No Way to Treat a Lady*, I would have had the detectives sit in the theater audience and see all of the costumes of the murdered on the stage—the priest, the fairy, etc. But I am not going to tell anyone else how to direct his picture.

Audiences

I remember seeing a London play called *Jolly Jack Tar*. During the action a bomb was planted on stage and I remember hearing a woman in the galleries shout to the actors: "There's a bomb in the box!" Audiences are very strange. I know their reactions so well I don't have to go to the theater anymore; the emotional anxieties are pretty well standard. And they do not necessarily relate to right and wrong. Those anxieties can be so powerful that, if you show a burglar in the bedroom and then cut to a woman opening her front door, the audience says to the burglar: "Get out!" They don't care about the fact that he is involved in a criminal act. When I made *Psycho,* I had a scene in which Tony Perkins tried to dispose of a body by pushing a car into a swamp. When the car did not sink under the water, the audience was pulling for it to do so, even though Perkins was the murderer.

Psycho.

Mystery vs. *Suspense*

I have made only one mystery and that was *Murder,* from a play by Clement Dane. It was a real whodunit. I feel that mysteries are fine in books, when you can spread the clues throughout the story and then reach the climactic moment when you find out that the butler did it. But I don't feel it works in a film when you have to wait the whole length of it for the surprise denouement at the end. It's like this: If you touch off a bomb, your audience gets a ten-second shock. But if the audience knows that the bomb has been planted, then you can build up the suspense and keep them in a state of expectation for five minutes.

Suspense

Mystery is mystifying; it is an intellectual thing. Suspense is an emotional thing. The audience does not necessarily emote when it is mystified, but it does emote with suspense. The point is to give the viewers information which the cast doesn't have. If you see a man with a club coming up behind an innocent person, you know more than the innocent person does, and suspense is created.

—1968

Roger Corman

Digby Diehl

    *Roger Corman is the perfect example of the director with less
honor in his own country than he enjoys abroad. Although he has gained
increasing respect from American critics, Europeans take him much
more seriously; he was the youngest director to have a retrospective showing
at the French National Film Institute.*

    *From his directorial debut, Five Guns West, in 1955 to Bloody Mama
in 1971, Corman made over 50 movies, of which the Edgar Allan
Poe films were the most widely praised. Newsweek admired their "stylish
cleverness" and found that he "shows a flair for Gothic weirdness that is the dark
side of America's sunny optimism."*

Q: You're known as one of the few professionals in the motion-picture industry who takes particular interest in young filmmakers. Why is this true?

Corman: Well, I've helped some in their first pictures, because I think it's worthwhile. When I got out of Stanford, it took me seven years of doing everything in the world to get going in films. I came out with all the honors and I got a job as a stagehand. Actually, first I was a messenger at 20th Century-Fox and then I was a stagehand at KLAC. So, anyway, I think it's a worthwhile thing to help a young person of some talent get his start in films. It's enjoyable and stimulating and I generally have made money at it—although recently the margin of profit has dropped. The ones at UCLA have gone far over budget and so I've decided to stop backing any new filmmakers until I can reassess the situation.

Q: Although abroad your films have achieved critical acclaim, your reputation in the U.S. is not so great. How do you explain this difference?

Corman: In general, I believe the standard of criticism in Europe is higher than in the United States. Film has been respected there as the twentieth-century art form for a much longer period of time than it has here. In Europe the critics are brought up in a different tradition and are taught to look for different elements. At the same time, however, there are American critics who are more perceptive, intelligent and informed—but they are in the minority. Ordinarily there is a great deal of snobbery from American film critics. They will accept a film directed by Stanley Kramer as a work of art before they see it, or a film from a European director, or even a low-budget film from New York. But they unloose their ire against a low- or medium-budget Hollywood production. Now, generally, I've gotten fairly good reviews in the U.S.—most often better in New York than in Hollywood; as a matter of fact, only in my last couple of times out have my receptions fallen off. When I was making the Poe pictures, I would hardly ever see an unfavorable review in either Europe or America. The only time I really began to be knocked was after doing *The Wild Angels* for American International. And, again, I can't say I was knocked everywhere: *The Los Angeles Times* listed it as one of the top ten films of the year! It seems, however, that when I turn to what I consider a truthful rendering of the American scene is the point where I run afoul of American critics.

Q: In your years of making horror and science-fiction films you must have developed some theories about the genre. You've been quoted as saying that your aesthetic is essentially Freudian.

Corman: Yes, specifically with horror films. To me the horror film is essentially the re-creation of childhood fear. The small child, alone in the world; he's worried, he's frightened, he depends upon the love and protection of his parents. But for some reason sometimes they are not with him. And at such times he can become very frightened. Now, as he grows older, these events are forgotten by his conscious mind —or he learns to cope with them—but he will usually carry some residual fears about some aspects of the world as an adult. I think it's the function of the horror film— and it's a useful function—to expose those fears and show they are baseless. The unconscious minds of most people have common underpinnings. After all, we've been raised in Western civilization in basically the same ways so there are similarities among us. I try to reach what I consider the uniform elements of the unconscious by building up a sense of suspense and then cracking through it quickly. It's the cracking through that reaches the subconscious for a moment, and it reacts. Very often, if it's done correctly, you'll get a scream from the audience—for you've affected their unconscious—followed by a little ripple of laughter, which is when the conscious mind takes over again and says to the unconscious, "Okay, you didn't need to scream." And this is why in my later films I added humor and made essentially comedy-horror films. These are a lot of fun to make but are also challenging—like a complex piece of music.

Q: Can you give me some specific examples of this theory from your films?

Corman: Okay. Say *The Pit and the Pendulum. In* that, Vincent Price is awakened in the castle by what seems to be the voice of his dead wife. Before this happened, we've set up several elements—that his wife may have been buried alive, that her ghost may still walk the castle, etc.—so that we've, as it were, sowed the ground. He wakes up and instantly he's frightened. And the audience begins to sense a little fear with him. He walks down the hall, trying to find the source of the voice, in other words, trying to investigate. At the same time, the audience is saying with him, "Find out what the secret is," but they're also warning, "Don't go any further down the hall." There are other elements working as well. I think the actual movement down the hall is another kind of fear-attraction combination. It's like a young boy dying to find out—"dying" is the right word I think—about sex. He's drawn irresistibly to it, yet at the same time he's frightened because he knows it's going to change his life. He doesn't know yet if he's going to meet the test adequately, yet he must meet the test. Now, the movement down the hall, I'd say, is to a certain extent the symbolism of the vagina. It's generally dimly lit in our films, which may add to it as well.

Q: So the secret he's trying to discover is the primal secret.

Corman: Right. There's a theory that mystery stories are always an attempt to solve that primal secret. Very often what's going on down the hall, behind the door, has with it the question "What is father doing to mother?" It could be murder—because it sounds pretty violent: the bedsprings are bouncing around, he hears cries, and that's pretty frightening to him because his parents represent the only security he has in the world. Anyway, back in *this* hallway, Vincent Price is proceeding further and further. Soon the audience begins to be caught up with him. We have point-of-view dolly shots moving backwards on his face. Once we get into it, I try to keep all the shots moving, so the audience is with him at all times. He goes down the stairway, into the underground crypt; it appears that the voice has been calling to him from his wife's tomb. He breaks through the bricks and pulls the coffin open and his wife sits up quickly and looks him straight in the face.

I've seen the film a number of times and at that point the audience has never failed to scream—and *really* scream! And then they laugh a little bit and it's all right, because they know you did something to them. And the laughter is always apprecia-tive laughter, because that's what they came for. When they bought their ticket, that's what they paid for—they didn't know what that moment would be or exactly what was going to happen, but they came for the moment when they were going to scream and, whether they knew it or not, they came for the moment when some part of a childhood fear was going to be exposed, after which they were going to be told, "It's okay."

Q: When you were at Stanford, did you study psychology?

Corman: I took a number of psychology courses, but my degree is in engineering. But, of course, I've also read a great deal in psychology.

Q: When you talk about a Freudian aesthetic, how is this translated into filmic terms?

Corman: Well, film is the best medium in the world for a Freudian aesthetic because the unconscious predates language; it seems to deal with predominantly visual images. We dream primarily in images and therefore using the motion picture enables you to create an experience closely related to the unconscious—particularly as we know it in dreams. In a movie theater you sit back, passively, in a darkened room. A passage of light appears before you and you concentrate your attention on it as you would on a hypnotist. You are in a near-dreamlike state and your conscious mind relaxes because of your surroundings, breaking down some of the barriers to the unconscious. But the beauty of the form is that your conscious mind can still function on a critical level just as you react to it on an emotional level.

Q: When you take a Poe story, how extensively do you work it out?

Corman: Most of Poe's works were extremely short so I would utilize them as the third act of a structure which I create to lead up to it. In *The Pit and the Pendulum* everything in the original story took place in that room containing the pit, the pendulum and the prisoner. We utilized that scene by taking a young man and bringing him to the castle of Vincent Price, and in the first and second acts we prepared for it. In the third he was in that room. With the art director I would work out say 80 to 90 percent of the picture's shots in advance, sketching them in the script on the blank pages opposite the text. I would then follow that—70 or 80 percent of the time. If there was any particular style or technique of working, it was of having as much time as possible, as much preparation, but then never be wedded to it. If I came to the set and saw a better way of working, I would always throw out the work that had been done before. If you become too rigid, you may get a very technically excellent result, but it may also lack life.

Q: Obviously it is easy to produce emotion on the screen by violence. But this can be done glibly, and I would be interested in knowing how you feel about resorting to such practices.

Corman: Actually there is very little violence in the horror films. Matter of fact, sometimes there's none at all. The essence of the horror is fear of the unseen—the image behind that door. Some of the most frightening sequences I've shot are simply a dolly coming up to a strange door and hearing some strange noise—not necessarily a violent noise. In *The Masque of the Red Death* there was no violence whatsoever. We were dealing with the plague, a perfectly natural phenomenon, and it was fear of death *per se*, not fear of any violence.

Q: In *The Masque,* Death was personified, much as it was in Ingmar Bergman's *Seventh Seal.* Did you get inspiration from his work?

Corman: Somebody once said I had, but all I can say is that I took my concept from Poe's story, which was written 100 years before Bergman made *The Seventh Seal,* and I believe that both Bergman and I took our inspiration from that story. I never started to do a series on Poe. I just wanted to do a version of *Fall of the House of Usher.* It was a success and AIP asked me to do another one. Poe's next two most famous stories were *The Pit and the Pendulum* and *Masque of the Red Death.* I couldn't decide between them, but finally chose the latter because *Masque of the Red Death* was very close to *The Seventh Seal.* And as the series grew, I always came back to *The Masque* as the logical film to do next, and I always rejected it in favor of a lesser Poe work because of the similarity to Bergman's film. Finally I had used up all suitable Poe material and had no choice. Of course, both *The Masque* and *The Seventh Seal* deal with the Middle Ages and in each the leading character confronts death as an individual. But in making my film, I tried as much as possible to avoid the similarities.

Q: Harold Pinter's plays and films emphasize the "something sinister lurking in the background" you mentioned earlier. Are you an admirer of his?

Corman: Very much so. In *The Birthday Party* there's always the feeling of a sinister quality out there—which is our modern world as I interpret it. And there is horror in the modern world, believe me. One time AIP asked me to do a prehistoric picture. The beauty of it was that they would let me alone to do pretty much what I wanted as long as I stayed within the scope of the type of film they wanted and their budget limitations. I came up with a very strange film with Bob Vaughn called *Prehistoric World,* and as you began to follow the story and learn about the tribe the young man belonged to, you could hopefully see the growth of religions built around strange beliefs, superstitions and fears. And at the end, you found that it all took place in the *future,* that the world had been destroyed by an atomic bomb, that the man was *rebuilding.* And just as his original beliefs came from attempts to cope with a world he didn't understand, he was now doing the same thing in a different world. Part of it was contaminated and his religion told him it was an "evil" area—that devils were lurking there. I think that we were dealing in the film with the same kind of sinister element you mentioned— but in a different way.

Q: Does science fiction fit into your theoretical framework for horror films?

Corman: I think that they represent different aspects of the same basic drive: to know the unknown. If you say that there is a superior civilization on another planet, you are answering the same basic question as if you say the spirits of the dead can come back and haunt us. In each case you are seeking to discover what is out there, either in the stars or in the world around us. The finest example of science fiction I've seen in my life is Stanley Kubrick's *2001*. Kubrick was saying that, in moving beyond what we already know, we eventually enter a mystical religious experience. Just as in my film *Man with the X-Ray Eyes* what started out as a simple experiment in vision ended up as a kind of quasi-religious parable. The man had to pluck out his eyes at the end because he had seen too deeply and too much, and could not stand it.

Q: Many of the New Wave filmmakers cite you and Hitchcock as being heavily influential. Why should you be coupled that way?

Corman: Of course, as mentioned, both Hitchcock's and my films are heavily psychoanalytic in their use of symbols. In *Psycho,* for example, Hitchcock uses a great sexual symbol with that old house on the hill. A house is accepted traditionally as a female symbol. And at the same time he had a long, low motel that pointed straight at the house. Guess what that is? And the whole interaction was built around Tony Perkins, playing a man *and* a woman, moving back and forth between the phallic symbol of the motel and the feminine symbol of the house. In many of Hitchcock's films he used the male symbol of a train. Now, on a train you are able to put people in a contained environment *but* with an ever-shifting background—which is a good enough cinematic reason for setting his films on one. But Hitchcock continued putting his people on trains after the time when everyone traveled by plane. An airplane is not as clear-cut a symbol as a train—you can't have it go through a tunnel, for instance—and so he had to resort to wild excuses explaining why someone in a film took a train when nobody takes trains anymore. In *Psycho* he came up with the magnificent substitute symbol of the motel—which, if you look at it quite clearly, has no relationship to reality. I mean the whole thing is a sound-stage affair, which is in keeping with a fantasy film. If you want to keep the fantasy, you don't want to show the real world.

Q: What do you call the type of film you're doing now?

Corman: AIP likes to call them "protest films," and so many have involved motorcycle gangs, people just call them "motorcycle films." But I only made one motorcycle film—the first one—*The Wild Angels*. I never intended to initiate a cycle. (No pun intended.) I've done nothing more or less than take a hard, objective look at life in the United States today. The Hell's Angels represent the dark forces in society that people don't like to talk about—that they don't like to admit are there, but which are always with us. They're part of a movement of people who have no part in a technical society—who are frozen out. Formerly these people might have been field workers or janitors. But such jobs are being automated now, and I think we have to anticipate a future when a large part of our society will be unemployable. It is beginning to be that right now.

Plus there's something else. The Angels have their own society, their own mystique, and they talk about how they don't want to be part of our society. It's partially because they can't be a part of it because they are not capable of functioning within it on any reasonable level. It's therefore natural to drop out and say the former society is no good. But if you come from a society, you will take most of its values with you. And, one more thing, if some advertising executive can say, "I want out of this rat

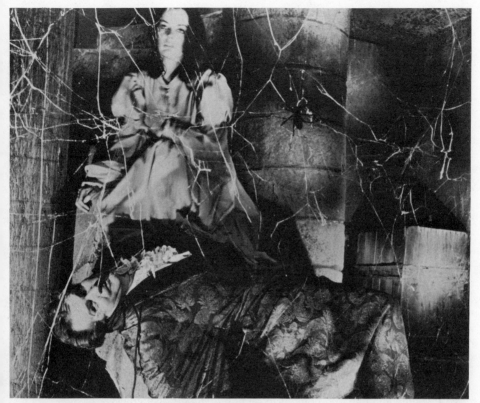

The Pit and the Pendulum.

The Wild Angels.

race; it's not good enough," how much easier is it for some guy who can only hope for a job as a garage mechanic to drop out. And to a certain extent, he's right. Why should he spend his life doing that? So I think the Angels are symptomatic of something in society today—and a growing something, too.

The Trip was the same way, only it dealt with the taking of LSD. I think that discoveries come about in the world when they're needed—not through any divine operation—but simply the mind of man turns to the problem at hand. I think one of the problems "at hand" will soon be growing leisure, and it's very possible that LSD or later chemical discoveries will be there so that people who work two or three days a week can spend most of their time tripping out. After all, how many pro football games can a guy who's free from his job watch until he says, "I just don't want to see another pro football game."?

Q: Thematically, do you connect *The Trip* with trying to know the unknown?

Corman: Yes. Both *The Trip* and *The Wild Angels* show us possible projections into the dark side of society and possible ways society may go in the future. People don't like to talk about these elements—except to put them down in an unsavory way—and both those films were highly criticized. Yet they both were shown at film festivals, so I believe there must be something there.

Q: What are your plans now in terms of future filmmaking?

Corman: Well, I haven't directed a film in a year—which is the first year since I started when I haven't directed at least three. It's partially a relief—that reassessment I mentioned. I got tired and simply said, "Enough! I'm tired." I financed a couple of films in this time and have a deal with United Artists on some projects. But I haven't anything definite at this moment. I would like to work along the lines of *The Wild Angels* and *The Trip,* possibly not with such sensational subjects, but simply on something which has relevance to human beings today in our world.

Q: Would you like to do one of those multimillion-dollar epics?

Corman: I would have no objection. I'm not snobbish and I have nothing against that kind of film. Should a particular picture call for that kind of budget, I'd be happy to work within it.

Q: What is the total count of your films to date?

Corman: I'm not certain; I lost track somewhere along the line. But as a producer, I've done over 100. As a director, I must have done over 50.

Q: Where would you say that the greatest improvement is needed—or the greatest advance could come in the Hollywood film?

Corman: The greatest opportunities for the director will come as the studios and the financiers learn more and more to leave him alone and let him make the film he wants. A lot of the executives would be making films if they could—for it's a lot more fun and profitable to be making films than to be an executive. But the executive must not tell the filmmaker what to do. Now, this then puts a burden on the filmmaker who can no longer say: "The front office wrecked my film." The responsibility is squarely on his shoulders. He makes the film and he stands or falls by it. And the front office sticks by this decision: if he makes a good film, hire him back. If he makes a bad film, fire him. I think operating under those conditions, the filmmaker will understand where he stands—he will live or die on the quality of his work—and the quality of his work will, at last, be his.

—1969

Don Siegel

Siegel, the actor, in *Play Misty for Me*, with director Clint Eastwood.

Leonard Maltin

Like Corman, Don Siegel was "discovered" several years ago by French film critics and their American disciples, who put him in the front rank of directors. Siegel has certainly earned his reputation: over a period of years he has managed, within the restrictions of low budgets and unprofound scripts, to make good, solid, expert films which stand the test of time.

After freelancing for many years ("Freelancing with me means not eating," he says) he signed a long-term contract with Universal, for which he made an impressive string of films: Madigan, Coogan's Bluff, Death of a Gunfighter *(completed by Siegel),* Two Mules for Sister Sara *and* The Beguiled, *in addition to three features for NBC.* Dirty Harry, *on loan-out to Warner Brothers, followed* The Beguiled.

Q: What was your first job in the film business?

Siegel: I carried cans of film, in the film library at Warner Brothers. The first thing I ever did was splice a reel of sunrises, which became sunsets—I couldn't tell where the frame line was. I thought when I was working in the film library that I'd be handling books on films. I had no idea that I'd be handling film.

Q: How did you progress from there?

Siegel: It was very difficult, because the head of that department, Walter DeLeon, liked me and we used to look at film all day long, to pick stock shots, with horrendous hangovers. As far as I was concerned, it was the best job in the world, and I never wanted to leave. But he felt guilty. He felt that I had a certain amount of talent, and he really kicked me out and got me hired as an assistant cutter. Otherwise I would still have been there. The big break I had was when I went down to Stage 5, which was a big special-effects stage, and I became head of the insert department, which meant that I had a crew. I had an operator, an assistant, a grip and an electrician. Well, that's a very dangerous thing to stick in the hands of anybody, because after shooting endless inserts, I began to get in trouble with the front office. I'd go to a director and say, "Look, why bother to shoot Bette Davis getting out of a car and going up the steps? I'll shoot it for you." So I'd save him time. It was very illegal, and nobody knew what I was doing, but actually the various directors were terribly pleased. The next step was a very important one. They had no montage department, so I started one. This is the one phase of the motion-picture business that gives the audience some credit for intelligence. It's a very imaginative job, a creative job, and that was great. There was a rule when I started that montages had to be silent; well, that was ridiculous. Why did they have to be silent? So pretty soon I was shooting scenes. I was a real pain in the neck to the studio. Montages are very expensive, and I did montages in every picture they made—*Yankee Doodle Dandy, Sergeant York, Confessions of a Nazi Spy,* you name it. I shot more footage than any director on the lot.

Q: How did that work? Did you still have to approach each director?

Siegel: A script would come out; it says, "He looks for work, and is turned down everywhere." I'd rewrite that, and it might come out four pages long. I'd take him in to, say, a series of people shaking their heads, and feet walking, and doors shutting. Then I'd have to take that montage script to the director and to the producer. I made one error, with Mike Curtiz. I took it to the producer first, who initialed it at the end. It was very funny, because Mike read it, and he's saying, "Marvelous—how do you do that? *Wunderbar,*" going all the way down, gets to the bottom of page four, sees the signature of the producer, and becomes enraged, wraps it up in a ball, and throws it off the stage. Now, I had to go and get it retyped, and get him to sign it before the producer signed it!

Q: When were you doing the montages?

Siegel: Let's see, I started in 1934. I'd say it was about from 1937 to 1942. I was still doing them even when I was doing second-unit and then I had a very good assistant, a fellow who was in the cutting department, Jimmy Lester.

Q: How did you get into second-unit work?

Siegel: Well, it was a very natural step. You almost couldn't separate the two. I did a great deal of second-unit, and I have a certain ambivalence about it. It opened doors for me to become a director. But, at the same time, it gave me a reputation of being an action director. That phrase—I prefer to think of it as a stigma—is with me to this moment.

Q: You did two shorts that won Oscars. Did that lead to feature film assignments?

Siegel: Yes. Well, you know, when you've worked on something that wins an Academy Award, they don't quite know what they've got. So in self-defense they gave me a project that nobody else wanted. I didn't want it, but I was told to do it, so I

Siegel directing Shirley MacLaine and Eastwood in *Two Mules for Sister Sara*.

With Geraldine Page during the production of *The Beguiled*.

did. It was called *The Verdict,* my first film—a very pleasurable experience for me, because I met two great guys, Sydney Greenstreet and Peter Lorre, with whom I got along famously. I had known Greenstreet slightly because of some montage work. One story occurs to me. I was called in to the head of the studio, Jack Warner, and he was very angry with me. He couldn't understand why I was not doing my job, and why I was getting the actors to come up and bother him when he was very busy. Apparently Greenstreet and Walter Huston, unbeknownst to me, on separate occasions had gone in and said, "You've got a young fellow on the back lot you ought to give a break to." I was very pleased, obviously, that they had done this. So I did *The Verdict,* and I did *Night unto Night,* which I really didn't do because I fell in love with the leading lady. I didn't have any idea what I was doing, and I think it shows when you look at the picture. Then I did another with her called *No Time for Flowers;* the picture was a total disaster financially, and I thought that the attitude of the producer was dishonest. We were in Vienna shooting a picture that took place in Prague. Every time I'd be shooting outside they'd say, "Oops, you can't shoot that," or "Oops, that's St. Stephen's Cathedral." And I'd say, "What am I doing here? Why am I not on the back lot?" I think that if the producer—who is alive and kicking and won't like this—had had some confidence in the property and director and cast, it might have been a much better picture. He might have made a lot more money.

Q: In the 1950s you worked with Walter Wanger. He had a reputation for being a creative producer, didn't he?

Siegel: Yes. He inspired one, and he educated one. For example, on *Riot in Cell Block 11* I knew nothing about our penal system. He had my desk so loaded with books that, if I had read everything, I never would have directed the picture; I would have had no time. He took me to Alcatraz, where we sat down and talked to the warden, and to San Quentin and Folsom. Well, I found myself giving lectures on criminology and exposing the vicissitudes that exist in our prisons. I was a surprisingly well-educated director on that subject, where normally I would have just been on the surface. On *Invasion of the Body Snatchers* it was inspirational working for him, because he recognized that the world was peopled by pods (the human-looking mongoloids who appeared in the film); even in the very studio that we were working in we realized that our superiors were pods. So it was a very pleasurable experience working with him. He was always in there thinking, coming up with bright ideas. Jerry Wald was that way, too.

Q: You did a lot of low-budget films in the 1950s. Do you think there's a good side to working under pressure, with a limited schedule and budget?

Siegel: Well, it will give you ulcers, indigestion. I don't know what the good side is. I think it's horrible to have to choose your shots economically, and not indulge yourself. You show me the bigger, better director and he'll be the one who wastes more film. Any great director shoots a tremendous amount of film; therefore, the vocabulary that he has to choose from is much greater than mine, and he can experiment more. But I don't like wasting film. I don't like shooting any sequences that are going to be cut out. You know, all of a sudden everybody's brilliant. You shoot the picture, and now they say, "Look, we can go from there to there, and take out that sequence," and everybody says, "Sensational." There goes four to six days' shooting. Why not take it out of the *script?*

Q: What about shooting television films?

Siegel: I've never done it. I've shot films for television, but I don't know what that means. I shoot them as films, starting from the very first film that was ever shot for television, *The Killers.* I think what they generally mean by television filming is that when you're making a two-shot; instead of shooting very loose, you shoot very tight. Well, I am anyway. But *Stranger on the Run, The Hanged Man,* they're films.

Q: And the shooting schedules?

Siegel: They're tight, they're tough. It's like shooting a C picture or a B-minus. You have a terribly impossible schedule, with a great amount of discipline. There I have an advantage, because I don't waste film, whereas a director who is "fatter" than I am would have trouble bringing it in in 18 days, 19 days, whatever. I've done a film in *nine* days, and I hope it's never been seen by my present associates.

Q: You produced a TV series, didn't you?

Siegel: Yes, *Jesse James.*

Q: Did you direct any of the shows?

Siegel: I directed the pilot. I worked for a very fine executive producer, David Weisbart, who was also my producer on *Flaming Star.*

Q: How did you happen to become a producer?

Siegel: Because I couldn't get a job as a director, and this was an opportunity for me. I had a decent track record as a director of pilots, so I realized there was no money in directing television, and that the cushy jobs were the producers' jobs. The producer is much more important than the director in television. The director comes in, does a three-day assignment, then he's gone—no postproduction; they can't afford it. So I produced and directed the pilot, and then became the line producer, which is a stupid, thankless job.

Q: Did you work with directors?

Siegel: Yes; it was interesting, because I thought, "Nobody's going to tell me anything about directors." So I hired them all, and I found out I didn't know anything about directors. How did I know about directors? So I made many mistakes. But out of it there was some fun; I gave directional opportunities to Curtis Harrington, Larry Peerce, Dick Colla. It only lasted one year, thank God, or I'd still be there.

Q: How did that lead to your present alliance with Universal?

Siegel: I had left them to take this job. I was with Universal and I had a remarkably successful career with them, in a short time, but I wasn't happy. I did *The Killers,* and several pilots that sold—*Destry* and *Convoy*—*Convoy's* the one that broke my back, it was so stupid. Anyway, I managed to get out by being my usual unpleasant self, and then I went to 20th. Then I said, "What's the big deal? Why was I unhappy at Universal? Is it any better at 20th?" So when the series was over, and I needed a job, Universal—through Jennings Lang—put me under term contract, which I didn't want, but which I'm still under. At least it gave me an opportunity to direct.

Q: The films that have resulted have been awfully good. I think what sets them apart more than anything is their professionalism—they're tightly made, entertaining films.

Siegel: Well, I had the advantage of all those years in montage, so that I was able to make a great many mistakes. I was able to contort the camera and do infinite experiments with the camera. Upside down, throwing it, anything. So I got it out of my system. Whereas, when I look at some films of my peers, I think they're still experimenting. I'm not self-conscious with the camera. If anything, I'm trying not to make the audience conscious of the camera. I have lots of little tricks you're taken into sometimes, so that you don't know the camera's moving.

Q: How would you describe your relationship with the cinematographer?

Siegel: I don't lean on them; that is, I don't use them for setups. But I do want their enthusiastic support, and I recognize that they know better than I do how to get what I want. I think that many cinematographers are frustrated directors. They should become directors, so that they'll be happy to go back to what they can do best, which is shoot film.

Q: Do you prefer producing your own pictures to working with someone else as producer?

Siegel: Essentially, I'm extremely lazy. Out of sheer laziness, I prefer to produce my own pictures, because it's less work. I don't argue with the director, I encourage the director, and I find it a lot easier. I don't exactly know what a producer does.

Q: What about the administrative duties?

Siegel: They can be handled very well by the production manager, who generally does them anyhow, or a unit manager. My trick in dealing with the studio is to start out making it appear that I'm going to beat the schedule. Then they forget you, they actually forget you, because you're obviously doing fine. If in the first three days of shooting you fall behind two days, *boing!* goes the computer. The picture's got a 40-day shooting schedule, and they figure it will take 75 days, so they're going to watch you like crazy. That doesn't follow. There might be many, many reasons why you're falling behind in the beginning that have nothing to do with how long it's going to take you to shoot.

Q: Is there one picture of yours that gives you special satisfaction when you look back on it?

Siegel: When I finish a picture, I'm really finished with it; I've had it. You must realize that, being an editor and following through on postproduction, I see my pictures in various forms, hundreds of times. So I'm bored. When I finish a picture, I never want to see it again. I think *The Beguiled* is definitely one of my favorites. It was the most enjoyable film I ever made. There are many reasons for it; one of the reasons is that the cast was so enthusiastic about the film, and so was the crew. We realized that it was a sharp departure from anything I had ever done. The picture that has given me the most pleasure, after it was out, is obviously *Invasion of the Body Snatchers,* because I received more recognition for that. Also, it's *about* something, and most of my pictures, I'm sorry to say, are about nothing.

Q: How does it feel to be the center of a cult?

Siegel: Pleasurable. I don't quite understand it, but I like it. I don't know why it was so late coming. But you must realize that it's a temporary thing at best; next week it will be whoever-it-is. I don't know how it's lasted this long. And I think they're going to be more and more critical of me, because as my pictures get bigger, they're not going to like me so much. My pictures *are* getting bigger. Now that I'm making more money, I'm an easier target. I think, too, that the fact that I'm getting along with the management is going to be my downfall; my cult followers are not going to like that at all. And to them I say that I'm doing the films the way I want to do them—it's just that they're *letting* me do them.

—1971

John Frankenheimer

Frankenheimer with Tuesday Weld.

Russell AuWerter

John Frankenheimer was one of the earliest directors to make the transition from television to films. At a precocious age he became famed for memorable dramas on such series as Climax and Playhouse 90. After 125 live television shows, he directed his first film, The Young Stranger. Other films include All Fall Down, The Manchurian Candidate, The Fixer, I Walk the Line, The Horsemen.

Q: When and how did you decide that you wanted to be a director?

Frankenheimer: I used to live in the movies when I was a child and, like every kid, I had terrific Walter Mitty dreams of being in movies and working in them—for all the wrong reasons obviously. I started acting when I was about sixteen in prep school and continued on through college. I wanted to be an actor. That's what I really wanted to be. In college I directed Noel Coward's *Design for Living* in the round and it was a disaster. The leading man entered and tripped over the wife of the head of the English Department. I did two years of summer stock, during which time I acted in about 20 or 30 different plays. When I graduated from college I went into the Air Force. The Air Force started a motion-picture squadron and anyone who had any type of theatrical experience or film experience could apply. So I applied and was accepted and came out here to Burbank, California (over at Lockheed Air Terminal) and started making documentary films for the Air Force—most of which were pretty ludicrous—like, they didn't know what to do with the men so they'd send them out to make films about asphalt or Hereford cattle just to keep the guys off the streets. Right away I found this more interesting than acting—the whole idea of what to do with the camera and learning about film. While I was in the Air Force I decided what I wanted to do when I got out was to get into film in some capacity. Of course, that was in 1952 and 1953 when everybody was being laid off in Hollywood—very similar to today. It was the invasion of television. Needless to say, I couldn't get a job, and so a gentleman I had met suggested that the thing I should do was try and get into live television. I ended up at CBS in New York in July as an associate director and the following year I was made a director.

Q: What were the greatest lessons or advantages you found in working in television?

Frankenheimer: To start off with, the basic thing I think you have to work with, whether you're working with television, theater or film, is story. I directed over 125 live television shows, each of which had a different script. I had a chance to work with writers on script problems, on the whole business of how to make a script work, which I think is terribly, terribly important. Secondly, I had a chance to work with a great many actors (literally thousands)—all different types of actors—all the way from Sir John Gielgud to Evelyn Rudie. I learned a great deal about cutting in live television because, after all, the live-television director certainly had the final cut. That's what went out on the air and all of our shots, contrary to what some people thought, were always preplanned. Some directors preplanned all of their shots before they started rehearsals. I didn't. I would rehearse and work with the actors for about a week and a half, and then I would decide how I wanted to shoot the show. What we were in essence doing was, on the air, functioning as film editors—I mean deciding what was going to be in close-up, what was going to be in two-shot, what we were going to dissolve, what was going to be in master shot and so forth. And also the experience and the confidence that you gain in yourself—I don't see how you can get that any other way but working. You can't get it discussing it. You can't get it in school. You can't get it sitting around swimming pools, talking about the great movies you are going to make.

Q: What were the disadvantages to working in television?

Frankenheimer: I don't know that there were many disadvantages, to tell you the truth. I think that perhaps, in terms of today's films, we bothered too much about content and form, in other words, acts one, two and three. Today the film seems to be going more and more toward the plotless type of picture. Perhaps we worried too much about this. I don't think so. But I don't see that there were any disadvantages to working in live television. I really don't. Look at the number of directors who came out of live television who are working today in film, like Ralph Nelson, Delbert Mann, Sidney Lumet, Arthur Hiller, Jack Smight—a lot of people.

Q: Were there any particular individuals whom you worked with during the days of live television who had a particularly strong formative influence on you?

Frankenheimer: There were certain individuals who had a great meaning on my career, as such, and they were men who had confidence in me—you know, at a time when I was a kid, at a time when I was certainly an unproven quantity. I would say chief among these people was Martin Manulis, who produced *Climax, Playhouse 90* and so forth. He took a chance on me—I'd only directed three or four shows—and brought me out to California to do CBS's biggest dramatic show, which was *Climax* at that time, and then *Playhouse 90.* Bill Dozier was also a great help in my career— he was head of drama at CBS in New York at that time; he and Hubbell Robinson, who was vice-president for programming. These were the men who promoted me from associate director to director. I would say that certainly they had a tremendous influence on my life because I was only one of 50 associate directors at CBS in New York, and certainly the youngest one.

Q: You directed your first television show at the age of twenty-four and your first feature film at the age of twenty-six, and were regarded as sort of a *wunderkind.* Was there any disadvantage connected with this—either then or later?

Frankenheimer: There was no disadvantage to it. I never suffered from the fact that somebody said, "Well, he's only twenty-four or twenty-five, so we shouldn't really listen to a word he's saying." I found it very difficult doing my first film, but that had really very little to do with my age, I think—it had to do with the setup I had to do it under at the time. I never found that it was a disadvantage to be young. I'm now forty, which means that I've been a director for 16 years. I think all the experience helps. I don't think it hurts in any way.

Q: How do you go about finding properties?

Frankenheimer: You have to, first of all, I think, know what interests you as a person and what you believe in. Sometimes you create properties, as in the case certainly of *Grand Prix.* That was created by me because I wanted to do a film about motor racing. I've always had a tremendous love for the sport and interest in it. I called my partner, Eddie Lewis, and said, "Listen, we've got to do a film about motor racing and I don't know what to call it—it's about Grand Prix racing." He said, "Well, let's call it *Grand Prix.*" That's how that happened. *The Manchurian Candidate* was something that George Axelrod and I decided we wanted to do together. We had been working on the script of *Breakfast at Tiffany's* and then when Audrey Hepburn was cast in the picture I was fired, because, of course, she had never heard of me— I had directed a lot of television but only one film—so I was canned. I was very upset about it, and so was George. So we said, "By God, we're going to get something that we control ourselves so that nobody can be canned." It was George's idea. He said, "Do you know a book by Dick Condon called *The Manchurian Candidate?*" I didn't, and we went across the street to a bookstore—this was in New York—and bought two copies of it. We both read it that afternoon and decided that we both wanted to do it. We bought it the following day. *Seven Days in May* came about through my meeting Edward Lewis. The two of us were going to do a television show for the American Civil Liberties Union. The show never worked out from a budgetary standpoint—but we did get to like each other and know each other. Eddie had just finished reading the galleys of *Seven Days in May* and asked me if I wanted to do it, and I read it and did want to do it. *Birdman of Alcatraz* was something I'd wanted to do when I was doing live television. As a matter of fact, at one time we owned the rights at CBS and the Bureau of Prisons said to the network, "If you do this, we'll never cooperate with you again on anything that you might want to do." As I look back on it, it was a godsend that we didn't try to do that show live—I mean, the birds would have been up in the rafters as soon as we finished the first commercial. It was a property that Harold Hecht and Burt Lancaster owned, and I had worked with them on a picture called *The Young Savages*. Out of that relationship came *Birdman of Alcatraz*. They asked me if I wanted to do it and, of course, I did. *Seconds*, again, was an idea that I believe in very strongly, which is you are what you are and you can't erase your past. When we read this novel by David Ely we decided that we wanted to do it ("we" meaning Edward Lewis and myself).

The Fixer was something that had the same theme, really, as *Birdman of Alcatraz* —which is the dignity of man, the fact that man is capable of many, many things. *Gypsy Moths* was a film about choice—I believe that you do have choice in life. I don't think that you are just a victim of your environment. Unfortunately it was sold as a film about sky-diving, which it really wasn't at all. You find properties various ways. Some you create, some you are lucky enough to have somebody come to you with, and others you find.

Q: You mentioned that one of the advantages of working in live television was working closely with writers. Do you still maintain a close working relationship with your writers on your feature films?

Frankenheimer: Very close, yes.

Q: How do you work with a writer?

Frankenheimer: You work with every writer differently. What you usually do is talk with the writer and make sure that you both want to make the same movie, because often a very talented writer may have a completely different idea about what to do with material than you have. In that case, either you have to be convinced that he is right or you have to convince him that you're right. And you have to find a writer with whom you have a common approach to the material. I usually work very closely with a writer before he starts to write—just describing what I think I would like to see. Then I let the writer write the first draft. If he has a problem, I'm there when he wants me. But I don't like looking over his shoulder at every word he is typing. Then after the first draft, we really work very closely. I mean literally scene by scene, line by line. Through the following drafts we work this way. And then I like to have the writer with me when I'm shooting, as much as possible.

Q: You have been an actor and you have worked with a tremendous number of actors, and I'm sure you have handled them in many different ways. Have you developed a special way of approaching and working with actors?

Frankenheimer: No. The only approach that I've got to working with actors is the realization that every actor is a different individual. Just as you can't have a relationship with two individuals exactly the same way, so you can't with two actors. It depends completely on the actor. Some actors need much more help than others. With some, it's best to almost leave them alone until you see what they themselves are thinking about a character. In the first place, I think that 60 percent of directing is casting. I think that you have to cast the right actor in the right role. I find that actors, the good actors I've worked with, have a tremendous amount to contribute and I don't want to stifle that creativity before they get a chance to use it. In other words, I don't want to impose a rigid pattern on the actor before he has a chance to really explore the character and find out what it's about. Sometimes out of rehearsal you get beautiful things which you never dreamed would happen. By that I don't mean that a director should not do his homework. I think you should always come in with a plan of what you want to do with a scene, but let the scene go and don't use it unless you have to. I believe in rehearsals, especially before you start shooting, if you possibly can.

Q: Is film a director's medium or is that a cliché?

Frankenheimer: The trend seems to be that the director is more and more artistically in control than he used to be. I think there are a lot of reasons for this and think that one of the big reasons is that the well-known American directors have kind of paved the way for those of us who have followed. Guys like Billy Wilder, George

tevens, Fred Zinnemann, John Ford—men like them really kind of fought our battles
or us with the studios and with executives to the point where it's a lot easier for us
ow. I hate to see young guys who have directed one movie throwing aside all the
ork that's been done by men who have forgotten more about film, in many cases,
an these guys are ever going to learn. To me it's terribly easy to be a young genius
d come along and direct one movie. It's what happens after your third and fourth
ovie that counts. In other words, what I'm talking about is a body of work. When
u say that film is a director's medium I'd love to believe you, but I can't really go

Frankenheimer directing Tuesday Weld and Gregory Peck in *I Walk the Line.*

along with it. I think you have to fight for everything you get and I think that there is no great director who can make a great film out of a lousy script. I would say that film is a collaboration between many, many people. Basically a director is dealing with over a hundred people a day, a hundred varied personalities a day. It's up to him to provide some type of leadership for these hundred people.

Q: You have made your last seven pictures with the same producer, your partner Eddie Lewis. What is the working relationship between you and your producer?

Frankenheimer: We always collaborate with script and also with the final editing. Eddie stays away pretty much while we're shooting the movie. He lets me shoot it the way I see it. And then I cut the film the way I see it. The first cut is completely mine. He never even sees it until I have the first cut. Eddie will look at the film and then recut it completely his way. Then I'll look at his version and we'll discuss both versions and usually it ends up as a mixture of both of our cuts.

Q: What films or what directors do you think are having the greatest impact on today's audiences?

Frankenheimer: That is a very difficult question to answer, because I think that these things go in fads and phases. It seems that the one common denominator for all the films that seem to be terribly successful today is that there is terrific honesty and truth to them. I think that is what young audiences care about. I don't think they give a damn about great photography. I don't think they really care that much about "the well-made movie," because, if you look at some of the films that are really "making it," they're terribly made movies from a technical sense. But they do have a basic honesty that appeals to the young audience.

Q: How would you summarize your directing style or your directing technique

Frankenheimer: I think that my directing style or technique changes with the subject matter that I do. I don't think that you can be married to a style and impose that style on everything that you do, because I think that it limits your growth. The style of *The Manchurian Candidate,* which was almost baroque, is certainly quite different from the style of *Grand Prix,* which was very large—it was the first commercial film to use the split screen—and we used Cinerama because we wanted to get the whole feeling of the Grand Prix through to the audience. The style of *Grand Prix* is very different from the style of *I Walk the Line,* which is a very intimate story of two people. My approach to directing is to first try to know as much about my subject matter as I possibly can. I really have to do a great deal of research, usually in terms of the period or of the location, that I can relate to. I do a lot of research by looking at photos. For instance, for *I Walk the Line* I looked at all the Dust Bowl photographs, all the Dorothea Lange photos and so on. Sometimes you can find a photograph and you say, "That's really what I want my movie to look like." I spend lots of time with my art director and my cameraman and assistant director going over what we want to do so that they can contribute and also so that they know exactly the kind of movie I want to make. I think it's very important that those three men know as much about the movie as I do. We have to decide what the look of the picture is going to be—that is always decided before you start shooting, what look you want. I try and stay away from—and I think most directors try and stay away from—the type of photography that you can take a frame out of and put a stamp on and mail home to your mother as a postcard. I don't make that type of movie and I don't like to make travelogues. You use a location for what it does to your story, not for the simple reason, "Gee look, Ma, I'm in Tennessee (or wherever)." I preplan the way I'm going to shoot locations as much as I possibly can—again with these same three gentlemen mentioned before. I think I could summarize it by saying I hate surprises on a movie, except in terms of rehearsing scenes with actors. I hate to be surprised by having somebody say, "Gee, I didn't know we wanted to do this." I think you have to be terribly well prepared. Out of the conversations you have with your assistant director, with your cameraman, with your art director comes really the style you're going to use in the movie. Naturally, everybody goes into something preconditioned by their own experience, but you try to be as flexible as you can in terms of the material.

—1970

John Schlesinger

William Hall

John Schlesinger's career began in a manner similar to Frankenheimer's:
he started out as an actor, then directed documentaries for British
television. His first feature was A Kind of Loving in 1962. He won both the
Academy and Directors Guild Awards in 1970 for Midnight Cowboy.
The following interview took place during the shooting of
Sunday, Bloody Sunday.

Q: How did you manage to capture the atmosphere of New York and America so vividly in *Midnight Cowboy?* You really did seem to get under the skin of the country.

Schlesinger: I think it's really a question of a total approach, of how one approaches being a director. One of the things that has interested me more than anything else in life is to observe. I was trained to observe by being both a documentary film director, working very quickly on TV, and being a stills photographer—and a very keen one. Early on I started trying to capture the essence of something in a split second.

One of the things that any director can do if he so chooses is to store up a fund of observations. I draw on it all the time. I don't necessarily go around with a notebook—though I did in some places in America for *Midnight Cowboy.* But you store things up, and then perhaps realize the possibilities of merging sound and vision in a film.

For instance, I walked past the Waldorf-Astoria once. I was in the street, but I noticed the extraordinary vivid sound of the clattering of knives and forks coming from a window above. It seemed an acute contrast with the atmosphere in the front of the Waldorf.

It's a tiny, simple thing, but I stored it up. I spend my life noticing these points. There's a terribly low standard of observation used in the cinema, I think.

Q: A lot of people were surprised that an Englishman was able to make such a vivid commentary on the American scene.

Schlesinger: I know. Everyone's astonished that an Englishman should make *Cowboy.* Why? I can't understand it. Every year since I first went to America as a student and drove across the whole country, I've taken a portable radio with me. I never go to America without my radio. You learn so much from it—and find so much you can use. It just seemed to me, even as a student, that one day I might make use of what I heard, just as I'm using in this film [*Sunday, Bloody Sunday*] an image I saw on Fifth Avenue last year.

It was a lovely sight! There was this doorman standing in the rain under a huge umbrella, looking for a cab for two customers. He was obviously an ex-opera singer reduced to being a doorman. He sang for his clients! When he couldn't get a cab for them he just stood there in the pouring rain, singing to them. I've transferred that scene to England, and it'll be in the film.

One uses all sorts of things. I keep my eyes open all the time. You've got to.

In a new country it's easier. When you're in a familiar place, routine surroundings, you often can't be bothered. It's too hot, or you're too tired, or whatever. But it's then that you must force yourself into all sorts of new experience, however trivial it may seem. It's all grist to the mill in the end.

Q: Has this observation become instinctive to you now?

Schlesinger: I think so. It's no use going around in a closed car with a chauffeur all your life. Very often I go by bus or subway, in order not to get used to being closed in. You know? Otherwise you don't ever keep in touch.

Q: Fair enough for modern films. What about period pieces like *Far from the Madding Crowd?*

Schlesinger: If you're preparing a historical film I think it's quite usual and right to send someone out to research something. But only up to a point. One has to get used to examining old prints, say, to handle them oneself. Something comes through. You mustn't sit on the sidelines too long.

For instance, Breughel is one of the most marvelous painters I know when it comes to observation. His skating works are simply wonderful. I tried to use that kind of observation in *Madding Crowd.*

Films of John Schlesinger

A Kind of Loving, 1962.

Billy Liar, 1963.

Darling, 1965.

Far from the Madding Crowd, 1968.

Midnight Cowboy, 1969.

Sunday, Bloody Sunday, 1971.

Epics become epics because they lack detail. They become shallow, without any depth or character or place. You get some of the parts, without the whole. We were very painstaking in *Madding Crowd*—but it didn't bring them in. I think the story was too slow. The film I'm doing now is full of relevant details.

Q: Do you have any feeling for what the public wants? Do you know what to give them?

Schlesinger: I really don't know what the public is attracted by. Why were people attracted to *Cowboy*? I think it touched something in everybody—for the need to make human contact with someone else in the face of fantasy that becomes adversity. I know the attitude of a lot of people before we made it was: "It's a blue movie. Why do it?" Why, there was even someone high up in the distributing company [United Artists] who went around openly saying: "It'll never be shown."

Q: What was the biggest problem you came up against in filming *Cowboy*?

Schlesinger: It was very difficult to get the flashbacks to work. One was constantly fighting against the problem of losing objectivity. I just wanted emotionally to start the journey of the Cowboy, and to use flashbacks to support this: I had to close my ears to all the people who said: "I don't think audiences will understand the objectivity of it." It's very difficult to stay faithful to the original idea if you're working for a long time on a film. In *Cowboy* the cutting seemed to take forever. It didn't work the first time, and we were very worried.

Q: How did you get off the ground initially with Dustin Hoffman and Jon Voight? Did you discuss the whole approach individually with them, or try to bring them together early on as a team?

Schlesinger: When I met Hoffman he had read the book and was obviously already thinking deeply about the character. We discussed the whole thing in terms of his character as Ratso. He said he wanted to go to a place to talk with me, a place where, if Ratso had been a success in life, he might have been, say, headwaiter! So we found ourselves in an Italian restaurant in Hell's Kitchen, talking about it over dinner. After that we went to a pool hall nearby, then ended up at an all-night hamburger joint on Forty-second Street.

We got into conversation with the strangest people, including one man we both felt was a potential killer. He had an overt politeness, even charm, but a tremendous inner violence. Hoffman had on a dirty old raincoat—it was very interesting to see the way he melted into the background, to become part of the environment.

Then he accepted the part. We did makeup tests on him to get that look of illness in his face. His teeth—we gave him false ones. People don't take enough time normally to prepare for films. I'm vitally concerned about details, however long they take to get right. The time to do it is before you start.

Voight was shaky on his Texan accent. He had never done one before. So we put him with a Texan and kept them talking together for hours. Then we went down to Big Spring, Texas, to absorb the atmosphere there. All this preparation took about two months, before we were ready to roll.

The tragedy is that an actor can be given the soft-glove treatment and start to cut corners. Hoffman, for instance, took the trouble to rehearse with every one of our candidate cowboys. I don't know if he would do it now.

I've worked in exactly the same way on this film, *Sunday, Bloody Sunday*. It's an original [he worked on the script with Penelope Gilliatt] and we rehearsed for two weeks before the first shot.

Q: How do you rehearse?

Schlesinger: I use rehearsing not as we all know it, like "You go in this door, or through that window." But I use the term more deeply, to plumb into the lives of the people you're examining. For instance, we had a scene where Hoffman accused Voight of dressing up as a cowboy. I thought: "There's something missing." We thought perhaps they would say things like: "You don't wash. . . . How often do you have it off? . . . Do you masturbate?" Things like that to lead up to it. We recorded all these open thoughts and listened to the tape and then tried organizing it so we could get it all in somehow.

A film has to have a life of its own, and this is what we try to bring out right from the start. I don't believe in a film being a blueprint, you know? As exact as that. I think I know what I'm trying to do. We don't go on the set and say to each other: "What are we trying to do?" But we've got to stay constantly aware that something may change.

I don't consider filmmaking as an eight-to-five job, and then go home and say: "Christ! I'm tired, I need a drink!" Of course, you are tired and you do need a drink. But a director has to keep going all the time he's on a film, and one of the problems is the limitation of a director's life: How long can he keep up that sort of energy?

Q: Warners has announced that you will direct *Day of the Locust* for them. How do you feel about working in Hollywood?

Schlesinger: It's all a bit premature, because I want to take a good long holiday this year, about four months off to tour Japan and the Far East. I've been working nine years with only the odd two-week break, and I figure if I can't take a holiday now, when the hell can I? I'll deliver *Sunday, Bloody Sunday,* and then head east. Next year I plan to film *Hadrian,* which is a fantasy about a writer who imagines he is Pope Hadrian VII. I usually like to do one film about every 18 months, not more.

But when I do get to Hollywood, I don't think I'll feel any differently about working there than here in London or Bray. I think it's changed now, from the days when the front office was breathing down your neck. I don't consider I would be working in conditions that would limit me. I may be wrong—I've never worked so close to the front office before!

I've never shown rushes, as a matter of course, in my entire career to the front office. And United Artists has never ever asked me to show them either tests or rushes. The first thing they see is the fine cut.

Once, when we wanted some more money on *Madding Crowd,* we showed selected rushes to MGM. Why don't I show them? Simply because I don't think anybody else is in a position to judge a film except those who are closest to it. I want everyone to see the film who is working on it. In America on *Cowboy* I found very few of the unit who would put themselves out to see it.

Everyone on my film is totally welcome. On this film the rushes are absolutely crammed with people from all walks of the picture, electricians, props, the lot. I find that marvelous. It's very gratifying.

In America, I remember one of our operators wanted to be paid overtime to see what had been photographed!

Q: You have said you prefer making films about losers than about winners. Why?

Schlesinger: Heroes just don't interest me a bit. The goody who is really a ——— would interest me! I don't believe there are any goody-goodies. They don't exist. And I want my films to mirror life. If there is any common thread in my work, I suppose it is that I'm basically very interested in people, and on the whole, people don't lead basically happy lives. You've got to work bloody hard to be happy.

I'm interested in the difficulties people go through. I'm not really interested in success stories. I'm much more intrigued by failure. I would prefer to study a coward than a hero.

Q: What difference have the Academy and Directors Guild Awards made to you?

Schlesinger: It's made me more paranoid! But really, I suppose it's made no difference in my life. It was very nice, of course, to be recognized by one's colleagues. It's a recognition of one's efforts. But in the final analysis awards aren't that important.

Jon Voight, Dustin Hoffman, and Schlesinger during the shooting of *Midnight Cowboy*.

I don't think one should set great store by them, and I'm suspicious of people who do. I was glad I was working on something when it was announced that I'd won the Oscar for *Cowboy*. Otherwise, it would have made the choice of the next film very difficult. The fear of what is expected of one as a result of Establishment accolade is a genuine one. It would be silly of me not to admit it. You're as good as your last picture, and if it doesn't make money—you're out.

It's the most short-lived industry in the world! It's filled with petty people and unsuccessful people who are struggling to keep their heads above water. The people who are the most successful are the most generous. They can afford to be!

Q: We talked about Hollywood. How do you feel about working in America generally?

Schlesinger: Artistically speaking, I found on *Cowboy* that I had some excellent people working with me. I worked with rather a mixed bag, actually—I had some of the best and some of the worst people I've ever been with. But freelance crews are always better than studio crews, because you can hand-pick the best of the bunch. I had a studio crew. On this film, now, everybody's interested—and it's not a very easy film to be interested in. There's an awful lot of chat! The basic difference between American and British crews is that American crews are prepared to work longer hours. They get paid very well for it, but there's never a problem on overtime.

Q: Is there any basic message you are trying to put across in your films?

Schlesinger: I don't think I can pontificate about my pictures. If people come away feeling they've learned a little more about other people, that's fine. Or that they've got a little more knowledge or understanding.

I'm not interested in politics. I don't want to preach. But if one goes through all the agony of making a film, you want it to say something at the end. I always say I want to make a mad comedy, but I don't think I want to unless underneath it all there's something important to say.

The actual making of a film is nothing short of dire agony for me. It's a sad thing to confess, but I don't enjoy making a movie. I never have. The preparation is fine, lively and stimulating. When you see it beginning to jell—that's the exciting time. But I find it such a difficult business living up to the way I thought it should go, to try and get it up on the screen, that it becomes a painful operation. That's why I hate talking about it.

A film is an animal of change. It may not turn out to be the same thing you talked about. So you lay yourself wide open.

Q: Which of your films gives you the greatest pleasure to remember?

Schlesinger: I remember the first and the last: *A Kind of Loving* and *Midnight Cowboy*. They come close to what one sets out to make in the first place, and they are my own personal favorites. *Loving?* Because I think it worked.

The least successful for me now is *Darling*. I think it is the one that's dated most quickly. But at the time, I adored making it and was very pleased with it.

With *Billy Liar* we could have taken the whole thing a lot further. With *Cowboy* they were both extraordinary and interesting characters, a bit larger than life. They fascinated me. From the moment I read the book I just knew it was the film I wanted to make.

Q: It sounds like you eat and sleep the film while you're making it.

Schlesinger: I do, six days a week. But now I've adopted an absolute system. The routine is this—I get more and more depressed as I go on making a film. I avoid seeing the stuff cut and I try to escape completely on Sundays! I can't work seven days a week. In fact, I find it incredible that someone like Kubrick can. I don't know how he does it. Then, when it's all finished, I take the next plane out of the country. After two weeks away I can come back to the editing, refreshed.

Q: How do you feel about having to work in color now?

Schlesinger: I'd much rather make *Sunday, Bloody Sunday* in black and white. But we're now a slave of the box, TV. It's very sad, but it'll go on until someone makes a great success in black and white, and then everyone will go back to it.

We're in the hands of the people who think everything must be in color. But the public will take what they're given. Actually, I'm glad that in the end I made *Cowboy* in color—we needed all those garish lights. I think that usually color glamorizes everything very highly. I don't want anything to get between me and the public. It's also extremely difficult to control the color tones in mass printing—the system is usually so bad. There are more quarrels between directors and laboratories than anyone realizes over the quality of prints!

Put it this way: I'd rather see a TV newsreel in black and white than color, and interviews, too. I've got a color TV in my basement and a small Sony black-and-white upstairs. When the newsreels come on, I always go upstairs to see them on the tiny black-and-white screen.

Q: Any thoughts on your own future?

Schlesinger: I'm rather stale now! As I said, nine years on the trot is a long time without a real break. Ask me again at the end of the year.

—1970

59

Robert Altman

Altman puts the final touches on apparatus for filming Bud Cort in flight in Houston Astrodome for *Brewster McCloud.*

Russell AuWerter

Few directors have had such varied careers as Robert Altman. After leaving the Air Force he wrote radio scripts, magazine articles and screen treatments in Hollywood, then moved to New York to attempt plays and novels. During this time he earned a living from such occupations as tattooing dogs for identification purposes. For eight years he turned out industrial films in his native Kansas City before returning for another go at Hollywood.

Altman wrote, directed and produced his first film, The Delinquents, *for United Artists in 1955, then began a career in television, directing such shows as* Kraft Theater, Bonanza *and* Combat. *In 1957 he made* The James Dean Story. *His second feature was* Countdown, *followed by* That Cold Day in the Park *and* M*A*S*H, *the movie that established him as a major director. He was interviewed during the preparation of* McCabe and Mrs. Miller.

Q: Was it a surprise to you that M*A*S*H was such a box-office success?

Altman: Hell yes. I think the reason the picture is really such a big success is that it doesn't alienate any audience. All the people who would not see Easy Rider will see M*A*S*H. The people who are very "hawkish" think it's a funny dirty war comedy.

Q: How has the success of M*A*S*H affected your career?

Altman: I had a hard time getting M*A*S*H. Now everybody overcorrects. I don't think I'm any different now. Everything is offered to you. It's made me a success, both in my profession and financially. If I wanted to sign deals, I could just say, "Yeah, I'll do this and do that." I could lock myself up for three or four years and not do half the pictures and pick up 150,000 dollars a year and just lie on my bed up here.

Q: Do you feel any disadvantages in this success?

Altman: Any success is a disadvantage. It's part of the whole thing. In the first place, everybody gathers together in failure. I have a lot of people who work for me. I do not work alone. I have, really, a staff, or a crew, or a group, or whatever you want to call it, that fluctuates between six and ten people, who are with me on all the pictures I do and with me on a lot of pictures I never get to do. When things are going badly, they're like a rock. They stay together and they'll do anything. Success makes you more frightened. You have a tendency to want to copy yourself. You start making a comparison of the project you're doing with the project that was successful. You kind of get set up for the critics. You say, "Gee, now they're going to be after me. Before, they were on my side." It's like being a politician. It takes on political implications. It's popularity and being able to deliver.

Q: How did you first become involved with the M*A*S*H project?

Altman: It came to me after the screenplay was written. The novel of M*A*S*H was written by a Richard Hooker. It was sent by the publishing company to Ring Lardner, Jr., to write a foreword about. Ring saw something in it and sent it to Ingo Preminger, who used to be his agent. Ingo went to Zanuck at Fox and made a deal to buy the thing and to have Ring Lardner, Jr., write the screenplay. They got the screenplay done—the first draft—and sent it around to about 15 directors. Everybody starts with a list. They say, "Well, let's get Kubrick." They then go for Nichols, or Arthur Penn. Finally they got down to me. A lot of guys turned it down. Most people weren't available. They didn't want to go with a picture like this with one of the solid (I don't want to call them "old-timers") directors like a Zinnemann or a David Lean. So, immediately those people are knocked off the list. You get down to where what everybody is searching for is a director who will really allow them to sell their package, or can attract stars, or can attract something. I read it and didn't like it. But I saw in it the opportunity to do something I had been working on for about five years, which was a World War II farce. It wasn't about the medical thing, but it had the same basic philosophy. I had a meeting with Ingo in my office and I told him what I felt about it. I told him I felt it would have to be very loose, very rambling. Anything that even looked like plot had to come out. Anything that looked like construction had to come out. I talked for a long time and I said, "If you agree with me, I'd like to make the picture with you." He said, "I agree." He backed me 100 percent, right down the line, and that's really how it got done.

Q: What was your next step? Did you turn your team or group on to the project? How do you work when you're starting from scratch on a picture?

Altman: Some I got hired by Fox and put on it. We take a project and we start out in the very simple terms of the way you would approach any picture. Sometimes it will be a very explicit plot line and sometimes it won't. Nobody really knows what his job is. They all know what it is, but it's not confined to any area. What happens is, as the thing starts settling in, everybody kind of finds out what they do. These guys will do a different kind of thing on each picture. On one film they may pick up the visual look and work on that more. In another one they may get into logistics. During *Brewster McCloud* I said, "Who's been watching the budget?" because the wings in *Brewster McCloud* came out right on budget. It wasn't like Leon Erickson—who designed them and built them—he doesn't think about money one way or the other, which is good. And they said, "Ross has been watching the budget." Well, Ross was the second assistant editor on *M*A*S*H* and he was on *That Cold Day in the Park* as the assistant on the dressing and the look of the film. He's sitting there on his own, running this thing, going into Leon and saying, "We can't spend this," and "We should do this," and he's keeping a running thing on the budget. Nobody asked him to. I didn't even know he was doing it. Those are the kinds of things. And it's not that unique. It happens in major studios sometimes, I don't think enough, but . . . If people become really enthused on a project, you'll find that you've got a lot of artists working for you that you never see. Like, we've been doing research on *McCabe and Mrs. Miller*. My secretary, Ann, has gone to librarians, she's getting some private diaries about whores and she's compiled it. We're getting all this research, which is truth. It's now about at a stage where we will turn around and reverse it and say, "Okay, these are all the things people wrote about; now let's look behind the lines and see what really went on."

Q: With all these production people utilizing a great deal of freedom and creativity, what brings things together? Is there a periodic shape-up? Do you use conferences? How do you keep all those things in touch?

Altman: There is a lot of waste. Every time we try and tighten it up, we lose. In each picture, it seems like some guy gets too successful and tries to go and do it the way it's done other places. There is a lot of waste in mistakes and there's a lot of double effort and occasionally there's total loss in the thing. But there still is that enthusiasm. Going back to *Brewster,* I saw some license plates come up for all these automobiles that we used in the picture. I said, "Jesus." They were marvelous and we featured them. One license plate was "DUV 222." They all related to birds and yet you really don't notice them— except you do. I said, "Who did that?" It was this guy. Yet he didn't come and say, "Hey, look what I did." It was never brought up. We were building a city up in Vancouver. This is just an absolute true fact: Warren Beatty came into town and we went up together. I wanted to show him the location. We drove up to this little site and there is a guy up to his waist in dirty water and he's pulling a log through the thing and he's got a beard and tattoos on him. He's my art director on the picture. He was a carpenter two pictures ago. He says, "Hi, Bob" and waves and he smiles (this is gratuitous). I said, "Hey, you're gonna do my bridge after all," because we had an argument whether we would have a bridge across the water. And he came up to me and said, "I figured out a way to make your bridge, because there are two trees that happen to be there that would work." He put a whole little structure in that allows for this bridge I wanted to be there. So he's up to his ass in mud and water building this bridge with some other guy, and I mean this is really hard work. Those people up there—and I know they're not on dope, so they're not just up there stoned—they really love what they're doing.

Q: Can you articulate your role in this whole process?

Altman: Yeah, I think I pull it all together, by starting it and by letting it happen. I know pretty much the picture I want to make. Most times I know how to articulate it, but I'm afraid the minute I articulate it it gets ruined. With actors I don't like to talk too early or too much about the thing. I don't want to know that much and I don't want them to know that much. I think that if I approach a film intellectually— and I can take anything in *M*A*S*H,* or on any picture and say, "Oh, yeah, the reason for this is . . ."—I can justify and rationalize. But when I do it intellectually, it is transmitted to the audience intellectually. But I think if it is transmitted emotionally, it's received emotionally. So the minute I know something works, I say, "That's right.

I know that's right." I just refuse to go into any more exploration of it. Now, it's impossible not to, which is a nice safeguard, because you do anyway. But I really avoid trying to overthink the thing, overstate it, to rip it down.

Q: Has your method of working evolved slowly or did you suddenly come upon this way of thinking?

Altman: I've always worked this way. You evolve each time. Each time you learn something. But I have been doing basically the same kind of thing. I must say it wasn't very popular either. I got fired for many years for doing a lot of the things that I'm now getting accolades for.

Q: Do you treat all actors differently? How do you work with individual actors?

Altman: Oh, yes. When I'm working with an actor early in the thing, I talk generally about the story or the look of the picture. In McCabe and Mrs. Miller, which we are doing in Vancouver, the thing I'm concerned with is the look of the picture. So I'll talk to them about what I think the picture is about. And I'll talk to them a great deal about what I think other characters are about. I'll talk to them very superficially about their character, until I get a response from them. Then at some time—I don't know when—I start saying "you" rather than "McCabe." Like when Warren [Beatty] and I flew up, I was saying, "And I think a guy like McCabe would come in and he would . . ." Now, by the time we got back, I was saying, "Maybe what you would do would be . . ." But I'm changing at the same time. I haven't got a clear-cut idea. I know what I want the picture to be. But that doesn't mean I know what I want this character to be exactly. I don't think that a picture would be the same with Richard Burton in it. You do the same picture with Peter O'Toole and it would be two different pictures. Everything moves. Many elements change.

Q: How does your approach, as you have been describing it, apply to casting? How do you approach casting?

Altman: I start off with all the clichés. My first two or three thoughts on every subject are just terrible. Because they are so on the nose. But I find I have to get rid of these. I have to say it. I also have to feel free to say it in order to get by it and get onto something else. I don't know how I cast. I really don't. I know how to say, "No, that's not right," and yet sometimes I can't tell anybody why. I cast very fast. I'll respond very quickly and in most cases make my mind up very fast to the character.

Q: You used quite a few actors in Brewster McCloud who were previously in M*A*S*H. It has been said that you have some kind of repertory group that you're working with. Is this a pattern that you consciously use?

Altman: I don't know. The guy who had the lead in Brewster McCloud had a minor part in M*A*S*H. It was his first film. When I was reading Brewster and first really going into it, I said, "Jeez, I don't think you could cast this picture," and I said, at that time, that I would do it if I could use this kid. I just never moved off of him. I think that you find security in people who like you and respond to you and know you and who you know work well together. I put together about 40 actors in a repertory group in McCabe. Most of them are Canadian, and I don't know any of them. I'm bringing a couple of the actors like John Chuck, who was the Painless Pole in M*A*S*H, and he played in Brewster. He said, "I want to be in your picture." I said, "Well, I can't, John, there aren't any parts. I'm putting together, like 40 miners and whores, and I'm not going to pay that kind of money." He said, "Well, I want to be in the picture." So he is taking a severe cut to come up and play a role that's unnamed. I'll probably build the group around him, but that doesn't necessarily mean that he'll come out of it.

Q: I read the novel M*A*S*H after seeing the picture and this made me conscious

Altman with Sally Kellerman on location.

of the fact that a lot of the lines in the film were thrown away or mumbled. In watching the picture I always had the feeling that there were things outside of the frame that supported the things that were in the frame. It was a great indirect buttressing.

Altman: Yeah. The real conscious point that we took in *M*A*S*H* was that if we had to go in for a close-up or underline a joke or a joke depended on a line reading or a word—we threw it out. That was the whole idea of having more going on outside the frame than was inside the frame.

Q: Did you do this with *Brewster?*

Altman: I don't know what I did with *Brewster.* I know the stuff is good in it, but whether the whole picture together is going to work or not is questionable, because this is an essay in a way, and the line is very funny. It's comic strip in many ways—a lot of it. I think it can be a hell of a picture. Really good. I know it's a better picture than *M*A*S*H,* because I think that was just timing. I think just everything got together. *McCloud* was a very funny picture. It wasn't an unhappy experience in any way, but there wasn't any fun in making the picture, because it was so spread out and I had so many actors down there [Houston, Texas] and I put them on for the full run of the picture. The script we went by was something that nobody really saw. I didn't do that for any dramatic reasons or anything. It was just that kind of vehicle. These guys would sit down there and they would have featured parts or starring parts. During the eight weeks we were there, they would work maybe half a day a week. Then one week they would work three days in a row. Actors are funny. They get very paranoid and they are sitting back and saying, "Jeez, I'm not going to be in the picture," because we were doing it in very fragmented style. So it got very rough.

Q: Did you cut it with a live audience finally?

Altman: I don't cut it with a live audience as much as I let anybody, within reason, see the film. We have big groups of people at dailies and you get responses. Each time I add more people to each screening and bring some of the people who have already seen it. This thing is like *M*A*S*H*, there's no story to it really. There is, but it's such a thin line we can change it and move around. *McCabe* I shot in sequence and it will undoubtedly be cut in sequence.

Q: What do you see ahead for yourself? What are the things that you haven't done that you want to do?

Altman: I really like making films. I like *MAKING* films. I like them to be successful, but . . . It's like each film is a lifetime. It really is. It's like a sudden whole thing. People talk about extending their lives with shots and monkey glands and all this jazz—I know people, including myself, who sit and do the same thing, wash the car every Sunday, and suddenly 20 years have passed and they don't know what's happened. Two weeks ago I drove through the Austrian Alps, I was gone for eight days. In four days I drove every road that can be driven from Innsbruck to Salzburg in an eight-mile radius. That trip seemed like it was a month. I'll talk about that, not now, but in two weeks from now. I'll say, "Hell, I know Innsbruck, Austria." And I was there maybe four days. It's like a lifetime. It's the very fact of doing something. When you go into a new film, you're going into a whole new experience of life, new people.

Everybody's up.

Everybody's high, a natural high. So you are aware of every moment.

—1971

George Stevens

Leonard Maltin

Everyone knows George Stevens as one of the important figures in American film, the director of, among others, Alice Adams, Swing Time, Gunga Din, Woman of the Year, The More the Merrier, I Remember Mama, Shane, The Diary of Anne Frank, The Greatest Story Ever Told *and two DGA Award winners,* A Place in the Sun *and* Giant.

But Stevens' career did not begin with Alice Adams, *his first dramatic feature. For ten years before his big break came he worked in the field of the two-reel comedy, as both cameraman and director, and later in the realm of the comedy feature. Many film buffs and historians brush over this phase of Stevens' career, which is a great injustice. Stevens' work in comedy shorts and features remains among the finest examples of both genres; his neglected* Boy Friends *shorts for Hal Roach are both delightfully entertaining and cinematically inventive—much more so than work being done by many current directors. His feature films such as* Kentucky Kernels *and* The Nitwits, *with Wheeler and Woolsey, are models of solidly constructed, genuinely amusing comedies.*

Q: How did you come to be a cameraman at the Hal Roach studio?

Stevens: I was really a kid at the time, and I had been interested in photography as a kid, as a hobby. I was in the theater world, but looking for a job in the film business. There were no unions, so it was possible to become an assistant cameraman, if you happened to find just when they were starting a picture. There was no organization; if a cameraman didn't have an assistant, he didn't know where to find one. And I learned a little bit about it; I was on a picture for four or five days. I had an opportunity to be on a set, and the assistant cameraman kept showing me things. One day I climbed the fence, knowing they needed an assistant cameraman. A couple of days later I was one, but the first day or two it was pretty disastrous. I knew something about photography, and I caught on quick.

When I stayed on with Roach, I started doing some things that they weren't doing, because they were very old-fashioned about the photography in their comedies. I worked first with Fred Jackman, who was making pictures with Rex, the King of the Wild Horses. I was cameraman on that, and he was director; his brother was cameraman. I knew about panchromatic film, and they didn't. I had bought the plates from England, a photo store there; we got some extraordinarily good effects, and he liked it. I finished those pictures, and there was nothing left to do but photograph comedies if I wanted to stay with Hal Roach. I hated two-reel comedies, but I got on the Laurel and Hardy pictures and that was great. Roach used to direct a picture every now and then, and he was directing this one. About noon he said, "You direct it." He would make one picture a year, and he would always pick the wrong story and get in trouble with it. So I said, "Not for me." I thought what he was doing was silly enough without my trying it. He insisted, and I said, "No, I can't do it, Hal." So he said, "Well, what do you want to do?" I said, "If you want me to direct a picture, let me get my own story, so I'll know what I'm doing." So I did, and it was *The Boy Friends* series.

Q: So you were writing as well as directing?

Stevens: Well, the first thing we did was with a chap named Warren Burke, a bright young fellow who had had a good part or two as a youngster and then there was no more acting for him. He came with me, and we put our first script together. We didn't know too much about it. I photographed it, and it was all right. The next one was terrible. We tried the wrong kind of story, one in which these people were supposed to be comedians rather than people. It was really bad. I had to make retakes on it, and they were the most painful things I ever did in my life. I knew the first thing we did was bad, the retakes were just as bad. I was so agonized, I don't think I ever made another retake on a picture. If there was something I was suspicious of, I'd fix it then. I didn't want the agony of having done something wrong in the first place, and bringing some poor people back with the confidence that you're going to do it better. If they don't rebel and say, "This is idiotic," then you know they're misplacing their trust. The whole thing is appalling.

Q: The Boy Friends comedies seem to have been designed more as silent comedies than talkies; they have great visual ideas, but little dialogue of note. Did you think of them in that way?

Stevens: Yes. The only pictures we were making at Hal Roach were silent comedies that spoke; it was just after the transition to sound. The first Laurel and Hardy pictures were really silent comedies. The script was written without any regard for dialogue. The situations were described, with maybe an occasional line. In the silent pictures they'd do the picture and then the titles would be written. Hiram Walker was the title man; he was very funny. So when the dialogue pictures started, the script was written, then it went to Walker, and he'd do the dialogue. So the three or four pages of script were here, and eight or ten pages of dialogue were here; it was sort of non sequitur. The dialogue was usually very awkward in the Hal Roach pictures, including the Laurel and Hardys. In *The Boy Friends* pictures all of a sudden somebody would stop and say something. We depended on situations and sight gags; we were inept with dialogue. The next thing I did was to think of the words as much as the visual aspect. Have you seen any of these *Boy Friends* comedies?

Q: Yes, I love them.

Stevens: Did you see the one with the glider?

Q: Many times.

Stevens: I haven't seen them since I made them. I was telling Hal [Roach] about this the other day. You know, we had no process shots, so how do you pretend this glider is up in the air? How do you get it up there in the first place? There was a cliff, where the top of Marine Del Rey is now, that had an edge where we could move along. We got two big sticks which they use to hoist girders. I hooked the glider on a 100-foot one, and the camera on an 80-foot one. We ran it along the edge of the cliff! It was absolutely terrifying, because when it would start to roll, you had the camera boom over you. At least the actor [Grady Sutton] had a glider!

Q: Your *Boy Friends* films were full of unusual shots. In a football scene you looked at a huddle up from the ground. That was something you just didn't see in other Hal Roach comedies.

Stevens: They were so simple. They shot here, and they'd move the camera there. I guess those shots (like the huddle) would look elementary now, because we've all seen that, but they hadn't then.

Q: Was there improvisation on those films?

Stevens: Almost totally. You'd have a scheme of what you wanted to do, that was all. Say Laurel and Hardy were getting out of a car and they go and ring a doorbell of this house. One of them would go to ring it, and he'd push the other fellow's hand away and say, "I'll ring it." He would ring it, but it would be the

Gertie Messinger, Grady Sutton, Edgar Kennedy (the cop), Betty Bolen, Mickey Daniels, Mary Kornman, David Sharpe in Stevens' *High Gear*.

wrong door, and an old lady would slam the door in his nose. By the time you'd get to the doorway, you'd have fun with the scene.

Q: How did you come to leave Roach?

Stevens: I got fired from Roach, because my films had been turning out better than they had expected. Roach wanted to do a certain kind of picture, like the kind he had started that didn't work. I did gag pictures, because with gags you could get laughs with people who weren't so expert as comedians. I did the football picture and the glider picture, and then one day somebody said that Hal wanted to see me. He told me a story he wanted me to do. I couldn't see it at all, and I'd just started on something else. So I thought it over, and I said, "Hal, I can't do it. I don't understand it." He told it to me again. I said, "Look, I'm working on something else." In fact, I'd previewed this football picture the Friday night before, and it got laughs like you'd get with Laurel and Hardy. He hadn't seen it, and this was kind of an obstinate thing on his part. He was going to do something a certain way. He said, "Now, this is what I'd like to see in this picture." I said, "Hal, I can't do it." A half-hour later the studio manager called and said, "George, I'm terribly sorry. I've got very bad news." I said, "What is it?" He said, "Hal wants to cancel your contract." It was a little shocking to me, but I said, "If that's the way it is, then okay." That finished me with the Hal Roach studio. It was during the Depression, and things were very bad. Everybody was on half-salary, and the other half went into the studio fund. But if you should leave, you'd get your back half-salary.

The first major Stevens film, *Alice Adams*, with Fred MacMurray and Katharine Hepburn.

They gave me a party because I was getting my back half-salary and nobody else was! It delighted Laurel and Hardy, and Charley Chase and the others. "Oh, you lucky so-and-so," they said. Nobody could get a job at that time, but they sent me out delighted, with my back half-salary. I put it in the bank in Culver City, and the building is still closed. Then Warren Doane, who had been manager for the Hal Roach studios, promoted Universal the idea of making two-reel comedies. Jim Horne, who'd made a lot of pretty good comedies, had left Roach, too. Warren got Jim Horne and myself to make comedies alternately. We didn't have much money; there was a small fee for the writer, a little better one for the director. So on Jim's pictures I was the writer, and I'd pick up that fee, and on my picture he was the writer, and he picked up the fee.

Q: What kind of shorts were you doing?

Stevens: We made story shorts. I started making shorts where I would write a story and use more realistic people. I made a picture with Raymond Hatton and Jimmy Gleason, a cowboy story with a baby. Then I did a picture with Frankie Albertson and June Clyde. They'd run for the regular time of shorts, and they were good. After a number of those, Universal wanted me to do a feature picture, to find out what would happen. George Sidney and Charlie Murray were at the end of the line [with their *Cohens and Kellys* series]; they had one picture left to do, and I did it with them. I had no contract with Universal, and they were talking to me about a feature contract. Then they closed the studio. That was the real depression.

But at RKO they had some comedies to make, so I made a deal to do six shorts. I didn't want to make them, but if I did, I could make a feature. Before I finished the six shorts, they had a feature picture they needed somebody to make; I made it, and then I didn't do any more shorts. There's a funny thing about the feature. It was a nice little story, and the writer of the script was pretty good; it wasn't my problem, as most of the others became. But the cast was filled with semi-stars, passé stars, not-quite people, and I said, "Why don't you let me fill in with some other actors under contract?" They said no, I had to use these people, and that was that. So I made the picture, and it wasn't bad. It wasn't until years later that I found out what had happened: RKO had contracts with six actors, each with one picture to go. So Louis Brock, the producer said, "I'll make a picture and use up all the contracts for you at one time." And that's exactly what happened.

Q: While you were at RKO you did some shorts with Edgar Kennedy.

Stevens: I don't remember how many I did with Ed, but I remember one where he shot a hole in the roof of a train, and it started to snow. We called that the *Happy Valley Express*.

Q: I wanted also to ask you about your Wheeler and Woolsey comedies. The end of *Nitwits* is a gag sequence borrowed from one of *The Boy Friends* comedies.

Stevens: I remember we did a gag with Wheeler and Woolsey where a kid tried to put together an ersatz machine gun, and we used berries instead of bullets.

Q: Did you find it a difficult transition from short comedies to feature films?

Stevens: It was the easiest thing in the world, because short comedies had to be laughed at. You'd go to the theater and if they didn't laugh, it was deadly. And I had had experience with shorts doing a story. Whenever I got a story into a short— if the story was light and convincing—the audience would stay right with you. You didn't have that awful void if they weren't laughing. So to go over into a feature story was very simple for me, very easy, because the story would work. The problem for me was not to seize a gag opportunity and thus deface the story by putting in some gag business. It was very easy for me to do that; I went for a gag many times when I shouldn't have.

Q: How did you get the opportunity to move up to such an important picture as *Alice Adams*?

Stevens: I did another little picture before that from Gene Stratton Porter's story *Laddie*. It was a pretty good little "straight" picture. Katharine Hepburn was a big star at RKO then, and the studio had this story *Alice Adams*. They were considering two directors, neither one of whom they knew much about. One was William Wyler, and the other was me. For some reason they talked to me about it, and I was very interested. They said, "Would you have a visit with Katharine Hepburn?" I said, "Well, I've got this comedy, and I've got to fix up these gags." I wanted time to read the book. I said, "Could we wait?" and they said, "No, because we have to make this decision between you and the other young director." So they said, "Let's make it this evening," and I said, "Okay, let's make it at her house, after I finish shooting." She was a young but grand lady in the studio, and I was shooting this stuff with guys falling into mortar and things. I thought, "If Katharine Hepburn sees this, she'll want to air the house out, knowing there's this kind of association." So I talked with Kate and I hadn't read *Alice Adams*, which was kind of ridiculous. But I wanted to make it and I knew enough about Tarkington to get by. She told Pandro Berman, the producer, "I don't know about that guy. He won't talk about the story." Berman said, "Well, he's a strange fellow; but if he wants to make this picture, he ought to make the picture, even if he has very little to say about the story." They agreed that I would make the picture, and we got along just fabulously. They had a very bad script, terrible script; it was long and didn't seem like the Booth Tarkington I'd read. So I started to read the book, and it was fascinating. We started the picture, and we shot it from the book. I worked with Morty Offner, who hadn't been on the original script. We'd dictate dialogue from the book for three or four pages and do that scene. We finally got a few days ahead. We were often changing it as we went along, until we got to the finish, and we did something a little different there.

As far as making a picture was concerned, I was on very solid ground with a book like that, with excellent actors. Grady Sutton even came into it. We had one casting difference. I wanted to use Frankie Albertson for her brother, and she despised the idea of his being her brother; she wanted a more classical New York actor. But that wasn't the family she was in; this was an American guy who didn't speak too well and got his hair cut in the wrong barbershop. So Frankie did it and did it very well, and she was rather happy with that. Film was never a problem to me as long as you had a story; if you didn't have a story, you were on some tenuous line of interest in keeping an audience with you on the basis of what might happen next—that's always difficult.

—1970

Richard Lester

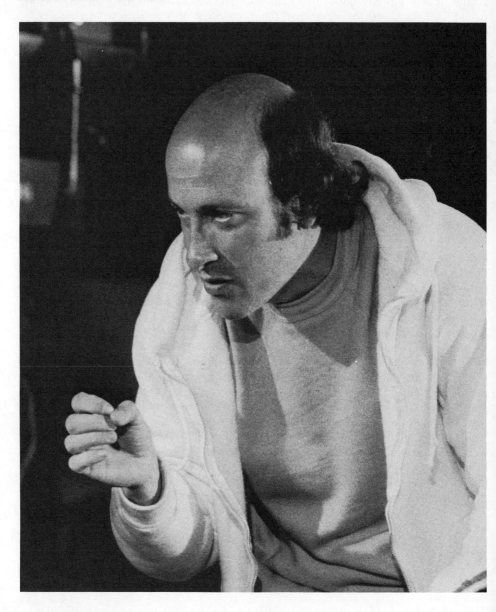

William Hall

Richard Lester was born in Philadelphia, got a B.S. degree in clinical psychology at the University of Pennsylvania and went to England in 1955. He worked on the "Goon" comedy shows in British radio and television before going on to commercials and feature films. His first hit was A Hard Day's Night *with the Beatles in 1964. During the making of* The Bed-Sitting Room *he talked about the influence that the more than 500 commercials he's made have had on his feature films, which include* Help!, The Knack, A Funny Thing Happened on the Way to the Forum *and* Petulia.

We have this sequence on a rubble heap in the middle of a pile of bombed-out ruins. It's quite desolate—not a blade of grass, not a green bush anywhere. No trees. Only gray rocks and bricks and dust. Two men are standing in the middle of the rubble. We go into them, and suddenly—wham! They're having a custard-pie fight, and a custard pie goes straight into the camera. It's slapstick on the surface, but you know the bombs have fallen, and underneath it's a different picture altogether.

Instant impact. I suppose I learned that from the commercials I directed, and a lot of that approach has rubbed off into my feature films. I had no film schooling in the accepted sense—most people come up through the cutting rooms or on the floor via assistant directors. I didn't. I learned through making commercials, and I was doing them at the rate of 80 a year for six years—and doing feature films as well. I must have done about 500 commercials in my life, and although now I don't get too much time, I still like to fit them in when I can. I made only two in 1967, and one last year [1968] for Carnation Milk.

I remember the first one I ever did—coming new from advertising. I was full of jolly ideas. I took five drawings that were unclear thematically, without any real link, and went to a Dr. Bernardo's Home and asked some kids what they meant. We taped their comments and got them to make up stories about the drawings. Then we made a continuous sound track of it, and went out and filmed their "story."

We were doing it for Cadbury's Coaster Biscuits, and we got three commercials out of that one idea. We had them munching biscuits up a tree and in a park—and although it won me an award in Hollywood, the commercials were banned in Britain! Someone pointed out that we forgot to show the kids brushing their teeth after eating the biscuits—at least, I think that was one of the reasons!

But in those early days we had a certain vitality that was not present in advertising. And commercials are nothing else *but* instant impact, aren't they? You're competing with a time slot, and you've got to make an immediate impression.

It isn't easy to say just where my commercial ideas overlap into my feature films. I'm influenced by all the films I've ever seen and by all the directors I admire. I'm influenced by everything that's happened to me. To try to tie anything down is virtually impossible. But ideas come to me at all times (and sometimes at no times), and while I think my feature films are more *personal* than my commercials, the best ideas come out of sheer unadulterated panic! I'm very much an end-of-the-fingertips filmmaker, and when I'm trying to get out of trouble, that's when the adrenalin comes splashing through!

That's why I leave a lot of filmmaking until I'm on the floor. Things happen— maybe someone breaks a leg and it's like a gift from heaven, and you've got three whole new scenes in the can!

Perhaps you remember the scene in the Beatles film *Help!,* where they walk into four front doors in a street of houses, and it turns out to be one room? Instant impact—and quickly forgotten. But it made its mark. One thing I learned from commercials was that people are always muddling up form and content. Form must always come next to content, although it's the only means available to a director to produce the content in a usable way. If it becomes a stylistic exercise, and there's an indication in some commercials today of this happening, then in terms of feature filmmaking you're always going to land in trouble.

The only time I've taken a stylized approach was in *Help!,* and that was because we had to use a series of audiovisual images. It was a biography of four living people, but we'd already shown their working hours in *A Hard Day's Night,* and we couldn't show their real private lives, either. So we had no recourse but to make the Beatles completely passive as performers and build a stylized film around them.

I work a lot by instinct, and then spend six months in the cutting rooms to complete the job. But to begin with I like working with a writer, preferably one man, because I'm not good enough to work on my own. Once behind the cameras, I always look through at least one camera for every shot, because I usually work with three, and I like to be looking through one lens myself when someone's performing, to see what I'm getting.

This is where my commercial training comes in—as it does, I think, when we have to improvise. Audiences, and critics too, rarely seem to realize why a scene might have been made the way it has. Sometimes it isn't just for effect, but through necessity. Like in *A Funny Thing Happened on the Way to the Forum*, which isn't a favorite film of mine. So much of what people call technique or style is simply getting out of trouble.

That scene with Buster Keaton running away from the camera—we didn't know how ill he was, and it was written as a continuous shot. But after four steps, he's out of breath. We had to bring in a stand-in, and the result was: close-up of Keaton, long shot of the stand-in running, then another close-up of Keaton—and I'm accused of having a "jumpy" attitude toward filmmaking! Yes, sometimes "creating a style" is just desperation. I certainly deny having a "zany approach."

But I'm quite proud of some of those early commercials. The After-Eight Chocolates, for instance. I did all of them from the beginning and I was faced with a new project and an image which needed to be put over. This is what pleases me—when a problem is present and solved.

In the After-Eights the problem was: these things are going to cost four shillings [50 cents] a packet and are bloody expensive! How are we going to sell it? In terms of making a film image, we decided to go for the fake classy stuff—dinner jackets among the pseudo-luxury. It was half-a-dram world, and half what people who had no money imagined luxury to be. It was a callous attempt—and it worked. They sold out after the first commercial!

But it's quite clear that commercials do have a very short span for the director in which he is fond of them and pleased with what he has done. It's natural, I suppose.

What struck me most in the early days was knowing that in order to make full-scale feature movies you had to know everyone's job. You have to understand lab techniques, how to lay a musical score, and so on. Although my commercials career and feature-films career started together—even if they were shorts at first, like the *Running, Jumping and Standing Still* film, which was like a day and a half's direction —commercials are a marvelous way to learn, because everything is scaled down; the problems are the same, but there are fewer people and things to juggle with. I had a blanket contract to start with, enabling me to choose the times I filmed, as long as I delivered up so many in a year.

I remember doing the most expensive commercial ever made, for Braniff Airlines. Don't ask me what the cost was, but we had a 12-foot model of the Concorde, and people flying around with "Jet Packs." We shot it for seven days in a small studio near London. Most of my commercials have been made in Britain.

If someone said to me, "When you're shooting, how do you set things up, how do you cut it?" I couldn't explain. It all starts to meld in the cutting room and that's why I take so long between finishing shooting and finishing the film. It's rather like self-analysis: you find out a whole lot about yourself deciding what to keep in and what to leave out!

The great thing about commercials is that you can always find the time for them. If a big feature project comes up, you can take it, which is something that doesn't apply if you're stuck with a TV series. I'd like to go on doing them, when I have the time, but films seem to take longer and longer. They can be fun and creative; and people look down on commercial directors less than they used to!

A Funny Thing Happened on the Way to the Forum, with Zero Mostel.

Besides this, although I've had commercials banned, I've never had one frame cut from any of my films—except for *How I Won the War,* which was censored in France, and that's only to be expected.

One commercial that might have run into trouble was a Grant's Whiskey short I did in 1960, to be sold in the Middle East. We tried to make it seem like an aphrodisiac! It went down very well, that one, and because it was about the time of *Last Year at Marienbad* it was done in that vein.

My favorite commercial? Apart from the After-Eights, I like the Acrilan wool piece I did which showed an almost continuous 60-second track of a Siamese cat stalking through a house and being elbowed off a bed. That wasn't easy to set up, but it was very satisfying in the end.

Commercials taught me a lot. I feel I must go on doing them, because it's the best way to learn what's going on that's new. One example was the running of a 40-second piece of film through the camera several times, with different scenes being impregnated on the same piece of celluloid. We learned that you have to use proportionately less exposure each time you run the film through. It's not something I invented, but something I learned. Similarly, if you need to get the lettering on a cigarette showing up clearly in close-up, but also want to show a couple holding hands in the background, you would think, "Christ! How do I do this?" Then you realize you can use half a dozen different lenses, and maybe a fish-eye with the cigarette almost touching it.

But basically, in terms of technique I'm using the same approach to feature films as commercials; getting up in the morning and trying to produce images that fit a pattern in a form acceptable to the conventions of filmmaking. I know I'm untrained in terms of schooling—I've never been on the floor of anyone else's film. I know people say I'm an unconventional director.

But the truth is that I'm only unconventional to everyone else, not to myself.

—1969

Gordon Parks

Bob Thomas

Gordon Parks came to direction with strong credentials. He was a star photographer for Life magazine, wrote novels and memoirs, and composed pop and serious music—the Munich Symphony Orchestra recorded one of his symphonies in 1972. His first feature was The Learning Tree, based on his autobiographical novel. It was followed by Shaft, which turned out to be a huge financial success for MGM. Parks was interviewed as he put the finishing touches on Shaft's Big Score a few days before the press preview. Because Isaac Hayes had declined to repeat his scoring job on the sequel, Parks took over the assignment. He completed the score, including two songs and a new theme, in two weeks and three days.

Q: When did you first start thinking about being a director?

Parks: I believe I first started thinking about it when I was assigned by *Life* to cover Roberto Rossellini and Ingrid Bergman when they were making a film on the island of Stromboli. That's when I got the first bug. Actually, the thing that propelled me toward directing was when I was covering a crime story for *Life.* That's when I realized the limitations of the still camera. I was on an assignment in Greenwich Village, answering a call where someone had been murdered. The police cars were there, with their lights circling around the buildings, and people were scurrying about. I shot the scene with a 28 mm lens, so I had a wide-angle view. But I realized that I missed the real essence, the real drama of the story.

Q: That's when you began thinking seriously about directing?

Parks: Yes. I concluded that if I wanted to capture moments like that one in the Village, I would have to make movies.

Q: Had you seen films throughout your life?

Parks: Yes, but only as a spectator. I was never what you would call a film buff. I didn't have enough time to see many movies.

Q: Did you have any favorite directors?

Parks: Not really. Favorite pictures, yes.

Q: Did you have any other motivations about becoming a director?

Parks: I had some feeling about the type of film Hollywood was making, particularly in regard to how the black man was portrayed. Once I had an assignment for *Life* that took me far into the Northwest Territory. It was so far north that the people had never seen a black man before. They looked at me with wonder. The Indians especially didn't know what I was; they asked me if I was a member of another tribe. They were surprised to see the white people greet me at the train as if I were someone important.

While I was there, they showed a lot of movies. Some of them portrayed the black man so badly that I thought something should be done about it. That was about 1945.

Q: What was your first filmmaking experience?

Parks: I had done a story for *Life* about a Brazilian boy from the *favela,* the hillside slum in Rio de Janeiro. The doctors had said he would die within two years if he didn't leave the place. The layout made quite an impression. Readers sent in a total of 100,000 dollars to help the boy, and I received letters saying, "You've got to go back and bring that boy out."

So in 1961 I returned to Rio to make a short film about the boy; it was called *Flavio.* I found out that other people were beating up on Flavio's family because of the fact that they were getting out of the *favela.* I had two other cameramen, and we stationed ourselves at strategic positions to catch the action, and to record Flavio coming for water and doing other things.

I also did two documentaries for NET, *The Diary of a Harlem Family* and *The World of Piri Thomas,* about a Puerto Rican boy in New York.

Q: How did you feel when you started your first feature, *The Learning Tree?*

Parks: I was just a little disturbed by the first movement of that camera. It's like the beginning of a basketball game, you know—there's the toss-up, and you have a feeling of apprehension when the ball comes down and the fury of battle is on.

Yes, I was concerned about that first shot. But I was determined not to let the crew know it.

Q: What was your first shot?

Parks: It was what I wanted it to be: a high crane shot. That would establish me as a director, I thought. Bernie Guffey, the cameraman, was great about it. He said, "You want me to go up there with you?" I said I'd appreciate it. When we got up there,

Parks with Estelle Evans on *The Learning Tree* set.

I said, "Which way should we go—right or left?" He said, "You're the director; you decide." It felt good having Bernie there.

Q: Since you came from photography, did you find yourself concerned with the visual aspects of the picture?

Parks: Yes. I had confidence in my being able to handle the visual aspects. That was good. Because I was confident that I could deal with how the picture looked, I was able to spend more time working with the actors. If I had to learn both the visual aspects *and* directing the actors, I don't think I could have made it.

Q: Was your confidence ever shaken?

Parks: Just once. Bernie and I had some confusion over one shot. The subject matter was in the shade, and there were flowers in the foreground under full sun. I wanted to use a screen to soften the foreground flowers, and Bernie said it couldn't be done.

Shaft.

I didn't see why not; I could certainly take such a shot with a still camera. "Bernie, I'm afraid I'll have to shoot it my way," I said. "But I'll shoot it your way, too." When we saw the dailies, he said, "You win." I replied, "You had me worried; if there was that much difference between still and movie photography, I'd be in trouble." That gave me confidence to follow my own instincts.

Q: Did you find any difficulty working in a fictional context?

Parks: No. The documentary approach that I had used in films was more difficult, because you had to shoot what came along. The fictional situation gave me a chance to set up.

Q: What about dealing with actors?

Parks: That didn't bother me. I had worked with such stars as Ethel Barrymore, Lionel Barrymore, Edward G. Robinson and Laurence Olivier in photographing stage plays for *Life*. Because it took less time for costume changes, we generally shot the play backwards, starting with Act 3. The actors would get confused and say, "Where am I?" So I gave them directions.

Q: Was your feature debut made easier because *The Learning Tree* was autobiographical?

Parks: Certainly. I felt much safer because I knew the subject matter.

Q: What happened after *The Learning Tree*?

Parks: I went through a period when I was offered similar projects. The feeling of the studios seemed to be: "Okay, he did a beautiful memoir, but could he direct a fast-paced melodrama?" My answer to that was: "If you saw the photo stories I've done on Harlem crime, the Black Muslims and other contemporary subjects, you'd realize that I can do something besides a memoir."

Q: Then along came *Shaft*.

Parks: It was a happy accident. It put me in a position to prove that I could make an action picture.

Q: How did you approach *Shaft*?

Parks: I knew that this was the type of film that had holes in it. If I wasn't careful, someone was bound to discover the holes. So the thing for me to do was to make it as fast-paced as I could so there was no chance to see the holes. I played everything twice as fast as I normally would. I pushed my actors as fast as they could go. It helped them, especially the inexperienced ones, and gave better pace to the whole picture.

I intended *Shaft* to be more serious than the Bond pictures. I wanted nothing in the picture that a man couldn't do. I stuck to that, even though I had a man falling out a three-story window over Times Square and Shaft being lowered by block and tackle and crashing through a window. A man could do both those things.

But really, there was no serious intent with the film. Vincent Canby hit the nail on the head when he said, "It's a great Saturday night movie." If I had it to do over, I think I would have had one or two less episodes and concentrated more on character buildup.

Q: Did you have enough time to shoot *Shaft*?

Parks: Yes and no. As I was preparing the picture, Herb Solow [then MGM production chief] got nervous about my shooting in the New York weather and he ordered the whole company to California. So we had to pull camp. I knew I wouldn't shoot it in Hollywood, and I tried to convince Solow to let me return to New York. I let him think I would do it in Hollywood if he insisted—even though I was determined not to.

I won my fight; [Jim] Aubrey decided in my favor. Then I had to get the whole film ready to go in less than two weeks. I still brought it in 200,000 dollars under budget—at 1,200,000 dollars.

Q: How did you manage that?

Parks: I learned how to save. I worked fast. I showed the cameraman what I wanted, and he showed the operator. We did the scene, and if the actors were right and the cameraman was satisfied, why shoot another take? I like to do one take.

Q: Did you have any qualms about doing a sequel to *Shaft*?

Parks: Yes. I thought if I did another *Shaft* that wasn't better than the first one, I'd be guilty of making a fast buck. I had to convince myself that I could make a better show the second time, one that was improved visually and better written.

I think I succeeded with *Shaft's Big Score*. It is much more professional, with better use of the camera and better use of the actors. Everything is on a much grander scale. The second one cost 1,800,000 dollars.

Q: What about more *Shafts*?

Parks: I suppose I could go on and on making them, and MGM wants one more. I'll probably do it—if I can also do three pictures of my own. I don't want to go down in history as the guy who directed *Shaft*. I know that's a good way to make a lot of money, but there are other things to worry about, things like aesthetics. After all, when I was a photographer, I didn't do one kind of subject. I'd do a crime story, then I'd go off to Paris to cover the fashion showings, or to London to photograph royalty.

Nor do I want to be known as a black director. I'm a director—period. I think I've proven enough as a black man of my interest in black causes. But I don't want to wear that on my coat sleeve every time I make a picture.

If I want to make an all-white musical, then I should be free to do so. If I want to make another *Shaft*—okay. If I want to do something serious about the black revolution, wow—that's me!

But it should be entertainment. A black director has a certain obligation to the public, white and black. That is to entertain. He shouldn't try to bend them down to the everyday problems, unless he can do it in the context of entertainment.

I'm a director-photographer-composer-author. Why must I be known as a *black* director-photographer-composer-author?

Q: Do you have any advice to black youth who want to become filmmakers?

Parks: The mistake that black youth make is that they get so involved in their blackness that their art suffers. I tell them that they must not let their blackness stand in the way of expressing themselves. If they persist in that, they will be shunted off into black pictures, no matter how great their talent. I don't want that. If a *Ryan's Daughter* comes along, I want to be given a shot at it. It might not be what I want to do, but I want to be able to say no.

—1972

Mel Brooks

Brooks directing the "Springtime for Hitler" number in *The Producers*.

Franklin Heller

*Many consider Mel Brooks one of America's funniest men. But he is
serious about the art of direction. He is also serious about the responsibilities of
a director, having served on the National Board of the Directors
Guild of America.*

*Brooks won early success as a gag writer for radio and television,
later applied his comedy talent to records (The Two-Thousand-Year-Old Man),
acting and talk-show appearances. He turned to film directing
with* The Producers. *His second film was* The Twelve Chairs.

Q: You write, direct and sometimes act, too. Do you consider yourself an *auteur?*
Brooks: Yes.
Q: What is your definition of *auteur?*
Brooks: I think it's a mispronunciation of "author." It's really a French word for
"filmmaker." That is, one who gets an idea which is usually rooted to his basic philosophy of life. It may be as simple as *Stolen Kisses*—a remembrance of nuances past that
had a great deal of meaning for Truffaut. So I guess I could say that an *auteur* really is
a man with an idea, a concept, a philosophy, who takes that idea from the vapor of
inception to the final coalescence of it on film.
Q: What do you think is the difference between a director and an *auteur?*
Brooks: The difference is that a director who is working for a living simply does
the job, which may not be akin to his philosophy, but it is not inconsistent to have
the same man being both. The key word is "hunger." If you are hungry and nobody
will buy your original idea, you might get lucky, direct a Kellogg's cornflakes commercial and take home a few boxes.
Q: Did you always want to be a director?
Brooks: Not really. But I was forced to become a director. Basically I am a writer
and every time I spoke to an actor about the script, the director would kick me out
for interfering with his people. So in self-defense I became a director. Now it's my
turn; I kick writers out. You know, it just occurred to me, I'm not a nice person.
Q: Was it hard to convince people that you should direct *The Producers?*
Brooks: About as hard as it is for a Jew to check into the Cairo Hilton.
Q: How did you manage?
Brooks: Well, I changed my name to Kabal el Sharif. First I went to all the big
studios with the script under my arm. "Hah!" said the big studios. So I thought of a
marvelous plan that I got from a friend of mine, who shall be nameless—*Mario Puzo.*
What I decided to do was cut off the grills of their Rolls Royces and place them at
the foot of their beds so that when they awoke the next morning they would all be
terrified and hire me to direct the picture. But what I actually did was say, "Maybe
next time," and then made the rounds of all the independent producers in New York.
Luckily, through a mutual friend who shall be nameless—*Barry Levinson*—I was introduced to Sidney Glazier, an independent producer who had just won an Academy
Award for his short film *The Eleanor Roosevelt Story.* Sidney had just ordered coffee
from the Hello Coffee Shop downstairs. He was sipping from a full container of
coffee—dark coffee; he always liked dark coffee—when I got to the "Springtime for
Hitler" number, and I related that portion of the story to him. He choked. He literally
choked on the coffee. I mean I had to slap him on the back to get the coffee out of
his lungs, his nose, his eyes. Finally, he got up from the floor, stuck out his hand
and said, "Kid, we got a picture. And you're going to direct it."
From there, Sidney went to every studio and every garage in America to try to
get a distributor. He did raise a half-million dollars privately, but even with a budget

of only a million, he couldn't raise the other half because they simply wouldn't go with me as the director or with the title, which was *Springtime for Hitler* at that time.

Anyway, Sidney went all over and couldn't get arrested. Finally he went to Joe Levine, who had just put a lot of money into *The Graduate* and was loath to put up any more money until some started coming back. Joe is a very simple, straightforward man. He said, "Listen, kid, do you really think you can direct a movie?" I said, "I know I can." He stuck out his hand and said, "Okay, kid, go to it." I am very grateful to Mr. Levine for that foolish gesture and, of course, to Sidney Glazier, who was the first person in the business to have faith in me as a director.

Q: Looking back on all the things you have done, what was the most satisfying?

Brooks: I started in show business as a drummer in a borscht-belt band. I loved playing the drums. Then I became a comic, and I liked being a comic very much. After that, I worked as a writer in television and I liked that, too.

I liked writing *Your Show of Shows*. I stayed with it too long. We all stayed with it too long. Especially Sid Caesar. Ten years. It's too much, but it was a damn good show, and I am very proud of it. It was quite a challenge writing an hour and a half every week, live. It was impossible, but somehow we did it. I think you have to love what you do in order to get through it. But so far, the most enjoyable things were *The Two-Thousand-Year-Old Man*—the record—which I did with Carl Reiner. I mean, I really wailed. I could hear my antecedents. I could hear 5,000 years of Jews pouring through me. And the other big thrill of my life was writing and directing *The Producers*.

Q: Up to that time you were a writer. How did you feel about directing?

Brooks: Well, it was hard—very hard. Because there's a whole maze of technical things to surmount before you get through to the pay dirt. *The Producers* was a joyful experience, although I may have moved ahead cinematically with *The Twelve Chairs*. I think it is a much finer film, in terms of cinema. The shots are more beautiful and the whole ambience, look and texture of the film are more cinematic. But who cares about all that junk? It's really the spirit of the thing that counts. It's whether or not the performances smash across the screen into your heart or into your laugh box and live with you, remain with you.

Q: Would you class your films as farces?

Brooks: In a sense, yes. And in another sense, no. The terms vary; some say "satire." *The Producers* is technically a satirical farce. "Farce" simply means that the characters don't know what's happening and that we, the audience, do. Satire, on the other hand, is poking fun at something false, the better to expose it. So it's quite possible that something could be both satire and farce. One does not necessarily preclude the other.

Q: I understand both your pictures were on or under budget. Are you budget conscious?

Brooks: Well, yes, I am. I try to figure out with the help of Mike Hertzberg, who was my assistant director on *The Producers* and then was the producer of *The Twelve Chairs*, exactly what's happening and where we are going with the budget. I work very closely with Mike, because his judgment and his production acumen are valuable assets to me. Actually, a man like Hertzberg is the key to preparation. And preparation is the key to saving money.

Q: Do you believe in preproduction rehearsal?

Brooks: I pray to it. It's very important to me. You find a great deal in rehearsal, and it doesn't cost a penny. Every director should rehearse portions if not all of his picture before it is shot. There are a lot of surprises, improvisatorial gold. Occasionally a few personality clashes develop, which then can be coped with. I cannot say enough about the value of rehearsal.

Q: What professional forces are most helpful to you?

On a Yugoslavian shore with the title objects from *The Twelve Chairs*.

Brooks: I'd say money. Is that a professional force? I guess you mean the technical personnel. A rehearsal period cannot help with an assistant director or a cinematographer, so plenty of lunches and talks are necessary to find where your mutual neuroses meet and where they clash. What you want in the end is a fraternal relationship where you are the absolute boss. The editor is also very important. I am schizoid about editors. I love them and I hate them. The picture is very close to the director's heart and he is not getting paid after the shooting is finished, but he is ready to work from eight in the morning until eight the next morning cutting the picture. Within limits, I think an editor should spend as much effort and energy. A lot of editors like to go home at six o'clock. If you meet one like that, fire him.

Q: What do you think appeals to the largest audience?

Brooks: Physical comedy. It cuts across every class and it is international. With a minimal number of words, the audience knows what you are doing and saying at all times. I can't say enough about physical comedy. Oh, sure, I can: E-N-O-U-G-H—already.

Q: Do you test laugh reaction with audiences before you lock in the final cut?

Brooks: Previews are critical to the success of a comedy. It's easy to tell whether the funny parts of the picture are working. If it's funny, you'll hear laughter. If they are not working, you will hear nothing or boos, or maybe even the sound of spitting at the screen. But it's a little more difficult to tell about the serious elements of the film. One way is to watch if cigarettes are being lit up. If it doesn't look like Tokyo after Doolittle raided it, then they are paying attention. Also, if you don't hear a Vicks commercial, then you're doing all right.

Q: What's your next project?

Brooks: I want to do *She Stoops to Conquer* starring Gene Wilder.

Q: Do you have any specific approach to this classic?

Brooks: Yes, I do; it's called "madness." I am using the basic structure that Oliver Goldsmith has so beautifully designed and adding the insanities that I am committed to. Also, I think that it would be a great picture and "GOLDSMITH AND BROOKS" would look marvelous in lights.

Q: What's the best picture you ever saw?

Brooks: I am basically a comedy director, but, strangely enough, the best picture I ever saw is two. It would be a toss-up between Renoir's *Grand Illusion* and Ford's *The Grapes of Wrath*. They hit me the hardest, and neither of them, you'll admit, is a flat-out laff-riot.

Q: What are the laff-riots you admire?

Brooks: I would say some of the earlier English comedies have given me the most pleasure. *Kind Hearts and Coronets, The Lavender Hill Mob* and, of course, a few Italian beauties like Pietro Germi's *Seduced and Abandoned,* a truly enchanting film. And *Big Deal on Madonna Street.* A beauty picture. And, of course, almost any early De Sica has thrilled me. Fifteen or 20 years ago the name of Vittorio De Sica thundered throughout the land of film. Today not a whisper. He is simply not modish. Today it is Visconti. Go see Visconti's *Death in Venice* and *The Damned,* and then see De Sica's *Umberto D, Miracle in Milano* and *The Bicycle Thief,* and then we'll have a cup of coffee and talk about who is a genius and who is just Italian.

Q: When you came to directing your first film, did you get any surprises, something you had not anticipated?

Brooks: Yes. When we got on the set, everything seemed so different with so much light on it. I could see physical nuances that I never saw before. My training was not with close-up comedy, but with the whole body. And it was a big shock to me to see a close-up for the first time and realize how grotesque it was without being funny. I learned with *The Producers* to limit the number of close-ups. Also I learned when to cut away. This is critical. I saw the rushes and I said to myself, "Wait a minute, I'm tipping my mitt. I'm cutting to the joke. That joke should happen. It should be a surprise and I've pulled the rug out from under it by cutting to it." It's like saying to the audience, "Here it comes, folks." When you say that, you'd better have King Kong hanging from the Empire State Building.

Q: Would you say you work a great deal from instinct, then? And technical matters are not so important?

Brooks: Absolutely. It's dangerous to get a false sense of succeeding simply because the actors get the lines right, and a light didn't fall down and explode, or there wasn't a hair in the gate. Unconsciously you're really a traitor to your own better judgment. You've really got to stay with your own good nose. You must know—you must smell—whether something is really good or not.

—1971

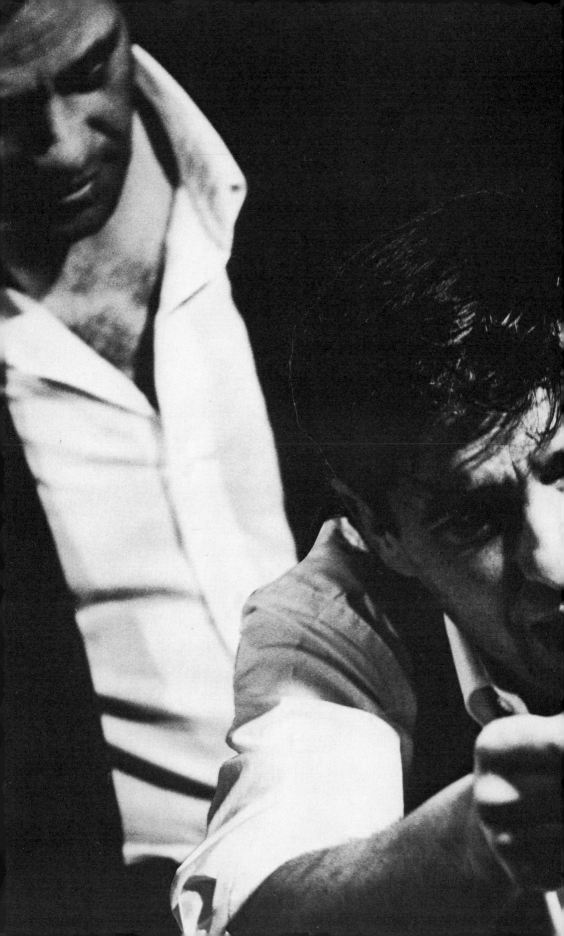

III.
The Director-Actor

"In most pictures I've directed myself. So why shouldn't I direct the entire picture?"

This was the reasoning of Marlon Brando, and so he directed *One-Eyed Jacks*, which is still well remembered by many critics.

Brando was following a tradition that has existed since the beginning of the cinema art. Many of the silent-film directors had themselves been actors—D. W. Griffith, Cecil B. DeMille, Charles Chaplin, Donald Crisp, Erich von Stroheim, Mack Sennett—and some continued to be.

With the advent of the big-studio era, the combining of the directing and starring functions became less frequent. But there were notable exceptions: Orson Welles, Dick Powell, Robert Montgomery, Gene Kelly.

Again, the film industry reverts to the patterns of its beginnings. The new era of films has brought a flood of actor-directors. Some, such as Jack Lemmon, Jack Nicholson and Paul Newman, have chosen to make their directorial debuts with films in which they did not appear. Most star as well as direct: John Wayne, Woody Allen, Sidney Poitier, Clint Eastwood, Elaine May, Alan Arkin, Cliff Robertson.

Jerry Lewis once expressed his own reasons for wanting to direct: "When I started in films in 1948, I started with a terrible frustration. I was dealing with some 120 people who were saying things and doing things that I didn't understand."

Soon Jerry Lewis was prowling along catwalks and through editing rooms, asking endless questions about how movies are made. He began making his own, and he has been doing it ever since.

John Cassavetes directing *Husbands*. Peter Falk is behind him.

John Cassavetes

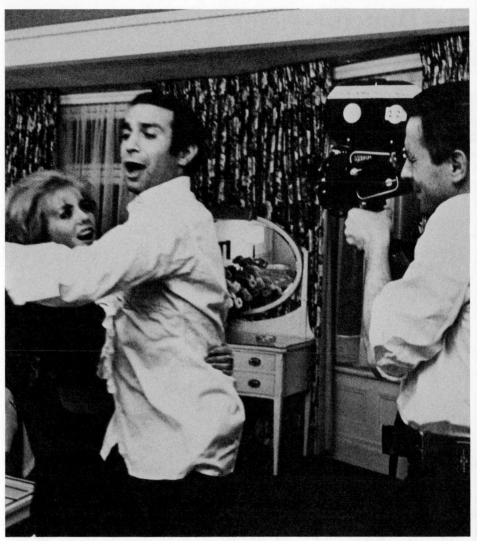

Cassavetes filming a scene for *Husbands*.

Russell AuWerter

With Minnie and Moskowitz *John Cassavetes completed his sixth film as a director. In four of his films—*Shadows, Faces, Husbands *and* Minnie and Moskowitz—*he had complete artistic control from story selection through promotion. Except for* Shadows, *which was almost a total improvisation, he also wrote the screenplays for these movies. His other directorial credits are* Too Late Blues *and* A Child Is Waiting.

As an actor, Cassavetes appeared in 90 television dramas, including his own series, Johnny Staccato, *and such films as* Edge of the City, The Dirty Dozen *and* Rosemary's Baby. *In* Husbands, *the story of three middle-aged, middle-class Americans on a spree in London, Cassavetes starred along with Ben Gazzara and Peter Falk. He was interviewed after its completion.*

Q: What were the circumstances of your decision to become a director?

Cassavetes: I never really decided to become a director. I had a lot of very talented friends who were out of work in New York. I was working and actors help each other. You can't recommend an actor to a director or a producer or writer—they have to discover for themselves what kind of an actor he is. So we got together and thought we would open a workshop. I found space on West Forty-eighth Street— the old Malin Studios. It wasn't to be a school. It was to be a place where people could just perform and I could invite all the casting people down to see these actors perform. Well, as it turned out, the actors were offended by this and no one showed up. I had rented the place for a year at quite a bit of money, so I thought I'd better take an ad in the paper. I took ads in *Show Business,* in *The New York Times, Daily News* and *Mirror.* People started coming in. Many, many people came in—from all walks of life—all wanting to be actors. I wasn't a teacher or a director—had no desire to be—only an actor, but I took the problems that were bothering me and used the people on stage to help me solve my problems, which were mainly how to make an entrance on a stage, how to interpret a part, how to mix improvisation with acting, how to start off a play properly, how to contact and communicate with an audience, how, once you got a laugh, to keep the laugh coming—all the problems an actor would face that I could think of. During the course of this we were dealing with improvisations. Actors would be on the stage doing an improvisation and it turned out to be very bad. I found out that by giving an actor some definite activity to do it would make him better. But it still wasn't very good, so we threw actors who were improvising into the midst of a written scene. What happened was that actors could not go on with the written material. I found that I couldn't go on. I found out that my study had to be deeper. As we made these discoveries, we started throwing away scripts and working more in an improvisational capacity. About that time we came upon a very good improvisation. And out of that improvisation, I said, "That would make a heck of a movie." I went on a radio program that night with a friend of mine, Jean Shepherd. While I was there I said I was going to make a movie and that all these people were going to make a movie—wouldn't it be terrific if it could be sponsored by just people. The next day 2,000 dollars in dollar bills came in. People from the Army came in and people with equipment came in. Shirley Clarke left some equipment for us. Other people brought in stuff. And they all contributed to this thing. We had 2,000 dollars, some equipment, a stage and actors. As soon as that came in the people started building sets. The picture that came out of this was *Shadows.* So it was, more or less, the desire of a group of people who wanted to accomplish something that started me off in directing, rather than my own personal desires.

Q: Why did you continue to direct?

Cassavetes: I enjoy it, because I can write and because I can keep a certain promise to an actor. And because I haven't stopped acting. We made a picture called *Husbands* and I'm in it, too. So it isn't really what kind of a part you have; it's important how well you play it. If you please yourself and you express something—good. As a director you have a responsibility to the picture; there's no doubt that *Husbands* is my picture. But if you ask Ben and Peter, *Husbands* is their picture individually. If you ask Al Ruban or Sam Shaw, the producers, it's their picture. We all make the film. The making of a film means that people go out and do the best they can to keep a rapport and an understanding and a feeling that what they have to say is more important than the way it's said by any individual.

Q: *Husbands* was the first film in which you directed yourself. Were there any special problems that resulted from this?

Cassavetes: Sure, a lot of special problems. It is very hard to see the scene when you're in it. But it was harder, I think, on Peter and Ben, my being in the scene, be-

Peter Falk, Cassavetes on location.

cause I could decide how I was going to play that scene and not worry about the direction of that scene, and they couldn't. The three of us are peers one moment, then suddenly they have to turn to me and say, "What do you think?" And they know goddam well I don't know anything more about the scene than they do, because I was in it, too. So we learned how to use our instincts. I would say to Peter, "How did it go for you?" and he'd say, "Fine" and then I'd ask Ben and he'd say, "Fine" and I'd say, "Fine" and that's the way we'd know.

Q: Would you direct yourself in another picture?

Cassavetes: I never say "never." I thought it was difficult and very strenuous, but I enjoyed it. In *Husbands* Peter, Ben and I were the idea of the film—the three of us acting together.

Q: You have written the scripts for the last two pictures you have directed. Is this a pattern that will continue?

Cassavetes: I wouldn't do a picture unless I could write the script. The reason for this is that making a picture or acting in a picture is a very personal thing. I just don't trust anyone else to do what I do. Not because I'm better than anyone else, but because I know that I'll put every last drop of blood I have into it—and not be concerned with the writing.

Q: There isn't a writer, whom you know of whom you would like to collaborate with on a picture?

Cassavetes: There are a lot of writers I would love to collaborate with on a picture, but I don't think they would want to collaborate with me. It's a very difficult thing—to say a writer is not important. Somebody writes a good screenplay—it's different from doing the kind of pictures that I do—where the actor is more important than anyone else. I wouldn't be concerned with what a writer felt. I would only be concerned that the actor who was portraying the writer's character was comfortable, was happy and was good. It's a very tough bargain to make with somebody who has an ego and who has been trained in a business where status is everything, to suddenly have a new level of work with new values that say the script doesn't mean a damn thing—rewrite it, do it again, rewrite it. Okay, let's improvise it. After improvisation, let's rewrite it again, then let's improvise it. And maybe we won't use anything. Maybe it will be background. I know that I'm willing to do that. I don't know anyone else who is. People say they are, but it's a hell of a lot of work.

Q: How involved do you get in the editing process?

Cassavetes: I think that's a very standard situation. Most editors are very good. On a picture like ours, with editors Peter Tanner and Tom Cornwall—the two English editors that we had here—it was just a matter of their getting used to the material and seeing it. They're in a business where they look at something and then they cut it. They are so expert that they can make it look good. But then they learn that that isn't going to work on a picture like *Husbands*. It's not that they're wrong and I'm right—it's just not going to work. It's a question of their finding that out through a long, hard process.

Q: Does the same apply to your cameraman, your art director and all the other production people?

Cassavetes: That's right. The best thing that could happen is for everyone to be highly involved. Once they're highly involved my job gets easier and easier. It takes a certain amount of time out of your life, to be highly involved, and most people are not willing to give that. Now, that's nothing against them. It's just that it doesn't work if they're not willing to give everything they have over a long period of time. It's an idea. Either the film is life and death to you or it's not. And if it's not, then you're no help. We're saying to ourselves—and this has its own pitfalls, too—that we have no limitations on the film. We can say whatever we want to say, whatever pleases us. Now, obviously if nothing pleases you, you ought to get the hell out. But, if something pleases you that can only enhance what we're working on.

Q: Ideally, then, you would like to be able to just concentrate on the acting and the actor?

Cassavetes: In the making of *Husbands*, yes. It's a story about three men, so it would be silly to concentrate on the landscape. It isn't earth's relationship to me that we're talking about; it's men's behavior in terms of themselves.

Q: Do you direct a nonprofessional actor differently from a professional actor?

Cassavetes: No.

Q: When you combine the two in a scene, does this create special problems?

Cassavetes: No. I think it's a stimulant.

Q: How do you use improvisation as a part of your directing technique?

Cassavetes: I think you have to define what improvisation does—not what it is. If you don't have a script, you don't have a commitment to just saying lines. If you don't have a script, then you take the essence of what you really feel and say that. You can behave more as yourself than you would ordinarily with someone else's lines.

Q: How important is high energy for you as a director?

Cassavetes: I think it's extremely important. For me it's everything. I gain energy by being comfortable. I get drained when I'm uncomfortable. I believe—and I think everyone else around *Husbands* does, too—that it's impossible to fail if people are given their head, if people are allowed to do what they know how to do and to do it with some kind of fun. I hate discipline, I despise it. If I walk on a quiet, polite set, I go crazy—I know there's something wrong because somebody has lessened himself in his own estimation and put either me or some actor above himself.

Q: Is taste in any way comparable to energy as a requisite for directing?

Cassavetes: You know, that's a word that's just evaded me all these years.

Q: How much of your directing is therapy?

Cassavetes: Therapy? For whom?

Q: For you or your actors.

Cassavetes: For me it's all the way. For the actors I hope it is. It's better than staying home.

Q: Is there any type of picture you wouldn't make?

Cassavetes: Yes, I think probably a musical or a situation comedy.

Q: Husbands is your first color picture. Did the change to color affect your directing in any major way?

Cassavetes: It caused me a lot of pain, because I see things in black and white, but Sam Shaw [associate producer of *Husbands*] assured me that the color, if we shot it in a certain way, would look as "hack" as anything else I've ever done.

Q: Did being an actor before being a director have any advantages?

Cassavetes: It makes it easier.

Q: Did being an actor before being a director have any disadvantages?

Cassavetes: No. But being an actor after you're a director has some disadvantages.

Q: Do you see yourself changing with each picture you direct?

Cassavetes: Sure. You have to fight sophistication. Sophistication comes to anybody who has been doing his job for a while. You have to fight knowing, because once you know something, it's hard to be open and creative; it's a form of passivity—something to guard against.

Q: What would you say to young directors who are just starting out?

Cassavetes: Say what you are. Not what you would like to be. Not what you have to be. Just say what you are. And what you are is good enough.

Q: Where do you see yourself in five or ten years?

Cassavetes: I see myself alive.

—1970

Paul Newman

Newman directing Joanne Woodward in *Rachel, Rachel*.

Digby Diehl

Paul Newman studied at the Yale School of Drama before acting in summer stock, television, and on the Broadway stage. After his film debut in 1955, a series of strong characterizations in movies such as Somebody Up There Likes Me, Cat on a Hot Tin Roof, Hud, The Hustler, Harper, Cool Hand Luke *and* Butch Cassidy and the Sundance Kid *earned him the title of America's Number One Male Movie Star. As director of* Rachel, Rachel *and later* Sometimes a Great Notion *and* The Effect of Gamma Rays on Man-in-the-Moon Marigolds, *he demonstrated that his talents weren't limited to performing.*

Q: Rachel, Rachel was in reality your second directorial effort. In 1959, you directed a short film at the Actors Studio in New York which was an adaptation of Anton Chekhov's dramatic monologue "On the Harmfulness of Tobacco."

Newman: I did that as an exercise for myself, really. I did it mostly to see whether I could handle a camera and direct actors. It didn't turn out as successfully as I would have liked it to, although it got a very good review in *The New York Times.* The audiences were divided pretty evenly between those who loved it and those who hated it. There wasn't much middle ground.

Q: Was the film commercially released?

Newman: It was commercially released in New York, but there was no market at all for a short. At 28 minutes, it was much too long, and I kind of suspect they thought that Chekhov was not all that interesting.

Q: When you made that film you must have had some notions about a personal concept of directing. Where did you learn most of your ideas about direction?

Newman: As an actor. Acting has always been pretty much of a community experience when I've been concerned. For example, I've only done one film since 1956 which has not had two weeks of rehearsal time in advance. I give two weeks of rehearsal to the studios for free, so they feel they're getting something for nothing and go along with it. But when you're working with someone like Marty Ritt or Stuart Rosenberg, they realize how valuable that kind of time is. During those two weeks it's really a community effort. Everybody crosses everybody else's lines, so for quite a while I've been directing myself, to a certain extent.

Q: Are there any keys to direction you've picked up through your experience as an actor?

Newman: Sure, the whole idea of an open line of communication. Joanne [Woodward] and I have a marvelous line of communication. It sounds academic but it's really very simple: active verbs. Once you give an actor the intention—an active verb—he can work variations on a theme. You can't play the verb "to love" and you can't play "lust." You can't play anything abstract as an actor, but you can play an action like "listen." Now, if that's the kind of character you're playing, a guy who really leans in to a woman and listens to her, then already you've got a quality of respect and attentiveness, so you get what you want as a director. Now, you can also say, "Measure her." Then it becomes a sexual thing. If that sexual motivation was in the character all the time, you've got a whole different thing going in the scene. The scene can look exactly the same, but that intention is going to color everything that happens.

Q: Rachel, Rachel is a film that seems to clearly have your personal stamp upon it. But considering the subject matter, a thirty-five-year-old spinster, I can hardly see how you identified with the film.

Newman: I told Joanne right at the very beginning of rehearsal, "I want to make one thing very clear: there's only one person who can play this part—that's me." Seriously, I know those ladies. The funny thing is, the script was turned down by all the major studios, because they felt it was too tiny an experience, when in reality it's a huge experience. It doesn't deal with nobility, not with a fall from grace (there was no grace in the lady). It deals with the problem that most of the individuals in our lifetime deal with: loneliness. Loneliness, and the struggle for change, which to me is the most important and noble effort of the story.

Q: The focal point of this change seems to come in Rachel's discovery of sex. Yet this section of the film seems much more blunted and implicit than other elements.

Newman: I decided to do it that way for a very specific reason. In terms of the progression of Rachel's initiation, she has allowed herself to fall into a certain pattern of existence and, suddenly realizing the limitations of that existence, she opts for a change. Now, at that particular instance, a wrench is applied in her life, which is the tabernacle sequence. As she is forced into that maelstrom, I gave Joanne one word for the character: "resist." I didn't want it to come out as something that was so overscale that she would have been crushed, yet there is maybe ten percent of volition in her acts. When she gets down on her knees, and she sucks in experience—sensation, rather—into her body, the change is made. Now, that is interesting, because in that act she realizes that she is capable of sensation. She has a line later, "I never thought that anything could grow inside of me." There is a continuing symbolism of death throughout her existence. And suddenly she is forced into a pattern of life. Right after the mistaken pass that Estelle makes to her, she reaches a point of readiness for Nick. When we got to the actual love scene, it was truncated because I wanted it to be a very clumsy kind of thing. And that's why the camera wouldn't go hand-held; we had a stable shot there. Most importantly, I wanted her to look beautiful at that moment, and she was. You may not have noticed, but there was no music in the love scene. Although music was written for it, the scene struck me exactly right the way it was, and I didn't want to romanticize it.

Q: That doesn't sound like the kind of Method technique you use as an actor. Do you apply the same criteria to yourself as a director?

Newman: No, I was not aware of myself playing the role of director. Again, it goes back to the community experience; instead of coming to the director with my suggestions as an actor, I now am coming to the actors with suggestions. Camera work was where I thought I would be in the biggest trouble, but I gave them a single word: "eavesdrop." Eavesdropping was the key to my photographic concept, that is, if eavesdropping is a concept at all.

Q: Do you mean that was the whole conceptual framework for your approach to the film?

Newman: There wasn't really any pervasive conceptual idea because Rachel, Rachel didn't accommodate that kind of thing. I hadn't really worked out anything for the character except that her whole life was sort of pinched. Strangely enough, the picture laid itself out in "beats" very clearly to me. And each scene was something in itself that contributed to the whole.

Q: There was no further directorial program?

Newman: No. The main thing, of course, was to make the camera come to the actor. The actor works as closely as he can to the director's suggestions, and it's the cameraman's obligation to photograph it. The actors must have a lot of freedom and not be constricted by the camera.

Q: Which of the technical aspects did you find the toughest to master as a director?

Newman: I don't know what you mean by that, but in cutting—for me a very complex part of filmmaking—I found I had to be most ruthless. I was very fortunate to have an extraordinary cutter named Dede Allen. I feel that there are four major creative areas: the screenplay or the book—the actual framework; the actress, who gives that screenplay her personality; the director, who makes a conceptual and intentional contribution; and everything that is done in the cutting room.

Q: Do you think that your real interests may actually lie more in stage drama than in film?

Newman: I would love to direct a play. In fact, I might enjoy doing a play more than a movie. A movie—at least this last one—is 14 months out of my life for very little financial return. A stage venture would be considerably less time, but the big problem is really getting good scripts. Even when you have a good script, costs are so high for both theater and films that it is difficult to get control of a dramatic property in your own way. The managements of the major studios generally don't have that kind of vision. My film was turned down cold. I mean cold. With a major actress, me as director (an admittedly unknown quantity) and a first-draft screenplay from a book

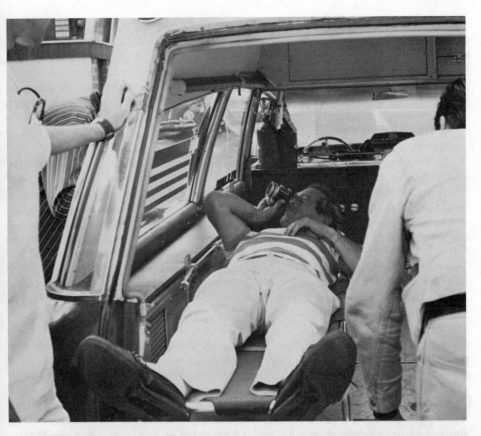

which had won the Governor-General's Award in Canada for the best fiction of the year, I offered them the *Rachel, Rachel* package for 55,000 dollars. And no one was interested. I wish that more motion-picture people would put faith in the tastes they believe in. If a person has a history of doing tasteful, and maybe even a few distinguished, films, then there's no reason why the studios shouldn't say, "Well, he's got some crazy vision of this film that we don't have, and we've just got to accept what he's doing on faith."

Q: The slogan is that movies are better than ever.

Newman: No, they're not. They're much worse.

Q: You mentioned that you have taken an option on Ken Kesey's novel *Sometimes a Great Notion.* Do you think that you'll be working on that shortly?

Newman: Sometimes is really a great book. A book about people. But I'm sorely torn, I must say, because I'd love to direct that film; yet it's also got a great part in it. You reach the obvious question: Can I do both? If I could get three weeks of rehearsal instead of two, and if we had enough preproduction work, which we never had with *Rachel,* I might. With *Rachel* I came to New York in May, hammered out the financial arrangements for the film, a location, then did my casting and was in rehearsal five weeks later. I'd never do it again, because there are just too many crises. And besides, you never seem to get free of the film.

Q: What do you mean?

Newman: Well, at the screening in New York I couldn't believe what a mess appeared on the screen after the lights went down. Wow! I shot up the aisle into the projection booth and the guy hadn't even run focus on the picture. And the sound— the scene with the recitation of the multiplication tables in the other room—you couldn't even hear them. I was so furious about the projection of the movie that I sent out an assistant cutter to Boston, Washington, Baltimore and Buffalo, when the movie first opened in those places, just to check projection. To check sound levels, and you know, it comes in at 1:85, and it's projected at 1:66, and either the characters are all walking around in the bottom of the screen or their heads are chopped off right above their eyes. It's really terrible, because we took a lot of care shooting that film, and those guys in the projection booths were killing it.

I guess Warren Beatty was the first guy to really do something about that. He used to go tour the country seeing *Bonnie and Clyde* and go screaming back to the projectionist. A friend of mine went to see *Cool Hand Luke* recently and the last half of the reel the sound went out. That audience really got the sense of a "failure to communicate."

Q: That reminds me, aren't *Rachel* and *Cool Hand Luke* despairing films of the same type? I get the feeling at the end of *Rachel* nothing's going to change. Maybe it's an open door . . . .

Newman: It's gotta be an open door. To me, it's an extraordinarily hopeful film. It's real. When she made that little tiny step, (A) to face sexual experience, (B) to have that child that was living inside of her, and (C) to allow that wrench in her life to happen—then I think she's capable of changing her entire existence.

Q: That's where I felt the hope had died, when there was no child, just the same emptiness inside of her.

Newman: That's interesting, because at the end of the film there was a good deal of inner voice, and I shot quite a bit more footage. Her subconscious voice was saying those poetic things like, "I'll always push the doors marked 'pull,' and pull the doors marked 'push,'" and so forth. The rough version I saw in the cutting room lasted five minutes and 20 seconds and I cut it down to two minutes, 15 seconds. You see, the problem of the picture was that the book was all interior monologue. Because we used no new conventions—I mean we've seen the voice-over, we've seen flashbacks and we've seen fantasies—all I could count on is that these conventions were used perceptively enough.

But in that ending of the film I was working from a written sequence to a visual design in which there were only three two-sentence ideas designed to create emotions. When I started cutting I left everything out except the emotional beats. You cannot start emotion and then go to something literary, and then go to emotion again, and then back to something literary. What happens is that it's like someone running a 50-yard dash in five-yard jumps. You start and stop and finally you end up with nothing. But if you create the way Chaplin created laughter, for instance, you would get a chuckle, and that would build into something else, and that would build into something else, and then the audience was never left off the hook.

Q: So you don't find any despair at all in the ending?

Newman: No, I find truth in the ending. There was some pressure on me to have Rachel not take her mother along. But I felt that wouldn't be real. It wouldn't happen that way. The mother is there, but now the mother has become the child, which is the way it should have been years ago.

Q: It's really a very antiheroic concept finally, isn't it?

Newman: Well, we said Hud was an antihero and we really misunderstood him, for the very simple reason that when you characterize Hud you give him all of the superficial graces that are supposed to be heroic. The so-called heroes of today, the movie characters and the politicians, all have that factor of external grace—really corrupt characters, but no scruples. The hero today is just a great con artist. They may have those beautiful faces, but the core of the matter is that they are really dull, foul people, because they have no morals at all. I don't know if Rachel is antiheroic, but at least she's struggling to change her life into something meaningful from an existence she had previously accepted without thinking.

Q: Do you feel that there is more control you can exercise over the kind of ideas like this that go into a script when you perform as a director rather than as an actor?

Newman: Both the actor and the director are always at the mercy of the screenwriter. They can't function except inside this framework. Right now the best scripts are the antiheroic scripts, and that's what I'm working with. Direction is just another part of the artistic process, and while I'm making movies, I suspect they'll be very similar whether I'm acting or directing.

—1969

101

Jack Lemmon

Bob Thomas

*Like Paul Newman, Jack Lemmon worked in summer stock, television,
and on Broadway before coming to Hollywood in the 1950s. Also like Newman,
he established a reputation as a fine actor in a variety of movies, among
them* It Should Happen to You, Mister Roberts *(Academy Award, best supporting
actor),* Some Like It Hot, The Apartment, Days of Wine and Roses, Irma
La Douce *and* The Fortune Cookie. *In 1971 he made his debut as
a director with* Kotch, *which won an Academy nomination for Walter Matthau.*

Jack Lemmon plopped into one of the overstuffed, floral-print chairs of the office of his Jalem Company. It was a compact place tucked in the rear of a two-storied building on North Robertson, in the heart of the interior-decorator belt. In the Hollywood custom, Lemmon's office is outfitted not like an office but a plush living room—deep, oversized couches, Matisse and Picasso prints, nouveau antiques, a desk at which he sits opposite Richard Carter, his onetime press agent and his partner in Kotch. Around the room are a few mementos of the Lemmon career—an award for this or that, an old playbill, a wooden plaque marked "Professor Fate" (from The Great Race). Also a megaphone with the initials in gold: J.L. That was the subject of our conversation: Jack Lemmon's debut as a film director with Kotch.

Like most movies nowadays, Kotch had a long, involved history. Dick Carter had read the book by Katharine Topkins, liked it, put in a bid for the movie rights. After treacherous dealings in the agency world, he acquired an option. He and veteran screenwriter John Paxton formed a partnership and Paxton turned out a screenplay.

Carter had originally planned the script for Spencer Tracy. When Tracy died, the would-be producer figured he needed a "name" director. He tried Mike Nichols, Arthur Penn and Paul Newman. No luck. Then, in February of 1969, Lemmon asked to read Kotch. "A strange thing happened to me while I was reading the script," Lemmon recalled. "From the very beginning, I could visualize the scenes depicting the relationship between the old man and his grandson. Throughout the rest of the script the scenes were playing in my mind, just as though they were on a screen. I must say I was walloped by the story. There was nothing in it for me to play; I think it would have been wrong for me to try to play the old man. After I finished reading it, I thought it over. I said to Dick, 'I love it. When you start making a list of directors, put me among them.' "

That was all Carter needed. He embraced the idea of Jack Lemmon as director. But even that wasn't enough to sell the package. This was in the era before Love Story, when production bosses turned thumbs down on anything that smacked of sentiment.

After several false starts, a deal was put together with Martin Baum at ABC Films. The star was to be Lemmon's co-star and close friend, Walter Matthau. Lemmon approached the chore with 25 years' experience as an actor, but virtually none as a director.

"Oh, I had directed a bit in stock, when the director got ill or something. But never in a major company. In the early days of television—and I mean the early days, late 1940s and early 1950s—I did five series at a time when nobody knew what a series was. I'd do a 15-minute show five times a week, and some of the time I'd direct, just to get the show on.

"Directing a feature had not been a burning ambition of mine, but it had been in the back of my mind. I guess every actor has the desire eventually to be a director. A lot of actors at various times in their careers realize that directing is more creative and less interpretive than acting. Well, acting can be creative if conditions are right. But 90 percent of the time, acting is interpretive.

"I think most actors have the desire to direct a film so they can have the decisions on what appears on the screen. That's the director's province. I had had a number of offers to direct in the past, but none had seemed right. Most of them were projects in which I would have appeared as well. I am leery of that. I have seen actors direct themselves successfully, and I've seen it done disastrously. I think for me it would depend on how secure I felt in the part.

"My big concern would be 'Who's minding the story?' I would worry that, if I said, 'Print,' I might be more concerned as an actor—that I had done my own part well—than as a director observing the overall scene."

With all the machinations of putting the deal together, Lemmon had plenty of time to prepare.

"That was good. I have found as an actor—and now as a director—that the longer you have to prepare, the better off you are. You can study a script and think you know how to do it. Then you're driving along one day and—*boinck!*—a light flashes on and you see something that you hadn't thought of before."

A large part of Lemmon's preparation was done in conjunction with his editor and his cameraman. He chose both with great care. His editor was Ralph Winters, who had worked on *The Great Race* and is "one of the handful of top editors in this town; more than that, I knew that we had a great rapport going for us, and that's important in a relationship as intimate as director and editor."

His cinematographer was Richard Cline, who had been an operator on the earliest Lemmon pictures at Columbia. "Not only is he a fine cameraman, he is malleable, not at all didactic. I knew he would work *with* me, not *at* me.

"The crew was all-important. I was vitally concerned with the selection of the set workers, because I've seen what can happen when you have an unhappy set. When the bubble isn't there, everyone is affected and you can't do good work. We had a helluva happy company—skillful, hardworking, predominantly young."

Lemmon participated in all the casting decisions, mindful of the problems that might arise with an actor directing actors. The prospect of working with Walter Matthau was reassuring.

"It wasn't just because I had acted with Walter; we're also very close as friends. We respect each other, and we know each other's reactions. I could anticipate how Walter would react, both as an actor and as a human being. I could say half a sentence to him and he'd say 'Gotcha.' It's the same kind of relationship that Walter and I have with Billy Wilder.

"Some actors think only of themselves. Not Walter. He's not that kind of scene-stealer who wants to give a bravura performance and will do anything to get his little bitty shtick across. He thinks about his own performance, but he tries to help the other actors as well.

"He and I are similar in our approach to acting. We realize that it is harder to play good material, because there are so many ways you can do it. Bad scripts are easy; there's usually only one way to do them."

Lemmon helped pick the locations, then he moved the principals into a Pacific Palisades residence for ten days of rehearsals in the actual set. When the scenes played satisfactorily, he ran them through for Ralph Winters and Dick Cline.

"My main concern was that the scenes should flow. I wanted to shoot as unobtrusively as possible, so that the audience would be unaware of camera angles and cuts and would concentrate on the people. The longer I could stage a scene, the better—as long as I didn't stage the actors for the camera. That takes some planning when you're shooting in a house where the walls can't be removed for a better angle."

Lemmon began production on the Palm Springs tramway. His reaction to his first day as a director: "Sheer, unadulterated fear."

Camera, power pack, lights, director, basic crew, extras and principals Matthau and Deborah Withers were loaded into the Alpine tram and transported to the mountain peaks overlooking the desert.

"It was madness. We had been assured complete freedom to use the tram, which wasn't true. We had been misinformed about the sun; it disappeared behind the peaks from time to time during the morning. And people on the tram were starting to get seasick. Walter was okay, but Deborah was changing color. Finally Dick Cline said, 'Either we'll have to change the filter or she'll have to play with white makeup for the rest of the picture.'

"Maybe it was good to begin the picture that way. I had to make the decision

Director Lemmon with actor Walter Matthau.

Lemmon instructing actress Felicia Farr, who is Mrs. Lemmon.

not to begin shooting, just to please the studio. I said to myself, 'Don't start printing until you're sure it's right.' So I waited. Once we started rolling, we were getting one and a half to two pages in a take."

There were other days when the limousine from ABC rolled up to locations with an emissary who inquired: "How come it's eleven o'clock already and you got no shots?" Lemmon resisted the pressure. He finished *Kotch* at 5:59 P.M. on the forty-fifth day of a 45-day schedule—"and I had half a can of film left, so I shot some extra footage of Walter on a bus—which I was able to use later." The film came in 15,000 dollars under the 1.6-million-dollar budget.

Like most first-feature directors, Lemmon was surprised by the amount of energy required. He rarely sat down and by midafternoon his legs began to fail.

Post-production proved a stimulating as well as enlightening experience.

"If an actor sees the same reel over and over again, he's bound to become bored. A director is different. He can stand the repetition because he is concerned about every frame.

"I think there are two dangers in the editing process. One is that you can become too protective of the material. The other is that the tedium of watching film over and over again might unconsciously make you want to tighten it. In that way, you can lose what you set out to do.

"I cut 30 minutes out of *Kotch,* then I put five minutes back. I think it's impor-tant in a film like this not to overcut. Here you are not worrying about the storyline as much as you are about the relationships of the people. I had a tendency to cut the scenes between Walter and Deborah in the last half of the picture. That would have been a disaster.

"Unless the audience digs the relationship between the two of them, what does it mean when she leaves at the end? Nothing. So I let their scenes run on, letting him just watch her as she makes a doll."

The first preview was in San Diego. It was a smash. It was the first time in the theater's history, the manager reported, that no one emerged to buy popcorn "or even go to the john." Previews in New Jersey and San Francisco went equally well. Only 22 seconds were cut.

"Don't touch another frame!" said Marty Baum. The film was rushed to a date at the Radio City Music Hall, and it proved one of ABC's biggest moneymakers.

Said Lemmon: "In a perverse way, that was my only disappointment in the whole experience—not having time to cut more. I think *Kotch* would play better with about four minutes removed."

Jack Lemmon spent about a year in preparing, shooting and editing *Kotch*. Besides his initiation fee to the Directors' Guild of America, the experience cost him a possible million or so he could have been earning as Jack Lemmon, superstar.

Would he direct again?

"Yeah," he said with eyes glowing, "if I could find the right material. And if I could work with a crew and actors that I loved. That's essential. Everything went beautifully for me on *Kotch*. I can't imagine what it would be like to have to direct a script I didn't believe in or with a cast and crew I didn't like.

"If the conditions were right, I'd do it again, anytime. I never had a better ex-perience in my entire professional career."

—1972

A Conversation with
Carl Reiner and Paul Henreid

Paul Henreid was born in Trieste, appeared in Max Reinhardt's theater, then in Austrian and British films. In 1940 he came to America, where he starred in many films, among them Now, Voyager, Casablanca, Song of Love, Devotion *and* The Spanish Main. *He has directed several films, including* For Men Only, Dead Ringer *and* Live Fast, Die Young, *as well as many television shows.*

Carl Reiner came out of Broadway revues and into memorable early television as sidekick to Sid Caesar and Imogene Coca on Your Show of Shows. *He has acted in films (*The Gazebo, The Russians Are Coming, The Russians Are Coming*), won Emmies as producer-writer for* The Dick Van Dyke Show *and written a book about his youth,* Enter Laughing, *which became a play. He directed the film version of* Enter Laughing. *His second feature was* The Comic.

Q: Do actors make good directors?

Reiner: Yes, certain actors do. Most actors who go into direction make good directors because they have learned their craft by paying attention. They often seek direction because they have been frustrated in their desire to express themselves fully. Usually the seed has been planted at one time or another when they have helped another actor. "Gee," the other actor says, "you'd make a helluva director!" Later, when the hair is falling out and the paunch starts to grow, the fellow starts to think, "Yeah, maybe I ought to try it."

Henreid: If they have been good actors, they should bring one important thing to direction: the understanding of an actor's problems. They should be able to suggest things that the nonactor is not in a position to do. For instance, a man like Carol Reed claims that he was a bad actor, yet he is able to communicate to his performer exactly what he wants. A director who had not acted, like a Michael Curtiz, would look at a scene and say, "There is something wrong here, but I don't know what it is." Eventually they would find out. But an actor-director might understand immediately that a gesture could take precedence over the word, or that tempo was desirable.

Q: Do actors have disadvantages as directors?

Reiner: Only in this respect: If an actor becomes a star strictly on personality or on instinct, then he probably won't make a good director. There have been certain stars, like Gary Cooper, who were marvelous performers but who couldn't examine themselves as actors. Directing would not be for them.

Henreid: The one disadvantage might be if the actor-director is a perfectionist acting-wise. He might persist if he does not achieve the perfection that he desires. When he is working on a television show or a short-schedule film, then he is not allowed such a luxury. He must keep the cost in mind and get the actors to deliver what is close to being right.

Q: When did you first have the yen to direct?

Reiner: I believe I've always had it. Even when I was playing with the kids around

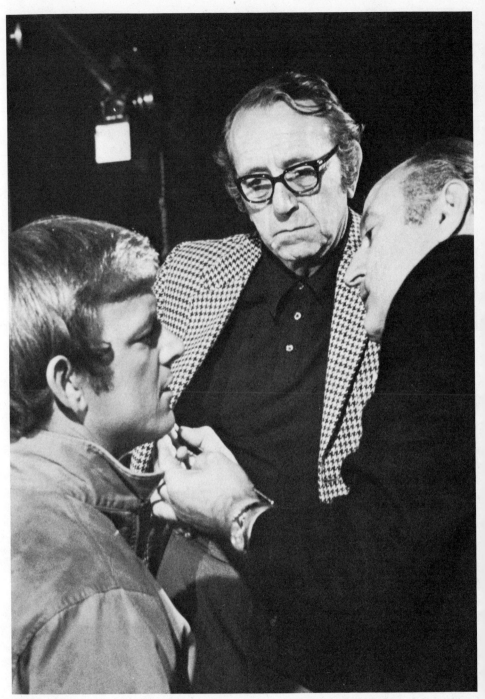

Paul Henreid oversees the makeup for actor Peter Haskell on the set of the television show *Bracken's World*.

the block, I'd say, "Let me be captain!" I had the feeling of leadership, that I could get the job done.

Henreid: I happened to be in Paris and to see a play of Sacha Guitry's, *Je t'aime*, which he did with Yvette Printemps. I was so much in love with the play that I didn't

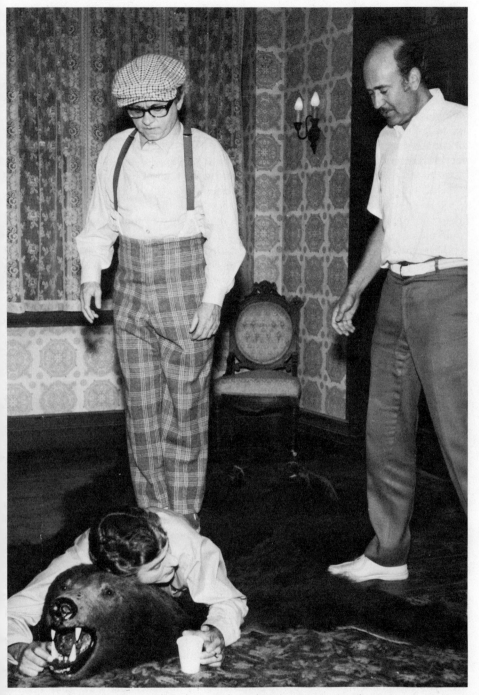

Carl Reiner rehearsing a scene with Dick Van Dyke and Mickey Rooney for *The Comic.*

want anyone else to direct it in Vienna, and besides, Guitry gave me strict rules about how to stage it. So I directed it myself. After that, I became so busy as an actor that I didn't have the time to think about directing.

Q: What was your motivation in becoming a director?

Reiner: I don't know. I suppose it may go back to the early days of television, when actors sometimes directed themselves. The director was pretty much involved with the technical aspects of getting the show on the air, and the actors did improvising on their own. I'd say to another actor, "Hey, wouldn't it be funny . . . ?" And often it was funny.

Henreid: I became a director out of the knowledge of any film actor with experience and background that the work of the director before, during and after filming is more creative than anyone else's job, except the writer's. And by collaborating with the writer as to what finally appears on the screen, the director's creative function is complete. I discovered that the director is able to change a performance not 100 percent, but at least 60 percent, in the cutting process. And during filming his attitude and spirit are reflected in the final product, apart from his actual direction.

Q: Did you have any trouble convincing people you could direct?

Reiner: No, not at all. Most people, if they think they can direct, inspire a confidence in other people. I would trust any actor who was thoroughly convinced he could direct.

Henreid: Not much. Because when I started, I was in demand as an actor, and producers said, "We want a film with Paul Henreid, so we might as well let him direct it."

Q: What was your first directorial job?

Reiner: The first real direction I did was at Georgetown University, where I volunteered to direct the play in our French class. My first professional job was on Sid Caesar's summer television show. He owned the package, and I directed sketches on the show. When I was producing and writing *The Dick Van Dyke Show* for television, I could have directed it. I knew the material, and I knew the actors better than anyone else. Many times I stepped in and solved staging problems that had seemed difficult. The cast kept asking me when I was going to direct. I said if I directed the show, then I couldn't produce and write it. And in television comedy the producing and writing are vital. My first real film direction was with my play *Enter Laughing.*

Henreid: I became terribly interested in film when I was under contract at Warner Brothers, and I spent a great deal of time between picture jobs in cutting rooms, dubbing rooms and other places where I could learn the production process. I had been interested in photography all my life, so the photographic aspects came easily to me. Later, the director on a film I was making didn't work out, and I finished half the picture. My following picture was an independent, *For Men Only,* and that was the first time I got credit as a director.

Q: What is the attitude of actors toward an actor-director?

Reiner: When an actor gets over forty and still is functioning in his profession, he gets a certain respect from his fellow actors. The actors I worked with knew what I had done in the business; they had confidence that I wouldn't let them fly in a rickety plane.

Henreid: Most actors are pleased and happy to have a director who has had experience as an actor. The only exceptions are those actors who feel you are in competition with them. They think: Here's another actor telling me what to do. But it is only the unintelligent or less talented actors who react that way. They are the ones who live in fear of delivering a performance and look for excuses not to appear: their hair is not in place, their lipstick is awry. There are the insecure ones who don't enjoy the process of acting; they only enjoy the result.

Q: Can actors direct themselves?

Reiner: Rarely. I can't. And I suspect that whenever an actor does direct himself, he has someone he respects watching over what he does. That's what I do.

110

Henreid: Yes, they can. But an actor is inclined not to experiment when he directs himself. He is likely to pick the safe things to do rather than try his utmost.

Q: What gives you the most satisfaction—acting or directing?

Reiner: The most satisfaction I get is from directing something I wrote. I found this while directing my own play on Broadway. It was the most grueling, the most excruciating experience I have ever known, and yet the most satisfying. I felt that nobody could understand my baby. Nobody could direct it as well as I could have. Oh, if Mike Nichols were available, I would have accepted him. Otherwise I worried that some director besides myself might add the wrong ingredient and sour the soup.

Henreid: Without question, directing gives me the most satisfaction. The reason is the creativity. In the past year I have acted in several movies. None of them seemed to offer any particular challenge as an actor; they were nice parts, but not great characters. But last year I directed a film for *Judd for the Defense* called *An Elephant in the Cigar Box.* That one show gave me more satisfaction and happiness than all of the acting parts.

—1970

Director-Actors:
A Partial List

Philip Abbott
Don Adams
Charles Aidman
Corey Allen
Woody Allen
Joseph Anthony
Alan Arkin
Desi Arnaz
Jack Arnold
Hy Averback
William Beaudine
Busby Berkeley
Milton Berle
Abner Biberman
Richard Boone
Marlon Brando
Mel Brooks
Kirk Browning
Abe Burrows
David Butler
Edward Buzzell
Yakima Canutt
Richard Carlson
John Cassavetes
Gower Champion
Charles Chaplin
Dane Clark
William Conrad
Tim Considine
Curt Conway
Jackie Cooper
Bill Cosby
Jerome Courtland
Richard Crenna
Donald Crisp
John Cromwell
Robert Culp
Robert Cummings

Jules Dassin
Delmer Daves
Lawrence Dobkin
King Donovan
Robert Douglas
Howard Duff
Clint Eastwood
Blake Edwards
Robert Ellenstein
Jose Ferrer
Peter Fonda
Stan Freberg
Bert Freed
Paul Frees
Ben Gazzara
Karl Genus
Lee Goodman
Peter Graves
Larry Hagman
Alan Handley
Paul Harrison
Jeffrey Hayden
Russell Hayden
Franklin Heller
Paul Henreid
George Roy Hill
G. V. "Skip" Homeier
Dennis Hopper
John Huston
Lamont Johnson
Byron Kane
Garson Kanin
Elia Kazan
Brian Keith
Gene Kelly
Michael Kidd
Alf Kjellin
James Komack

Fernando Lamas
Francis Lederer
Jack Lemmon
Sheldon Leonard
Mervyn Leroy
D. Peter Levin
Elliott Lewis
Jerry Lewis
Norman Lloyd
Barbara Loden
Joshua Logan
Richard Long
Sidney Lumet
Ida Lupino
Howard Magwood
Karl Malden
James Mason
Elaine May
Darren McGavin
Don McGuire
Andrew McLaglen
Burgess Meredith
Ray Milland
Sidney Miller
Robert Montgomery
Harry Morgan
Howard Morris
Vic Morrow
Barry Morse
Ken Murray
Gene Nelson
Ozzie Nelson
Ralph Nelson
John Newland
Anthony Newley
Paul Newman
Mike Nichols
Jack Nicholson

Alexander Nicol
David Niven
Edmond O'Brien
Donald O'Connor
Jack Palance
Jerry Paris
Fess Parker
John Payne
Leo Penn
Joseph Pevney
Robert Peyson
Sidney Poitier
Don Porter
Stanley Prager
Otto Preminger
Denver Pyle
Richard Quine
Carl Reiner

Allen Reisner
Gene Reynolds
Martin Ritt
Cliff Robertson
Mickey Rooney
Coby Ruskin
Mark Rydell
Gene Saks
Dore Schary
George Seaton
Joshua Shelley
Vincent Sherman
Frank Sinatra
Richard "Red" Skelton
Paul Stewart
Ezra Stone
Barry Sullivan
Don Taylor

Danny Thomas
Marshall Thompson
Norman Tokar
Peter Ustinov
Ed Waglin
Charles Walters
John Wayne
Dennis Weaver
Jack Webb
Leonard Weinrib
Orson Welles
Richard Wesson
Crane Wilbur
Cornel Wilde
Paul Winchell
Bonita Granville Wrather
John Wray
Alan Young

A scene from Howard Hawks' *Rio Bravo*.

IV.
The Western

'A Western is a wonderful thing, because you take a group of actors who have acted on the stage or who have acted in rooms and now you take them out into the elements. You throw them against the elements, and the elements make them much greater as actors than if they were in a room. Because they have to shout above the winds, they have to suffer, they have to climb mountains.''

Anthony Mann, who directed *Devil's Doorway, Winchester '73, Bend of the River, The Naked Spur, The Far Country, Man of the West* and other films, was describing one of the joys and challenges of making a Western.

Other directors have found different reasons for making Westerns. The challenge of bringing new attitudes and dimensions to the long-established genre has attracted many directors—George Stevens, William Wellman, Fred Zinnemann, William Wyler, among others—whose main work was not in the Western form. Others, such as John Ford, Howard Hawks, Henry King, Henry Hathaway and Sam Peckinpah, have been closely identified with Westerns, although they have made other kinds of films, too. Both the specialists and the occasional Western makers have succeeded in keeping the Western the liveliest and most durable of American film forms.

In its celebration of the Western, ACTION polled a cross section of newspaper and magazine critics for their choices of the best dozen Westerns of all time. Results of the poll are on the following pages. Among the runners-up: *Gunfight at the OK Corral, Ride the High Country, She Wore a Yellow Ribbon, How the West Was Won, The Alamo, The Magnificent Seven, The Big Country, The Covered Wagon, Destry Rides Again, Will Penny, Rio Bravo, Support Your Local Sheriff, My Darling Clementine, Broken Arrow, Cowboy, Hondo, The Iron Horse, One-eyed Jacks, Union Pacific.*

The Great Dozen: A Critique

Judith Crist
So there you are, strolling down the main street of your moviegoing days—and suddenly it's shoot-down time. Not the annual end-of-the-year event, when you pick your own list of bests, comparing the incomparable and defending the indefensible and anticipating the hassle at the New York Film Critics meeting. And not the interminable questionnaire that perpetually pops up in the mailbox now that movies are revered in academe, that goes: "I am working for my doctorate in moviemanship at Oscaloochee Tech and will appreciate your listing the ten greatest cartoons of all time" or "the ten greatest trailers" or "the ten greatest greatest . . ."

No such luck. It's shoot-down—or showdown—time, a confrontation with a list of the 12 films cited most often by some 250 *other* film critics as "The Best Dozen Westerns of All Time," in a poll for ACTION.

Primarily there's the relief at not having been polled. It's the "of all time" that makes the difference, a realization of all the unseen Westerns from the days of silents, of all the films half-remembered from childhood, of all the "oaters" that pass the big-city moviegoer by. Then there's the definition of terms, of boundaries for the genre that latter-day critics suggest is not a genre, of aspects of the historic mythology that satisfies neither history nor myth. Of course, were the gun on the other fellow's hip . . . Well, stick to the theory that even when it comes to moviemaking or list compiling those who can, do; those who cannot, teach; and those who like to think they could if they would but are smart enough not to, criticize. Let's get to the list.

What's interesting about the "best dozen" is that the oldest film listed is the 1931 *Cimarron* and that three of the others were released last year [1969]. Is it that critics are weak in their movie pasts, that the films freshest in mind rate highest—or that 1969 was a bonanza year for Westerns? Just as a touchstone, I asked William K. Everson, as both film historian and top authority on Westerns, to provide his list of a top ten. In no comparative order, and after noting that he would really like to come up with a list of ten John Ford films, he cited two silents, William S. Hart's *Hell's Hinges* and *The Narrow Trail,* and then Edward Cahn's *Law and Order;* King Vidor's *Billy the Kid;* Delmer Daves' *Broken Arrow;* John Ford's *Wagonmaster, Stagecoach* and *My Darling Clementine;* Henry King's *The Gunfighter;* and Sam Peckinpah's *Ride the High Country.* Only two, *Stagecoach* and *The Gunfighter,* appear on the critics' list I'd go all out for perhaps half of it.

Appropriately, albeit alphabetically, *Butch Cassidy and the Sundance Kid* heads the "best dozen" list and *The Wild Bunch* completes it. After all, it was Butch and other Wild Bunch boys who inspired the first Western film, Edwin S. Porter's *The Great Train Robbery,* in 1903, by their holdup of the Union Pacific in Tipton, Wyoming, three years before. But beyond their linkage in subject, these two very different films demonstrate what has happened to the Western by the start of the 1970s; it has developed a sense of humor—and it has taken a blood bath.

Butch Cassidy, with William Goldman's original screenplay and under George Roy Hill's direction, is a particularly satisfying multilevel film, more than an "entertainment" in its dimension. It is essentially a humanization of the bad-man legend, the story of two nice guys whose time is over and who are left to face up to themselves a "a couple of two-bit outlaws on the dodge." The triumph is ultimately the director's for Hill goes beyond the wit and laughter of the script to show the end of the game the rot beneath the raucous surface insouciance. Among his many beautiful effects, hi slow survey of rolling terrain and flashing montage of city fun, the outstanding one

Butch Cassidy and the Sundance Kid 1969 George Roy Hill.

Cimarron 1931 Wesley Ruggles.

s his moment of truth, the turning point of his "entertainment." The two outlaws, ironically, have gone straight but are beset by bandits. Sundance has the sharpshooter's ool, but for Butch there is the horror of the first kill, the slow-motion death and vailing scream. And in Hill's hands a current cliché becomes a master stroke, and he myth of the charming bad man is shattered by blood.

Cimarron stands through the years as the epic of frontiersmanship, with Yancey mbodying the free spirit that adventured through it and Sabra epitomizing the inomitable spirit of the builder who took root. It's been imitated and even disastrously emade over the years, but nothing has matched Wesley Ruggles' original triumph in acing the decades (from the 1890 Oklahoma land rush to 1930) and tracing the

Duel in the Sun 1946 King Vidor.

The Gunfighter 1950 Henry King.

High Noon 1952 Fred Zinnemann.

Lonely Are the Brave 1962 David Miller.

The Ox-Bow Incident 1943 William Wellman.

Red River 1948 Howard Hawks.

Shane 1953 George Stevens.

Stagecoach 1939 John Ford.

True Grit 1969 Henry Hathaway.

The Wild Bunch 1969 Sam Peckinpah.

growth of a community, in keeping his canvas alive but uncluttered with characte
and subplot, matching the meaty fiction of Edna Ferber. Archetypal of the grow-old
along-with-me generational story, it's a romantic movie-movie that endures and is
perhaps, the best of the films that have attempted to trace frontier roots into twentieth
century society.

Duel in the Sun was a bad joke in 1946 and anyone who awards it any sort o
stature in 1970 has to be kidding. That producer David O. Selznick spent more on i
than on *Gone with the Wind*; that it was referred to variously at the time as *Lust i*
the Dust and "The Outlaw in bad taste"; and that King Vidor quit with the suggestio
that the producer "shove it" may be worth noting. Its one plus value—Walter Huston'

fine portrait of an evangelist—has been cut to shreds in the rereleases over the years. Its vulgar nonsense isn't even good for laughs anymore.

The Gunfighter stands as the classic study of the malaise of the professional gunslinger. Henry King's remarkable humanistic approach gives every aspect of this 1951 film an emotional impact that does not lessen in the face of countless imitations. Peck's tight-lipped immobility and inner turmoil as a man risking his life for a reunion with his estranged wife and child and his dream of a new life; Helen Westcott's almost stolid honesty as the hopeless wife; Millard Mitchell's compassion as the one-time gunslinger turned lawman; Jean Parker's warmth as a bar girl who knows the odds; Karl Malden's sycophantish familiarity as the bartender with an eye for the main chance are all concomitants in the vivid drama King orchestrates to the ticking of a clock and the gathering tensions in a town outgrowing its onetime tolerance of the gunman, and beyond these is the risk of a young punk making a fatal move. King's triumph is in bringing heartbreak to the end of a legend, in giving posthumous grandeur to a wasted life.

High Noon, on the other hand, achieves its stature by type rather than humanism. Fred Zinnemann's 1952 film is a masterpiece of precision even beyond its adherence to the classic unities, its tense pacing to the exact 80 minutes to showdown time. Only the theme ballad suggests a flesh-and-blood romance; there's no time for declarations of love or other emotions. Each character is representational, from Gary Cooper's man of self-imposed duty to Katy Jurado's worldly woman of surpassing understanding to Grace Kelly's prim but courageous Quaker to Lloyd Bridges' petulant "gunsel." Each townsman represents a moral viewpoint, a human attitude, as if each were labeled Fear, Prejudice, Self-Interest. It's the perfection of these embodiments, of each choreographed move to the climax, of every minute ticked off, that gives the film its enduring quality.

Lonely Are the Brave is a literal film of the cowboy's clash with contemporary civilization, his doom in a jet-age society where walkie-talkies and helicopters are part of a posse's equipment. David Miller's 1962 film is, in fact, too literal for my taste, its symbolism overt, its questioning of whether all free spirits must be tamed oversimplified, if only because the equation of free spirit and barroom brawler seems to be unjust to the anachronism of the itinerant cowboy. It is nevertheless an absorbing and interesting film, with Kirk Douglas giving an extraordinarily good performance and Walter Matthau simply brilliant as the sympathetic sheriff. My preference for a contemporary end-of-the-Western-era film would be *Hud,* wherein the final transition from living on the land to living off it is made and the roots are drilled rather than planted as the cattle are plowed under.

The Ox Bow Incident stands, of course, without peer as a story of mob injustice reinforced by its frontier setting. Its power is in its relative fidelity to Walter Van Tilburg Clark's novel; as a film it looks more than a wee bit arty. (James Agee remarked memorably that on first viewing he felt it suffered from *rigor artis;* his appreciation grew in retrospect.) It's that gnarled hanging tree, I suspect, that throws one off. But the structure of the film—the two wandering cowboys as passive witnesses, the three strangers picked up by a mob, the various interests and motives that dominate the crowd, the quiet murder and the shattering final disclosure—encloses a tense and impressive drama, beautifully cast and tautly directed by William Wellman, as powerful today as in 1943.

Red River remains, after 22 years, the ultimate epic of the cattle driver, with Howard Hawks making magnificent use not only of setting but also of theme to present the tough drudgery and courageous spirit of frontiersmanship. It has, of course, the "circular" plot of the epic—the return, for Wayne, to Red River after 20 years, to resolve his relationship with his adopted son, brilliantly played by Montgomery Clift, and to close the romantic circle of their lives. But it's the cattle drive itself, complete with stampedes, Indian raids and brawls, that provided the juice of the film. For myself, in recent years I've felt the film moves slowly and drags from time to time—an impression enhanced, perhaps, by my preference for *Rio Bravo* among Hawks' work as a human drama within the Western framework.

Shane remains the classic homesteader story, the Western concerned with the farmer rather than the cowboy. George Stevens' 1952 film also remains the prototype for the "mysterious stranger" who appears from nowhere to save the underdog before riding off into nowhere—and certainly Jack Palance set the standard for the evil, gloved gunhand. It's chic to put *Shane* down nowadays; I still find it unflawed in its picture of ordinary men establishing themselves, a picture romanticized by the advent of the knight in shining armor. It's Stevens' blending of grubby living with chivalric derring-do, his pitting humble folk against pure villainy, his being frankly sentimental and his doing all these things with cool that give the film an enduring quality.

Stagecoach is, of course, the nonpareil, the source from which all Western clichés seem to me to flow. This 1939 *Grand Hotel*-on-wheels is so perfectly structured, so immaculately cast and so beautifully directed that it would head my list of choice Westerns. Its morality is classic—the social outcasts (the outlaw, the prostitute, the gambler, the alcoholic doctor) and the heroes; the pillar of society (the banker) is the villain. A boyish John Wayne (in suspenders, yet), a glamorous Claire Trevor, a wonderfully sodden Thomas Mitchell—the foolish attempt to duplicate them in the recent remake only attested to their fine originality. And this was, of course, Ford's first use of Monument Valley to provide that unforgettable vision of the lonely voyagers on the vast salt flats. For action, beyond the Indian chase (so okay, smart Indians would have shot the horses and cut the whole thing short!), carries into a final shootdown on Main Street, with a genial lawman to speed the lovers on their way. Who needs Cinderella when John Ford can give us stuff like this to dream on?

True Grit boasts an old John Wayne as a "one-eyed fat man" and an off-beat plot, but beyond Henry Hathaway's clear detailing of an amusing story, this 1969 film seems to me to have dubious claim to classic rating. It's an engrossing film that cuts away from clichés by having an over-age hard-drinking lawman as hero, a teenage Miss Priss as heroine and a romantic young man (Glenn Campbell, idol of teenie-boppers and housewives) who, remarkably, gets killed off. But the film itself rates primarily as entertainment.

On its level I would certainly list Burt Kennedy's 1965 *The Rounders,* with Henry Fonda and Glenn Ford as two dumb contemporary cowhands; Sydney Pollack's 1968 *The Scalphunters,* with Burt Lancaster and Ossie Davis doing some of the dandiest and frankest interracial brawling we've had on screen; or—above all—Elliot Silverstein's 1965 *Cat Ballou,* the best Western spoof on record, with Lee Marvin's Kid Shelleen a sophisticated match for Wayne's Rooster Cogburn any day.

The Wild Bunch is simply not my cup of gore. I find this 1969 movie the epitome of the blood-lust slaughter-cult film, two hours of murder and mayhem wherein the innocents are killed by the bad guys, who are killed by worse guys, all to the tune of what Peckinpah cultists claim are "blood ballets" and pure thoughts about the evils of killing. They see this depiction of the last days of the last remnants of the old gang as a portentous comment on violence in our time, on the disintegration of a group, on a variety of things. It is, they claim, "a man's movie." As for me—I'd as lief drop in on the local abattoir for entertainment and look to the bloodiest spaghetti Western for social significance. Peckinpah did his best work on *The Westerner* for television, where the small screen and time restrictions disciplined him. I admire much of *Ride the High Country*—and hopefully find traces of his original talent in *The Ballad of Cable Hogue.* He has a feel for the age of the Western; I wish he had one for its people.

—1970

Sam Peckinpah

Joel Reisner and Bruce Kane

Sam Peckinpah earned his master's degree at the University of Southern California in drama, worked as an actor and director in the theater before moving to television. He directed segments of Gunsmoke, The Westerner, The Rifleman, Broken Arrow and The Dick Powell Show. His first feature was The Deadly Companions in 1961. Others: Ride the High Country, Major Dundee, The Wild Bunch, The Ballad of Cable Hogue, Straw Dogs, Junior Bonner, The Getaway.

There are 3,643 cuts in the original release print of *The Wild Bunch,* more than any other motion picture Technicolor has ever processed. Some of these cuts are three and four frames in length. They are imperceptible to audiences and only Sam Peckinpah really knows for sure that they are there.

When Peckinpah set out to make *The Wild Bunch,* many who read the script regarded it as just another Western—and not a very good one at that. Peckinpah had a reputation as a Western director. His series *The Westerner* is still regarded by many as one of television's finest moments. His second film, *Ride the High Country,* established him as a director of real talent. This early success was followed by a series of stormy encounters with producers who hired him for his skill and then bucked him because they wanted it their way. And with Peckinpah there can only be one way—his way.

> "People are born to survive. They have instincts that go back millions of years. Unfortunately, some of those instincts are based on violence. There is a great streak of violence in every human being."

Peckinpah is an unreasonable man principally because he demands an unobtainable kind of perfection from an industry which usually requires only commercial competence. Most producers are, understandably, in the business of making pictures for profit. Peckinpah makes his pictures for audiences and for several years he remained, as a director of motion pictures, inactive. It was only when producer Phil Feldman and studio head, Ken Hyman, took a gamble on Peckinpah that he was able to work again. They were forewarned. Peckinpah was difficult, tenacious, volatile. They were also aware, however, that he was among the most gifted American directors of his generation. The result was *The Wild Bunch.*

Peckinpah makes a picture via the process of elimination, frequently in the footage and almost as frequently in his staff and crew. There are those who would say that he fired as many people as there are cuts in the picture.

Explains film editor Lou Lombardo: "Peckinpah takes hold like a bulldog and doesn't let go of any aspect of the show. Most directors let the cutter go. Sam goes over every piece of film cut by cut and frame by frame. He's a perfectionist."

Lombardo, who did the initial cutting of *The Wild Bunch* on location in the remote Mexican town of Paras, remarked that Peckinpah gave him only a rough idea of what he wanted to see. "Peckinpah gave me my head on the rough cut for each particular sequence. Only afterward did he come in to adjust what I had done to conform with his vision of the ultimate structure of the movie. Not that he works with that tight a preconceived notion of what he wants. He builds metamorphically."

> "*The Wild Bunch* is about a bunch of guys that went to Mexico . . . and *The Ballad of Cable Hogue* is about a man who found water where it wasn't. . . It's also about God."

Peckinpah suspected from the very beginning of the project that the front office would ask to see the film. So he polished key sequences to perfection while simultaneously shooting the rest of the picture—a schedule which committed him to virtually a 15- to 20-hour-a-day job for weeks at a time. Peckinpah had outguessed the studio. They did ask to see film and the ten reels they saw were the ten reels Peckinpah wanted them to see—footage that was refined and polished and almost self-contained.

"Peckinpah took a gamble with me," continued Lombardo, "because he felt we were compatible. I'd never worked on a movie of this caliber before, but I had worked with Peckinpah, on a TV version of *Noon Wine*. It takes a special kind of person to work with the man. I'm a flexible guy. You're with him 15 to 16 hours a day. If Peckinpah asked the average editor for two more frames or three less frames day by day, sooner or later they'd wig out. But he needs this kind of perfection and if you're willing to give it to him—if you're willing to stretch yourself further than you think you are able—he can get things out of you that you'd never thought you were capable of. He's like that with his actors, too. That's why with Peckinpah they give such fantastic performances."

> "My idea was that *The Wild Bunch* would have a cathartic effect. No, I don't like violence. In fact, when I look at the film itself, I find it unbearable. I don't think I'll be able to see it again for five years."

One of these actors "who stretched himself further" is Strother Martin. In a scene for *The Wild Bunch* Martin, cast as one of the trigger-happy bounty hunters, was called upon to express extreme nervousness and impatience. As Martin explains: "In the first couple of takes, I guess I didn't give him the kind of intensity he wanted, so Peckinpah, peering through those god-damned mirrored sunglasses he's always wearing, began to ride me to such an extent that I became the nervous wreck the character in the picture was supposed to be. He kept telling me that I was screwing up his picture and holding up production. I could never tell if he was joking or being serious, because his voice is completely devoid of emotion and you can't see his eyes because of those god-damned mirrored sunglasses."

> "The myth of the noble savage is bull. Law and order and grace and understanding are things that have to be taught."

Peckinpah, unlike many directors, frequently expresses great admiration for actors and treats them with enormous respect and care, Strother Martin notwithstanding. This respect is frequently reciprocal. Robert Ryan remarked, "All the Westerns have been made. The only difference is style, and Peckinpah's style is extraordinary."

Cinematographer Lucien Ballard, who photographed three of Peckinpah's films, as well as a number of his television shows, describes a typical incident illustrating the director's attention to style:

"Before shooting *The Wild Bunch* we pored over movies and stills having to do with the Mexican Revolution. We were both very taken by the shallow, flat effect of these images. We selected our lenses in an attempt to recapture this same kind of visual texture."

Ballard reflects that Peckinpah's attention to the ambience of his films is an integral part of his technique. He remarked that, for example, while making *Ride the High Country* Peckinpah selected virtually every piece of clothing the actors were to wear, a practice he carried over through each of his projects.

"During the filming of *The Wild Bunch* he wanted to see the costumes for the extras," actor L. Q. Jones commented, "and the assistant director brought him only those costumed actors who would be seen in the foreground of the action. When Peckinpah asked where the others were, his assistant told him that hardly anybody would know they were in the shot. Peckinpah's reply was, 'I'll know!'"

While shooting, Peckinpah's closest working relationship is with his cinematographer. "Sam uses me both as his eyes and his sounding board," Ballard remarked. "I

Major Dundee.

can come up with specific suggestions and I know that he will listen to me and seriously consider them. If he picks up on an idea of mine and uses it and it doesn't come off, he'll never pass the buck. Peckinpah once told me that he accepts total and complete responsibility for his films."

When he is making a film, Peckinpah seems to care only about one thing—what is going to be finally realized on the screen. He will work under any kind of conditions at all hours to get what he wants.

"All I want is to enter my house justified."

"It's true, he does work ungodly hours," Ballard continues, "but no matter how many hours the rest of us put in, the chances are that Peckinpah will put in more. He might stop by after a day's shooting to have a few drinks with the boys, but long after they've gone to bed, he is up rewriting the script or preparing for the next day's shooting. He has enough guts to change a scene or rewrite it if it doesn't work, even if he has to do it on the set or in the middle of the night. I think that Sam must have rewritten half of *The Ballad of Cable Hogue* while he was shooting it."

Peckinpah's appraisal of his own work is a series of contradictions. "I don't like to futz with it—I want to get it on," he says repeatedly. Yet, according to Richard Lyons, producer of *Ride the High Country*, "If he had his way, he'd still be cutting that show this week."

> "I believe in the complete innocence of children. They have no idea of good and evil. It's an acquired taste."

"Getting it on" could well be translated from Peckinpah-ese to mean months of complex and often convoluting decision making: examining and reexamining a reel, reworking and recutting so that it will come out "the best way."

> "The Western is a universal frame within which it is possible to comment on today."

Peckinpah has worked and can work quickly. *Ride the High Country* was shot in less than a month and yet looks like a picture costing several times its actual budget, and is regarded now as an authentic classic of the Western genre. Trained in TV, Peckinpah is able to work against mind-splitting deadlines. Yet months after principal photography had been completed on *The Ballad of Cable Hogue*, he was still working on it. He could easily have shot another picture during his long postproduction period. Then, too, Peckinpah knows that his work is going to be judged and he wants that work to be what he considers to be the very best he has in him. Recently, when asked which directors he admires, Peckinpah quickly responded: "David Lean—he has freedom."

> "I'd like to be able to make a Western like Kurosawa makes Westerns."

There are those who love Peckinpah and those who hate him. Mostly there are those who have a love-hate relationship going.

Stella Stevens, who co-starred with Jason Robards and David Warner in *Cable Hogue*, says succinctly: "Sam Peckinpah is a man who expects excellence. If you can't give your best, he doesn't want you around. I don't blame him."

—1970

Henry Hathaway

Philip K. Scheuer

Henry Hathaway started as a child actor in 1907 and continued to act until 1932, when he began directing Westerns. He has long been identified with the Western genre through such films as The Ox-Bow Incident, Rawhide, The Sons of Katie Elder and True Grit. But his films have been diversified; among his other credits are Trail of Lonesome Pine, Lives of a Bengal Lancer, 13 Rue Madeleine, Kiss of Death, Call Northside 777, and The Desert Fox.

"It isn't so much that I stick to Westerns," explained Henry Hathaway, "as that there are not many people who are making 'em." He pointed his usual cigar for emphasis.

Hathaway, the director, was ensconced in his bungalow at Universal City, where he had been employed as a prop boy in 1915—"March 17, 1915, to be exact"—holding forth on an industry and an art whose very beginnings he had been in on, at least in the West. Even earlier, in 1909, he had worked as a child actor for the American Film Company. "And they were making Westerns, one-reelers, even then—usually at La Mesa, which is between San Diego and the Mexican border."

Hathaway warmed up on the subject—at first chronologically: "There are only so many stories and situations, after all. Even then they were about fences—the battle between the farmer and the cowman over water rights. From the one-reelers to *Shane*, in which bad man Alan Ladd was hired to come in and protect the farmer.

"In between, from the one-reelers they went on to two- and three-reelers, like here at Universal with Harry Carey. By the time they stretched to five, they were running out of plots; they even tried silents without subtitles. Then sound came in—a new way to tell the same story!—in talk. Then color, the CinemaScope and Cinerama, which used mechanical things to make it appear they were using new plots.

"But then suddenly there were no new crutches to fall back on, so they were forced to come up with a new approach. Not altogether of necessity but certainly happily, they found the public was more interested in interesting characters than old-hat situations, in what a certain character would do even in an old-hat situation.

"Out of this came, I think, the greatest advance in the Western picture in years—in decades. I mean *Butch Cassidy*, *The Wild Bunch* and *True Grit*—all character studies. *Butch* had two characters who might have been out of *Mice and Men*; one of the great relationships, George and Lennie, one bright guy and one dumb guy—I'm not saying a copy, mind you, but as interesting as the relationship of those two.

"Then, of course, there was that tendency in the early days to glorify the West—which got a little monotonous. Today we tell it as it is, or was.

"*The Wild Bunch* was about a gang of disreputable bastards who destroyed each other. In *True Grit* we made no attempt to make the leading character glamorous; in fact, we leaned over backward the other way. Duke Wayne played him as a fat old man with an eye patch; as a drunk, a thief and a killer—and you ended up liking him.

"This is something like what happened in other pictures—Wally Beery in *The Champ*, Emil Jannings and so on. But the Western was the last to get to it.

"Another happening is kids. They won't believe, like, two men making love in *Staircase*—in which Richard Burton and Rex Harrison were only playing at homosexuality, two guys camping and not very funny at that. But they accepted the truth —even though it was repugnant—in *Midnight Cowboy*.

"Also, one of the reasons the kids like *True Grit* is because they accept Duke as Mister Western.

"Then there was Kim Darby as the kooky kid; we picked her because if we had picked, say, the girl in *The Flying Nun*, no one would have believed her. Today you have to cast the people for what they are in it—not because of what star happened to be available—in *The Only Game in Town* they cast Liz Taylor, who becomes a cocktail waitress to make money to live. First, people know she doesn't have to do it, and second, she doesn't look it."

From realism in characters to realism in locations was a logical talk step for Hathaway. "When I read about the young filmmakers and their grand new ideas about going to real locations—well, I did that 40 years ago. In 1931—the first picture I ever made for Paramount—I wasn't allowed to come in the studio. Too expensive, I had to use the ranch for locations. And that went for interiors, too."

131

The location practice persisted through the years and some 80 features (he never directed shorts)—from *Trail of the Lonesome Pine*, itself a 1936 pacesetter, to such farther-east superthrillers as *The House on 92nd Street*, *13 Rue Madeleine* and *Call Northside 777*.

The kids, of course, also discovered the camera. "The subject matter itself suggests the style," he insists. "Trick camera work—trick photography, rather—has, I think, destroyed more movies than it's helped. It should only be used for an effect. Take the split screen: In *Grand Prix* it created a certain excitement in itself, as did the polo game in *The Thomas Crown Affair*. But no split screen ever helped a beautiful scene."

The moviemakers are also overboard on length: "It all depends again on type—*War and Peace* or *Napoleon*, sure—but two hours is a long time to hold your rapt attention."

The pale blue eyes of this veteran filmmaker fail to belie the ruggedness of his physique, even for a man who has passed seventy—or the vigor with which he defends violence on the screen. "Look, no one has used violence any more than I have—but it's always acceptable, to use a bad phrase, if it suits the occasion.

"In *The Lonesome Pine* I had a man shooting his own son—not only that, but emptying the gun till it clicked, till it ran out of shells. Walter Wanger, the producer, said it would never get by; but when Joe Breen of the Hays Office ran the picture, he exclaimed, 'He deserved it!' You see, the son had killed Henry Fonda in cold blood.

"Then there was Dick Widmark, who shoved the old lady in the wheelchair down the stairs in *Kiss of Death*. Darryl [Zanuck] forbade me to shoot it, but when he saw it in the picture he changed his mind. The point was that it would make the audience realize the depths of which Widmark was capable when he later threatened to get back at Victor Mature through his family.

"When the action really justifies it, when it creates an emotional justification, the audience will accept it. But the brutality must be an integral part, not just gratuitous."

Hathaway himself wasn't the only prop boy/man to make good on the Universal lot, Hathaway recalled. "For instance, Jack Ford and Willy Wyler." He started his own duties on the first flicker for which a set builder (Lee Lawson) was especially brought in—"only he was called a 'construction foreman' then." The picture was *Damon and Pythias*, and it boasted a chariot race led by Herbert Rawlinson and William Worthington.

Hathaway went from Universal to the Army to Inceville, which Goldwyn later took over, and worked till the strike of 1920. He eventually landed at Paramount for his first Western there—and stayed (or, as he grins, overstayed) 18 years. This record was topped by that at 20th—21 years.

Some of his later releases are *How the West Was Won* ("three episodes, about 80 percent"), *The Sons of Katie Elder* and *Five-Card Stud* ("wasn't very good"). He has proved versatile in every kind of film—like, as I mentioned, the late Michael Curtiz. Hathaway nodded vigorously: "The most underrated director in the motion-picture industry."

—1970

Burt Kennedy Interviews
John Ford

Burt Kennedy and John Wayne during the shooting of *The War Wagon*.

From The Iron Horse *in 1924 to* Cheyenne Autumn *in 1964, John Ford has proved himself the master of the Western idiom. Some of his greatest achievements in that form are* Stagecoach, Wagonmaster, My Darling Clementine, Fort Apache, She Wore a Yellow Ribbon, Rio Grande, The Searchers, The Man Who Shot Liberty Valance. *Ford was interviewed by Burt Kennedy, who has demonstrated his facility with the Western with such films as* Mail Order Bride, The Rounders, Return of the Seven, Welcome to Hard Times, The War Wagon, The Train Robbers.

Kennedy: I never saw *The Iron Horse.*

Ford: You weren't even born when I made that one.

Kennedy: I know. I have heard that *The Iron Horse* was your favorite picture. Is that true?

Ford: No. "The next one" is my favorite picture. Well, maybe there's one that I love to look at again and again. That's *The Sun Shines Bright,* a Judge Priest story by Irvin S. Cobb, who was a pretty damn good writer. I had Charles Winninger in that one and he was excellent. That's really my favorite, the only one I like to see over and over again. The only trouble was that when I left the studio, old man [Herbert] Yates didn't know what to do with it. The picture had comedy, drama, pathos, but he didn't understand it. His kind of picture had to have plenty of sex or violence. This one had neither; it was just a good picture. But Yates fooled around with it after I left the studio and almost ruined it.

Kennedy: The Quiet Man—That was a wonderful picture.

Ford: Yes. I like that one. There again I had trouble with Yates. He kept complaining, "It's all green. Don't they have any browns or blacks in Ireland? Why does it have to be all green?" I had a lot of fun with old Herb on that one. He wanted to call it *The Prize Fighter and the Colleen.* I felt that was an awful title because it tipped the story that Duke [Wayne] was a boxer. Well, Yates said that he had received lots of letters from exhibitors who told him that they preferred his title to *The Quiet Man.* I asked to look at the letters, and he showed them to me. "What a strange coincidence!" I told him. "All these letters have the same date and they say the same thing." Obviously he had sent out a letter that was practically mimeographed and asked the theater men to write in letters. And they did. But I still wouldn't go with his title.

Kennedy: I've made practically all Westerns, and I keep hearing the remark, "Why don't you change the mold?" Has that ever happened to you?

Ford: No one has ever told me what kind of picture to make. When [Merian] Cooper and I were starting our own company I made four or five Westerns in order to make some money. They were potboilers, but they served a purpose.

Kennedy: I love to make Westerns.

Ford: So do I. I like nothing better. It gives me a chance to get away from the smog, to get away from this town, to get away from people who would like to tell me how to make pictures. You're working with nice people—cowboys, stuntmen, that kind of person. You get up early in the morning and go out on location and work hard all day and then you get home and you go to bed early. It's a great life—just like a paid vacation. I love to make Westerns. If I had my choice, that's all I would make.

Kennedy: Have you seen any of these Spanish or Italian Westerns?

Ford: You're kidding!

Kennedy: No, they have them, and a few have been popular.

Ford: What are they like?

Kennedy: No story, no scenes. Just killing—50 or 60 killings per picture. . . . How do you prepare for a picture?

Ford: Well, you ask yourself a few questions: What are you going to say? What is your format? Right now I'm wrestling with a story about the OSS. I made a promise to Wild Bill Donovan on his death bed that I would make an OSS picture, so I've got to do it. Right now I'm wading through piles of reports and histories and trying to break it down into some kind of a format. I'm suffering from a wealth of material. But you try to get a format for each picture. For instance, on *She Wore a Yellow Ribbon* I tried to make it as Remington as possible, though it didn't quite come out that way. On another picture I might try to make it as if it were seen by Charlie Russell.

Kennedy: How did you happen to use Monument Valley for *Stagecoach?*

Ford: I knew this guy, Harry Goulding, who had a trading post there. Once he asked me, "Did you ever think of Monument Valley for a location?" I said, "Say—that's a good idea." He said, "The Indians are starving down there, and I'm starving. They're hocking their jewelry—the turquoise things they make—so they can eat. If a movie company came down there, the Indians could make some money and be able to live." I thought that was a good idea. I remembered Monument Valley when I had driven through there. So I took the company of *Stagecoach*—the first one, not the second one—down to Monument Valley and we left 200,000 dollars down there and the Indians ended up fat and sassy. It's a wonderful location and a wonderful place to live.

Kennedy: I was just down in Sedona [Arizona] shooting a picture, and I liked that location.

Ford: Yes, Sedona is okay, but it's too small, too confined. If I'm going on location, I'd rather go farther, to some big place like Monument Valley.

Kennedy: Did you ever have any trouble getting the studios to let you go to the right places?

Ford: No.

Kennedy: We're always bucking to go to a good location, but the studio always wants you to shoot it on the back lot.

Ford: I never had that. I wouldn't make a Western on the back lot. They could get somebody else.

Kennedy: Did you ever have any problems with big-money actors?

Ford: No, I never ran into that problem.

Kennedy: Well, you know, the actors now have their own companies.

Ford: No, I never had that. I wouldn't work with an actor's company. Oh, I did some pictures with Duke when he had his Batjac, but I wasn't working for him. I never had any trouble with actors; if anybody kicked up a fuss, I'd say, "Okay, we'll get somebody else."

Kennedy: What do you think of the various wide-screen processes?

Ford: I still like the conventional-sized screen.

Kennedy: So do I. I think the 1.85 ratio is the best.

Ford: You're right. It still has height and you can get composition. It's so hard to get good composition in a wide screen. I like to see the people and if you shoot them in a wide screen, you're left with a lot of real estate on either side.

Kennedy: I like to tell a small story against a big background. It seems to me that you did that in *The Searchers*.

Ford: Yes, and that was in the ordinary-size screen. But then, I still like to work in black and white.

Kennedy: Why?

Ford: You like spinach? It's all a matter of taste. But anybody can shoot color; you can get a guy out of the street and he can shoot a picture in color. But it takes a real artist to do a black and white picture.

Kennedy: Speaking of artists, I had Bert Glennon as cameraman on one of my first pictures. He kept telling me to look through the camera, and finally I told him, "I don't have to; I know it's going to be a good shot." Bert said, "Yes, but you won't have me every time on a picture."

Ford: Yes, Bert was a god-damn good cameraman. It's a good idea to get a cameraman you know well and can trust.

Kennedy: I use the same actors in pictures over and over again.

Ford: Yes, I did that, too. It's good to have actors you can trust, ones who will know their lines and be there.

Kennedy: I fight to get good actors in small parts. I find you not only get a better performance, but you save time, because they know their job.

Ford: That's a good idea. It pays to get good actors. I remember in *The Searchers* I had a scene where all an actor had to do was go through the door and take his suspenders off. I did the scene 35 times, and the actor still didn't do it right. I couldn't figure out what was wrong. Finally I asked him, "Did you read the script?" He said he didn't. I said, "For Crissake, don't you realize what you're doing? You're going to bed and leaving your wife outside with Duke Wayne." The actor said, "Christ I didn't know that. Most of us who play small bits never read the script. We just come in, find out what the director wants, do the part and leave." I shot the scene one more time, and the actor got it right in the first take.

Kennedy: Many times the studios will send actors only the few pages that they're involved in. That's a mistake.

Ford: Of course it is. Every actor is better if he knows what the hell the story is about. I always give everybody a script and we have a reading with the whole cast the day before the picture starts. I want to let all of them know what they're doing.

Kennedy: I find myself spending more time in the cutting room with the cutter after the picture is over, and I won't let anybody see the picture until I've made my final cut. I find if I stay in the cutting room, then the picture doesn't become the work of a committee.

Ford: You're right. You can't make pictures by committee. At one studio I had all the executives coming to the rushes, including the lawyers, and they started giving me lots of advice. I stopped that. I never let the cast see the rushes. I did that once, and the next day every character in the picture changed. One of the actresses said, "Oh, I look so old. Can't you put in a fade-back where I look young and beautiful?" After that I wouldn't let any actors see the rushes.

Kennedy: How much preparation do you do the night before shooting?

Ford: None. I come home at six o'clock in the evening and I'm through. I find it much better to get there in the morning for a cup of coffee and sit around and talk to the actors about what they're going to do that day. I figure I work hard all day and when I come home I deserve a rest. Nobody discusses pictures in the house. My wife never sees pictures; she only goes out at night to Anaheim to see the Angels play. Do you work at home at night?

Kennedy: No, no. I used to, but I've found that I got locked in and couldn't change my thinking when I got to the set and found things were not the same as I had expected.

Ford: Yes, you can walk into a set and find it altogether different. But if you have preconceived notions, you may lose the atmosphere entirely.

Kennedy: One thing I do—I'm awfully aware of wardrobe. I always see the fittings of any of the characters in the picture.

Ford: We all do, don't we?

Kennedy: No, I don't think so.

Ford: I guess you're right. I've seen some pictures that made me say, "Why in God's name did the director ever let the star wear that costume?" Or "Why did that woman wear such a dress?"

Kennedy: Is it true that you "cut in the camera"?

Ford: Yes, that's right. I don't give 'em a lot of film to play with. In fact, Eastman used to complain that I exposed so little film. But I did cut in the camera. When I take a scene, I figure that's the only shot there is. Otherwise, if you give them a lot of film, when you leave the lot the committee takes over. They're all picture makers; they know exactly how to put a picture together and they start juggling scenes around and taking out this and putting in that. They can't do it with my pictures. I cut in the camera and that's it. There's not a lot of film left on the floor when I've finished.

Kennedy: I'm the same way, too. I've never lost a sequence in a picture. I think my cut of *War Wagon* was only 18 seconds longer than the final release—the studio took out a scene with Kirk Douglas in his bare fanny. They don't have much film to play with when I'm finished either.

Ford: You know, I think you've been copying me, Burt.

Kennedy: You know, you're absolutely right.

—1968

V.
John Ford and *Stagecoach*

"My name is John Ford. I make Westerns."

That is the way he introduces himself on the rare occasions when he appears before the public. The self-description is not entirely accurate. His immense output of films, dating from 1914 to 1966, includes almost every movie form. But it is the Western for which he is best remembered, and justly so. With one astonishing achievement, *Stagecoach*, he elevated the Western to the level of art. *Stagecoach* proved that the Western was worthy of the talents of the most accomplished film-makers, and others began to undertake it.

The film is analyzed, by Andrew Sarris and Arthur Knight, in two essays in this section. Ford himself defies analysis. His grandson, Dan Ford, offered some insight in an ACTION article describing the problems of producing a television documentary about his famous grandfather:

"John Ford is not a cerebral man. He is guided by his instincts. The mind is used to file information, facts, and he is as retentive as an IBM 360. Driving outside Washington, D.C. one night, he had been sitting quietly for nearly an hour. Out of nowhere he remarked offhandedly, 'Lee must have had a hell of a time getting his troops through these swamps.'

"Despite his retentiveness, his decisions are based on instinct. Intuition, not facts, lead the way. In this fashion, he is an artist."

Stagecoach Revisited

"The coach is halted by the Ringo Kid himself."

"Mitchell slyly opening Meek's sample case of liquors."

Arthur Knight

"I still like that picture," said John Ford of *Stagecoach* in his published conversations with Peter Bogdanovich. And well he might. For those of us who saw it when it was fresh and new, it opened up new vistas of the West. Ford himself had just discovered Utah's Monument Valley, an area that was to become virtually the trademark of Ford's future Western opera. But more than that, he also managed to breathe fresh life into a fading genre. By 1939, the year of *Stagecoach's* release, the Western had become routine and formula. The 1930s spawned the Hopalong Cassidy series, and the "singing" Westerns of Gene Autry, Roy Rogers and Tex Ritter. Even Nelson Eddy and Jeanette MacDonald made "singing" Westerns, such as *Let Freedom Ring* and *The Girl of the Golden West.* "Big" Westerns, such as *Cimarron, The Plainsman* and King Vidor's *The Texas Rangers,* were few and far between—and almost as thoroughly conventional in their plotting as the "little" Westerns that came pouring forth from studios such as Universal, Columbia, Republic and Monogram, but on much lower budgets.

In addition, the studios had discovered the economic—and physical—benefits to be derived from rear projection. Second units went on location; the stars stayed in Hollywood and fought Indians from behind papier-mâché rocks, with Western buttes and skies flickering palely behind them. It was great for the budget, less effective for any sense of authenticity. Nor were the studio back lots and ranches much more effective. Any aficionado of Westerns soon grew terribly familiar not only with each studio's Western streets, but even with its prop rocks and phony mesquite. During the 1930s the "B" Western became the standard Western, tied to a star (such as Autry) who could be relied upon to drag in a steady, but relatively circumscribed audience week after week. To reach beyond that required the imagination and daring of a first-rate producer, both of which Walter Wanger supplied.

Wanger also seems to have had that special mastery of the elusive chemistry of casting which is the earmark of a great producer. Although Ford began his long career as a director of Westerns and made several outstanding works in this genre during the 1920s, his last was *Three Bad Men* in 1926. Obviously, Wanger had a good memory as well. John Wayne, a former USC football hero, had achieved overnight stardom in *The Big Trail* (1930), then was relegated to a dreary succession of "quickie" Westerns during the 1930s, until his career was resuscitated by *Stagecoach.* Claire Trevor, a star in innumerable undistinguished program pictures since 1933, was considered already over the hill when she was rediscovered by this picture. John Carradine, Berton Churchill, Donald Meek and Thomas Mitchell had all been used by Ford in earlier films. *Stagecoach* was far from an "all-star" picture. But it made stars.

What strikes one first on seeing *Stagecoach* again is the tautness, the impetus of the Dudley Nichols script. This is something that is lost completely on television, with its incessant interruptions for commercial messages from those used-car dealers who thrive on late-night TV. But taken as a piece, which is the only way it should be seen, *Stagecoach* builds at an inexorable pace to the inevitable climax. From its first shot, with a rider barreling into the cavalry camp bearing the information that the Indians are on the warpath, followed by the telegraph operator's discovery that the lines have been cut after the single word, "Geronimo," the Indian threat provides a canopy that hangs ominously over all the subsequent action.

Just as economical is the introduction of the passengers of the departing stage. Thomas Mitchell is being run out of town because he is a drunk, and he persuades Donald Meek to make the trip because he—Peacock, Hickock, whatever his name is—is a whiskey drummer with a caseful of samples. Pregnant Louise Platt hopes to join her husband, an officer with the cavalry stationed in Lordsburg; and gentlemanly gambler John Carradine joins her on a quixotic, chivalric impulse—she is a gentlewoman of the Old South, of a family known to him in happier days, and she just may need protection. The very proper ladies of the town escort Claire Trevor to the stagecoach because she is a prostitute (although the word itself is never used), and good riddance! Sheriff George Bancroft decides to ride shotgun with driver Andy Devine because he has heard that the Ringo Kid is headed for Lordsburg with intent to kill. Before the stage even leaves town, it is flagged down by Berton Churchill, a sanctimonious banker who is absconding with all of his firm's liquid assets crammed in a little black bag. And not much later—less than 15 minutes into the film, in fact—the coach is halted again, by the Ringo Kid himself—John Wayne. The cast has been assembled.

From that moment on, until the Indians are finally seen in a splendid series of pans from the distant stage to the warriors commanding the bluffs shot at very close range, the action might better be defined as interaction. Within the confines of the stagecoach Carradine curtly orders Mitchell to extinguish his cigar. It is offending a lady. He offers Miss Platt a drink from his collapsible silver cup, but denies Claire Trevor the same privilege. Churchill grumbles constantly because the accompanying cavalry will leave them before Lordsburg, and succeeds in alienating all his fellow travelers. Claire Trevor's compassionate attempts to comfort Louise Platt are coldly rebuffed. John Wayne offers Claire a swig out of the communal canteen before taking one himself.

These conflicting attitudes and purposes are neatly posited in two scenes. One is during a brief stop for lunch at an outpost where, still accompanied by the cavalry, the group votes to go on. Churchill dresses down cavalry lieutenant Tim Holt for not ordering his troops to accompany the coach all the way to Lordsburg in a "law and order" speech that carries strong overtones for today; and at the lunch table the "respectables" make quite a point of shunning the outlawed Ringo Kid and the fallen woman. Alignments begin to shift, however, during an enforced stop at Apache Wells, where Louise Platt has her baby. The drunken Doc is sobered by coffee—"strong, lots and lots of coffee"—and delivers the child with the help of Miss Trevor. Churchill grows boorish in his anxiety to get away, but is held in control by John Carradine. Meanwhile, in the film's worst scene, the Indian wife of the owner of the cantina sings a Mexican folk song while her accomplices steal all the fresh horses and ride off with them. When John Wayne, preparing to escape with the help of Claire Trevor, emerges at the break of dawn, the sky is already filled with the smoke signals announcing an impending Indian attack.

From there on, it is straight action. The hardy travelers decide to make a break for it— the only thing they can do under the circumstances, since they have already seen the results of an Indian attack on a partially fortified position at a previous rest stop. Wayne, after his attempted escape, is manacled. Louise Platt, after her accouchement, is weak and faint. The horses are holdovers from the previous day's hard ride. The Indians have not yet been spotted. Obviously, the odds are against the coach's ever getting through to Lordsburg. Even so, by this time, despite the mixed baggage that it is carrying, everyone in the audience is rooting for the stagecoach's safe arrival.

And now the Indians, high in the hills, see the coach snaking through a valley far below. They charge in pursuit, and the first premonition of their attack is the arrow that fells Donald Meek. The people in the stage fight back. Wayne, freed of his bonds, climbs to the top of the coach and handles a rifle with deadly accuracy. (At one point, two Indians seem to fall from a single shot of his.) When Andy Devine is winged and drops the reins, Wayne (or veteran stunt man, Yakima Canutt, doubling for him) performs the most hair-raising trick in the picture: Leaping forward from horse to horse, he mounts the lead horse, retrieves the traces, and guides the stage safely forward.

At the climactic moment, just as the last bullet has been expended and the Indians are closing in for the kill, the tide of the battle turns. In a scene straight out of D. W. Griffith, John Carradine places his pistol to Louise Platt's temple, then crumbles before he can fire it. On the sound track, while still holding on this scene, we hear the bugle call of the U.S. Cavalry sounding the charge. The cavalry sweeps in, the Indians are routed and the stage rumbles on toward Lordsburg.

Cinematically this should have been the end of the film, but the plot has dictated otherwise. The Ringo Kid still has his score to settle with the Plummer brothers in Lordsburg. Louise Platt must learn the fate of her husband. Berton.Churchill must reap his just rewards. Will Claire Trevor meet the Kid across the Rio Grande, or must she be consigned to living out her days in some crib in Lordsburg?

All of these questions are settled, albeit a trifle anticlimactically, in the movie's last ten minutes. The final shoot-out is managed in the approved Western style—

three against one, with virtue magically triumphant. But this shoot-out, for once, takes place in the deep shadows of the night, not at high noon. For a proper finale, Bancroft and Mitchell place John Wayne and Claire Trevor in a rig and, waving their hats in the air, send them off to Wayne's dream spread in Mexico.

So far, it would seem that we have been discussing the virtues of Dudley Nichols' script, not John Ford's direction. But during the 1930s, with Ford, Frank Capra and a handful of other directors, a tight bond often developed between the screenwriter and the director in what would seem to be the most productive of relationships. Ford, with his eye to the ultimate action on the screen, would cut ruthlessly on Nichols' dialogue; Nichols, who had worked with Ford on perhaps half a dozen pictures by this time, knew the kind of material that the Old Man could shoot best. It was a kind of collaboration singularly, and sadly, lacking in our films today.

But what of Ford? *Stagecoach* was, for him, his first trip to Monument Valley, and it was a case of love at first sight. Never before had its grandiose scenery been captured so crisply, so lovingly as it was by Bert Glennon's camera. But apart from these natural grandeurs, the camera was utilized in the best Ford tradition—functional, utilitarian, without frills. The camera is so still throughout most of the film that when it does move—a pan for the river crossing, the tilt and pan up to the Indians waiting on the bluff, the wild traveling shots during the Indian attack—the very fact of its movement enhances the excitement of these sequences. But the camera placement is also exciting in its stillness. Only Hitchcock, in *Lifeboat,* dared to work in such confined quarters, knowing that he could illuminate the complexities of his characters through the variations of his camera placements. Cutting, too, enters into it. Dorothy Spencer, who worked with Ford on this and many other films, once complained that when he gave her footage, all that she as the editor could do was to cut off the initial slates. Ford seemed to know precisely what would work and what wouldn't—and he eliminated what wouldn't before it reached the editing rooms, generally by calling "Cut" on virtually the frame where the cut would come.

This same precision governs Ford's camera positions. He painted a lot in his youth, he has said, and undoubtedly this experience sharpened his eye for composition. The odd thing is that his compositions, even in the cramped quarters of the stagecoach, are rarely static. Movements, however small—Mitchell slyly opening Meek's sample case of liquors, Wayne slowly raising his head to catch Claire Trevor's eye from under his dusty cowboy hat, Carradine passing his silver cup to Louise Platt—assume a larger importance, while in the long shots, the screen is fluid in the extreme. People move from light into shadow, walk menacingly close to the camera or group themselves into meaningful patterns. Ford can point his camera toward a door (as he does just before Tom Tyler, the leader of the Plummer gang, makes his final entrance into the saloon) and build a feeling of anticipation simply because the audience senses that part of his composition has yet to be fulfilled. His lighting, while always stark and dramatic, is rarely artificial. Indeed, there is only one sequence—when Elvira Rios sings outside the cantina while Louise Platt is giving birth inside—that could be described as false or "arty." On the other hand, the passage of time and the increased sophistication of film technology makes us almost painfully aware of the vast amount of rear projection used in this movie, and of the studio-construction quality to such sets as the "garden" in which Wayne declares his intentions to Claire Trevor.

Even so, this is a film that bears seeing, reseeing and studying—hopefully in a good 35mm print that does full justice to the crispness of Bert Glennon's magnificent black and white photography. So well has this picture stood the test of time that when *Stagecoach* was remade in 1966, with an all-star cast headed by Bing Crosby and Ann-Margret, its quarter-century-old ghost seemed to hover over every scene, every line of dialogue, almost every frame. And always to the disadvantage of the newer, slicker, gaudier, costlier version. The fault, dear Brutus, was not in its stars. . . .

John Ford on *Stagecoach*

John Ford on the set of a TV documentary on Ford.

I found the story by reading it in *Collier's,* I think it was. It wasn't too well developed, but the characters were good. "This is a great story," I thought, and I bought it for a small amount—I think it was 2,500 dollars.

I tried to sell it to the studios, but nobody was buying. After the studio heads read it, they said to me, "But this is a Western! People don't make Westerns anymore!"

"Sure, it's a Western," I said. "But there are characters in it. What's the difference whether it's played in the West, or wherever?"

I couldn't convince them. Finally I got down to RKO. The president of the company was a gentleman named Joseph P. Kennedy, who happened to be a friend of mine. I went to Joe and told him about the story and how much trouble I had selling it to the studios.

"What's the objection?" he asked me.

"Well, they say it's a Western," I said.

"Maybe it's about time they started doing Westerns again," said Kennedy. "I'll tell you what I'll do. I'll send it to the producers at the studio and see what they think."

So he sent it to the so-called producers at RKO—four men who also happened to be close friends of mine. One of them said, "I only do classics"—which was an expression he had learned only recently.

My answer was: "A story is a story, whether it's laid in the West or whether it's *Two Gentlemen of Verona.*"

Joe Kennedy couldn't convince his producers. He told me: "I don't know what the hell I'm paying these fellows for. I'm certainly not getting very good pictures from them. I remember when you came to RKO with a story about the Irish Revolution

"I assembled a good cast."

called *The Informer,* and none of those producers were interested in it, either. So the studio sent you across the street to shoot it on one set. That picture gave RKO a lot of prestige. Have you got a script?"

"I'm working on an outline with Dudley Nichols," I said.

Joe Kennedy said he'd like to see it. But meanwhile, I got a call from Walter Wanger, who had one more picture to make under his United Artists contract.

"I understand you've got a good story," Walter said. "What's it called?"

"*Stagecoach,*" I said.

"A Western, huh?" he said.

"Yeah," I said.

"Well, that might be a good idea," he said. "Is it exciting?"

"I think it is," I said.

"Okay, let's talk," he said.

So I sent him the short story and he said, "That's a pretty good story. I'd like to see Gary Cooper play the lead."

I told him I doubted that Coop would want to play in a Western like this one.

"I'd like to have a couple of top stars in it," said Wanger.

"I don't think Gary would fit the part," I said.

"I'm thinking of Gary Cooper and Marlene Dietrich," he said.

"I don't think you can go that high on salary with a picture like this," I said. "This is the kind of picture you have to make for peanuts."

"Have you got anybody in mind?" Wanger asked me.

"Well, there's a boy I know who used to be assistant prop man and bit player for me," I said. "His name was Michael Morrison, but he's making five-day Westerns and he calls himself John Wayne now."

"Why didn't the Indians just shoot the horses?"

"Do you think he's any good?" he asked.

"Yes, I think so," I said. "And we can get him for peanuts."

"What about the girl?" he said.

"Well, I think Claire Trevor is a helluvan actress," I said, "and she fits the part."

"Okay, go ahead and cast the picture," Wanger said, "but I'm leaving for New York. I'll be gone for ten days and when I get back, I'd like you to have the script ready."

So he went off and I assembled a good cast. Besides Wayne and Claire Trevor, I got Thomas Mitchell, Andy Devine, John Carradine. Wanger had a girl under contract, Louise Platt, who fitted into the picture. Then I got that wonderful character actor—what's his name?—oh, yes—Berton Churchill: he played the crooked banker. Donald Meek was the liquor salesman, and George Bancroft played the driver. Good cast.

I did the location scenes first. I had driven through Monument Valley, and I thought it would be a good place to shoot a Western. I used it for the first time in *Stagecoach*. There was a dry lake that was perfect for the Indian attack. We didn't have any camera cars in those days; we just put the camera on an automobile and shot on the run. It was fast. I asked the driver how fast we had gone, and he said 40 to 42 miles per hour. You wouldn't think that horses could go that fast, but they did.

The chase took two days to shoot. That chase—every half-assed critic says, "Why did it go on so long? Why didn't the Indians just shoot the horses?"

I tell them, "If the Indians had done that, they would have stopped the picture."

The real truth is that the Indians were more interested in the horses than in the white men. They fought on foot most of the time, and they needed horses. Besides, they were notoriously bad shots on horseback.

I did about four days on location, and then we went back and finished the picture on the Goldwyn lot. The script was not prolix; there were no long speeches. I shot it pretty much as it was written. Dudley Nichols was on the set at all times, even though he wasn't getting paid for it. If I needed a new line, we'd work it out together.

The shoot-out at the end was something I had done once before, with Harry Carey—I had done a lot of silent Westerns with Carey and with Tom Mix, but never a talkie. I used the same idea again in *My Darling Clementine*.

It went back to what Wyatt Earp had told me. Wyatt was a friend of mine—in fact, I still have his rifle in the corner of my bedroom. He told me: "I'm not a dead shot. I always walked up pretty close to the other fellow before I fired. The legend has it that I killed a lot of people. As a matter of fact, I never killed anybody. I shot people in the shoulder or in the leg, but I never killed them. I left that to my partner, Jones, who was a dead shot."

I made the picture for a good price—220,000 dollars I think it was. Came in 8,000 dollars under budget. Today you couldn't make that picture for under ten million dollars.

Duke did okay. He knew his lines, and he did what he was told to do. Of course, I surrounded him with superb actors, and some of the glitter rubbed off on his shoulders. But he's still up there with the best of them. He's god-damn good.

After I shot *Stagecoach*, I worked closely with the cutter. But there wasn't a helluva lot to do. I cut with the camera.

When the picture was put together, Wanger invited a few top people—brilliant brains of the industry who proceeded to say how they would have done *Stagecoach*. Sam Goldwyn said, "Walter, you made one mistake: You should have shot it in color. You should start all over again and make it in color." Douglas Fairbanks, Sr. said: "The chase is too long."

Then it was shown to the great producers at RKO. One of them said, "It's just a B picture." Another said, "It's all right, but it's still a Western."

Well, of course, the picture went out and hit the jackpot. It started a flood of Westerns, and we've been suffering from them ever since.

STAGECOACH

Producer Walter Wanger

Director John Ford

From the story "Stage to Lordsburg"

by Ernest Haycox

Script . . . . *Dudley Nichols*

Photography . . . . *Bert Glennon*

Art Director . . . . *Alexander Toluboff*

Set Decoration . . . . *Wiard B. Ihnen*

Musical Direction . . . . *Boris Morros*

Costumes . . . . *Walter Plunkett*

Music . . . . *Richard Hageman, W. Franke
Harling, John Leipold, Leo
Shuken, Louis Gruenberg*

Editorial Supervision . . . . *Otho Lovering*

Editing . . . . *Dorothy Spencer, Walter Reynolds*

Assistant Director . . . . *Wingate Smith*

Running time: 96 minutes

Released March 2, 1939, by United Artists

CAST: *Claire Trevor* (Dallas), *John Wayne* (The Ringo Kid), *John Carradine* (Hatfield), *Thomas Mitchell* (Dr. Josiah Boone), *Andy Devine* (Buck), *Donald Meek* (Samuel Peacock), *Louise Platt* (Lucy Mallory), *Tim Holt* (Lt. Blanchard), *George Bancroft* (Sheriff Curly Wilcox), *Berton Churchill* (Henry Gatewood), *Tom Tyler* (Hank Plummer), *Chris Pin Martin* (Chris), *Elvira Rios* (Yakima, his wife), *Francis Ford* (Billy Pickett), *Marga Daighton* (Mrs. Pickett), *Kent Odell* (Billy Pickett, Jr.), *Yakima Canutt, Chief Big Tree* (stunt men), *Harry Tenbrook* (telegraph operator), *Jack Pennick* (Jerry, barman), *Paul McVey* (express agent), *Cornelius Keefe* (Capt. Whitney), *Florence Lake* (Mrs. Nancy Whitney), *Louis Mason* (sheriff), *Brenda Fowler* (Mrs. Gatewood), *Walter McGrail* (Capt. Sickel), *Joseph Rickson* (Luke Plummer), *Vester Pegg* (Ike Plummer), *William Hoffer* (sergeant), *Bryant Washburn* (Capt. Simmons), *Nora Cecil* (Dr. Boone's housekeeper), *Helen Gibson, Dorothy Annleby* (dancing girls), *Buddy Roosevelt, Bill Cody* (ranchers), *Chief White Horse* (Indian chief), *Duke Lee* (sheriff of Lordsburg), *Mary Kathleen Walker* (Lucy's baby), *Ed Brady, Steve Clemente, Theodore Larch, Fritzi Brunette, Leonard Trainor, Chris Phillips, Tex Driscoll, Teddy Billings, John Eckert, Al Lee, Jack Mohr, Patsy Doyle, Wiggie Blowne, Margaret Smith.*

WHITE SCOUT: Apaches, Captain! The hills are swarmin' with 'em.

DOC BOONE: Take my arm, my dear. The tumbril is waiting.

WELLS FARGO AGENT: Howdy, Buck. Got that payroll for the mining company?
BUCK: She's back in the Wells Fargo box.

HATFIELD: I'm offering my protection to this lady. I can shoot fairly straight if there is need for it.

DALLAS: What have I done, Joe? Haven't I any right to live?

The stage rolling down a winding road into Monument Valley, the horses going at a good clip.

Behind the stage the detachment of cavalry is strung out.

CURLY: Hello, Kid.

BUCK: I took this job ten years ago so's I could get enough money to marry that Mexican girl.

family?

DOC BOONE: My friend is a whiskey drummer. We're all going to get scalped, Gatewood.

CURLY: I guess you don't understand, Kid You're under arrest.

RINGO: I ain't arguing about that, Curly. I just hate to part with a gun like this.

Now the stagecoach turns right on the road in front of Dry Fork Station. Blanchard leads his men left.

RINGO: My friends just call me Ringo. Nickname I had as a kid.

BUCK: Well, why don't you say somethin'? A man gets nervous settin' up here like a mummy, thinkin' about Indians!

RINGO: Looks like I got the plague, don't it?
DALLAS: No—it's not you.

Apache Wells Station at sundown as the stage comes lurching through the gate.

DALLAS: Mrs. Mallory, let me . . .
LUCY: I'm all right, thank you.

DALLAS: It's a little girl.

GATEWOOD: A sick woman on our hands!
That's all we needed!

CHRIS: I know why you go to Lordsburg,
Kid.
RINGO: You mean Luke Plummer.

DOC BOONE: Get me coffee—lots of coffee
—and black!

RINGO: You oughtn' go too far, Miss Dallas.
Apaches like to sneak up and pick off strays.

DALLAS: My people were killed by the Indians. I was just a kid.
RINGO: That's tough, on a girl. It's a hard country.

DALLAS: Why don't you escape, Kid?

CURLY: What you doin' out here, Kid? Oh, it's you, Dallas. You come along. Stick close to the reservation.

CURLY: Apaches?
RINGO: Yeah, war signals.

LUCY: She didn't go to bed, Doctor. I'm afraid she stayed up all night, while I slept.

The stagecoach appears careening along, Buck driving to get all he can out of the horses.

PEACOCK: Are we in a trap, Brother? Do you see any savages coming?

The view moves up and around to the rim of the canyon and we see a band of savage-looking Apaches.

GATEWOOD: The ferry's burned!

Buck is yelling at the horses and chucking stones, while Curly raises his rifle again to the canyon rim.

CURLY: Roll a couple of them logs into the water.

At the canyon rim an Apache falls from a ledge.

HATFIELD: Get down, Mrs. Mallory—way down. Keep her down, Dallas!

Ringo makes his leap.

The stagecoach is now going full speed.

Ringo is doing the driving now.

Thirty or forty Indians are riding furiously, gaining ground on both sides of the coach.

The cavalry comes sweeping in from two sides.

SHERIFF: I'm talking about you cleaning out your own bank, Gatewood. Just keep goin'.

Luke Plummer steps up to the bar and makes a sign with his hand to the bartender, who reaches under the bar and pulls out a sawed-off shotgun.

BUCK: Watch out, Kid, the Plummers are waitin' for you.

At the other end of the street, the Plummers come around the corner together.

DALLAS: It's all been a crazy dream! I was out of my mind, just hoping!

At the opposite end, Ringo is seen walking steadily ahead.

There is a crack of a rifle and he makes a dive for cover.

CURLY: Get in, Dallas. Might as well stick with the Kid long as you can.

THE END

The Company Remembers *Stagecoach*

"Only one actor could play it—Lloyd Nolan."

John Wayne, Actor

I had known Jack Ford for ten years, ever since I propped for him. One day he handed me a short story and told me to read it.

"Who do you think could play it?" he asked me.

"Well, there's only one actor I can think of who could play it," I said, "and that's Lloyd Nolan."

"Why, you stupid son of a bitch," he said, "I want *you* to play it."

And I was hoping like hell that *he* wouldn't say Lloyd Nolan.

Pappy wanted me, but nobody else did. There was a lot of resistance to my playing the part—and with good reason. After all, a theater could get me in a Republic Western for five dollars. So why should they pay 200 dollars for me in *Stagecoach?*

But Ford held out, and then [Walter] Wanger decided in my favor.

Was Ford tough on me? You bet he was. But I had learned about him when I was propping for him. Ford was very protective of his crews. But he did sometimes pick on certain members. Especially assistant directors. He was hell on assistant directors.

He did a pretty good job on me, too. I remember once in the beginning of the picture I had a scene where I was supposed to splash my face with water. I turned around and wiped my face with a towel, but I didn't seem to satisfy Ford. He made me do it over and over again, until my face was almost raw from rubbing it with the towel. Finally Jack Holt's son, Tim, said to him, "Jack, why don't you lay off the poor guy?"

Another time was the scene I had with Claire [Trevor] when I said goodbye to her and she went down to the whorehouse. I did the scene three times, and each time Ford said to me, "For God's sake, keep your face up! Don't look down!"

I couldn't figure out what was going on, because I had been looking straight ahead. Then I realized he was saying it to me, but he really wanted Claire to look up.

159

I'll never forget the preview. It was at the Village Theater in Westwood, and it was sensational! The audience yelled and screamed and stood up and cheered. I never saw anything like it.

I had sent tickets to my bosses at Republic. I saw them sneaking out of the theater afterward, so I knew they had come. But they never said a word to me. Finally, three or four days later, I saw one of them and I said, "How did you like *Stagecoach?*"

He told me, "Well, the boys and I went out and had some coffee afterwards, and we decided if they want Westerns, they'd better let us make 'em."

Stagecoach was a helluva picture. Only Ford would have the guts to stage a big Indian chase, and *then* take me into the town to finish off the business I had there. Any other picturemaker would have ended it with the chase.

What did *Stagecoach* do for me? It started my career.

"Ford set up the romance only by looks."

Claire Trevor, Actress

Stagecoach was my first picture after five years under contract to Fox. What a pleasure it was! Most of the pictures I had made at Fox were pretty dreary. I went from one to another, and we always worked long hours; I could never plan anything for Saturday night, because we were certain to be shooting late.

Then to make a picture with John Ford! Not only did we quit every day at five or six, Ford stopped shooting every afternoon so we could have tea!

For some reason, Ford was interested in me as an actress. I couldn't understand why, because I had nothing at Fox that would have shown any promise. He had wanted me for another picture, and it killed me that I couldn't do it. I had a cold and developed fever blisters above my mouth. He didn't believe me and sent for me. I kept my mouth covered while he insisted that I could work. "You can do it," he said. "Impossible," I said: "Let me see your face," he insisted. I showed him, and he said, "You're right."

So you can imagine how thrilled I was when he sent me the *Stagecoach* script. It was a very brief script. Not much dialogue at all, except that between Tommy Mitchell and Donald Meek. The rest was terse.

I did a test with Duke Wayne, whom I had never met before. *He* was testing, not me. Ford had us do the scene after the birth of the baby, about the only real scene we had together. The idea was that he was very respectful of me. He didn't know I was a hooker. Ford had us play the scene standing against a fence. At one point, Ford took Duke by the chin and shook him.

"What are you doing with your mouth?" Ford demanded. "Why are you moving your mouth so much? Don't you know that you don't act with your mouth in pictures? You act with your eyes!"

It was tough for Duke to take, but he took it. And he learned eight volumes about acting in this picture.

The cast was remarkable. Each one was an individual, each was remarkable in his own way.

Ford got the most out of all of us. I was absolutely mesmerized by him. One thing I realized during *Stagecoach*—that most great directors are inarticulate. Ford himself had a kind of radar. He'd say, "You know, Claire . . . you can't . . . that fellow isn't . . ." And I'd reply, "Yeah, I know." It all became very clear to me.

He could have said to me: "Claire, I want you to walk to the edge of that cliff over there and jump off"—and I would have done it.

Ford only yelled at me once. Once I came on the set whistling, as I sometimes did. Ford yelled: "Who's that whistling?"

"It's me," I said.

"Well, stop it," he said.

I thought he was kidding, and I started whistling again.

"For Crissake, when I tell you to stop, I want you to stop!" he yelled.

I was hurt and embarrassed. But I realized that I had probably upset him by interrupting what he was thinking about. It was soon forgotten. And I remembered not to whistle on the set again.

While we were making *Stagecoach*, I knew it was going to be good. But I didn't realize how great it would be. I didn't go on the beginning location. Ford said, "We got some good stuff down in Arizona," but he gave no indication what it was.

During our own scenes the actors didn't get any feeling of great drama; the scenes were too fragmentary. But it was all shaping up in Ford's mind. He knew how all the pieces were going together.

There was one scene I was looking forward to. It was the one where Duke finally says that he'd like to see me after the whole thing was over. Up to that time, Ford had set up the romance merely by looks that Duke and I had exchanged. At last I came to my chance to be romantic!

When I came on the set, Ford looked at the page and a half of script and said, "Too mushy." He threw everything out but two lines of dialogue. I was crushed.

Later I saw Ford at Goldwyn Studios when he was cutting the picture.

"It's going to be great," he said. "And you're so good that they're not even going to notice it. It'll go right over their heads."

He was right. *Stagecoach* made Duke Wayne, but it didn't do much for me. There are certain parts that command attention, like the one Jack Nicholson played in *Easy Rider*. I had mine in *Dead End* and *Key Largo*. But not *Stagecoach*. It was too subtle.

Yakima Canutt, Stunt Man

From 1932 on, I had been working with John Wayne in a flock of Westerns. When Wayne was hired for *Stagecoach,* he put in a good word for me with John Ford, and Ford sent for me.

"Well, Enos, how are you?" Ford said to me when we met.

That set me back on my heels. Hardly anyone in Hollywood knew that my real name was Enos. I said to Ford: "I see Wayne has given you the inside dope on me."

"That's right," said Ford. "In fact, he said so much about you that you're going to find it hard to live up to all of it."

Ford gave me the script to read, and I found it a darned good Western. I went back to Ford and told him some ideas I had about doing the stunts. I was going to hire the stunt men and ramrod 'em through the picture.

One of the things I started to discuss with Ford was a sequence in which the stagecoach came to a stream and saw the stage station burned by Indians on the other side. The script called for the coach to be lashed with logs and floated down the stream to escape the danger.

"You can forget about that," said Ford. "They tell me it can't be done."

"I don't know about that, Mr. Ford," I answered. "It seems to me you can do almost anything if you have enough time and money."

With Ford's approval, I went to work on devising a way to float that stagecoach. Some fellows over at Paramount helped me devise some hollowed-out logs which could be attached to the coach, two on each side. They had to be planned just right—big enough to float the coach, but high enough for the wheels to reach the ground.

Then I devised an underwater cable which could be fastened to the front lead tongue and pulled by an offstage truck on the other side of the river. It was attached with a pelican hook which could be tripped when the coach reached the shore. I had the six horses in regular harness, but hooked together so they could be towed along if they quit swimming.

Ford okayed my plans and sent me up to Kernville with a crew to test the rig. I got it all set up and telephoned Ford in Hollywood.

"Put eight people in it tomorrow and see if it works," he told me.

I did it, and telephoned him that everything went fine. "Okay, we'll be up tomorrow to shoot it," he said.

When the company arrived, everything was ready to shoot. I put on pads to double for Andy Devine as the driver. Ford shot the crossing in one take.

Afterwards he asked me: "Do you think Andy could drive it across?"

"Don't see why not," I said. "The way it's rigged, all he has to do is hold on to the reins."

"Okay, I want to do it again at closer range so I can see all the principals."

It worked fine the second time, too.

We finished the picture with the Indian chase on the flat lakebed at Victorville. I knew by now that Ford liked to shoot fast and didn't want any delays, so I planned everything as closely as possible. We had a lot of saddle-and-horse falls to do first. So the night before we started on 'em, I hired a farmer to disc 15 to 20 acres of the lake with his tractor. That way, we'd have soft ground to land on and get the job done faster and safer.

After we finished the falls, Ford said to me: "Yak, go get your warpaint on. We're going to do that Indian gag of yours, starting with the transfer."

This was a stunt I had first done in a serial and had repeated two or three times. The idea was to have the Indian jump from his pony onto the lead horse of the stagecoach and try to take the reins. The driver shoots the Indian and he drops to the tongue between the lead horses, drags awhile, then lets go, the horses and

"They tell me that stunt can't be done."

coach passing over him. It was kind of a tricky thing to do, because you only had two and a half to three feet between horses and you had to be flat to get clearance under the stagecoach.

First I did the transfer, and it wasn't easy. The pinto I was riding shied away from the team, and I had a long jump to make. I made it, and Ford said, "You'll never top that."

Next, we shot the drop. Wayne shot me from the coach, and I dropped to the tongue. Then he was to shoot me again, and I was to drop off. It was kind of spooky, dragging along and looking back at those horses' hooves. But they were running straight, so I let go. I kept my legs together and my arms flat against my body, and nothing hit. As soon as the coach passed over me, I did a little roll and got up, then fell back again and lay still. That was an added touch of my own.

Afterward, the cameramen weren't sure whether they had gotten the shot.

"I'll never shoot that again," said Ford. "They'd better have it." And they did.

Wingate Smith, Assistant Director

I remember the time we were shooting on location in Arizona, and we were all staying in the little town of Caliente. I got a call at three o'clock in the morning from a production man who said excitedly, "It's snowing! You'd better wake up Ford and tell him."

I wasn't about to wake up Jack Ford at that hour of the morning. I waited until the regular time to get him up, and I told him, "Jack, there's a lot of snow on the ground."

To my surprise, he answered, "Great! That's just what we needed."

We took the whole crew out in the snow and shot stagecoach scenes. Merian C. Cooper, who was back at headquarters, kept calling on the shortwave radio to ask Jack how he was going to use those scenes. Jack wouldn't say. For days he wouldn't tell his plan. Then one day he had a scene of the stagecoach coming into the station. He had Andy Devine deliver the line: "I took the high road, because the Apaches don't like snow."

That's the way Jack Ford works. The average director wouldn't have worked that day in the snow. But Ford did, and as a result he got some of the most striking scenes in the picture.

There was never any friction on a Ford set. The crew respected him, because they knew what Ford shoots, he uses. They might not have respected another director who made a lot of protection shots because he was unsure of himself. But they didn't mind taking orders from Ford. They knew he was doing the right thing.

Even when he seemed to be asking the impossible, they went along with him. There was no saying, "It won't work," to Ford. No matter how impossible it seemed, whatever he asked for *did* work. Like the snow sequence.

Actors always respected Jack Ford. Obviously. They all knew there was only one boss: Ford. They knew they had to be up in their lines; it was too easy for Ford to shoot over their shoulders if they weren't. The actors generally stayed on the set at all times, even on their days off. They'd say, "You never know when Ford will give me a plum." That was true. Ford was always coming up with plums for actors, bits of dialogue and business that made the scene stand out. That's how he got great pictures.

Ford could blow his temper on occasion. Often he would bawl out an assistant for something an actor had done. He had one assistant who couldn't understand it, and he kept saying, "Why did he bawl *me* out?"

It never bothered me. After Ford had blown his temper, he would come to you later and say, "I went a bit wild. Now, if you want to hold a grudge, go right ahead. But I want you to know I didn't mean it."

We got some great stunts in *Stagecoach*, and nobody got hurt. You couldn't get a better man than Yakima Canutt, and Yak doesn't take chances. Neither does Ford. Under the old system, if a stunt man didn't take his fall correctly the first time, he had to do it over again free. Usually the director placed the camera and told the stunt man to fall on a certain mark. If he didn't hit the mark, he had to do it over again.

Ford didn't work that way. He asked the stunt man, "Where are you going to fall?" Then he placed the camera accordingly. Ford never asks anyone to do anything hazardous or unnecessary.

Here's an example of the Ford luck. We were on location with *Stagecoach* and about to shoot the Indian chase. That morning a whole tribe of Indians came over the hill. They had smelled the snow coming and decided to move. I talked to the chief, and he agreed to let his braves work in the picture. The production company wanted to pay them two dollars a day, but Ford insisted that they get the regular wage. That's one of the reasons the Indians made him an honorary chief.

"That morning a whole tribe of Indians came over the hill."

Walter Reynolds, Sound

I built and made all the sound effects on *Stagecoach,* and I did all the dubbing. It was a grand show, and I was delighted to be working with such a great director as John Ford. He was a very definite man. Once Otho Lovering had shot some second-unit work, and Ford disagreed with him on it. Lovey stood his ground. So Ford sent the prop man, Sammy Bricker, to the restaurant for a silver platter with a cover. Ford lifted the cover and a hot potato was sitting there.

"Okay," said Ford, "you can handle anything—let's see you handle that!"

One thing I remember about the shooting. John Wayne was having a lot of trouble with a scene he was doing with Claire Trevor. He just couldn't get it. So Ford told him: "Just raise your eyebrows and wrinkle your forehead." Wayne's been doing that ever since.

In those days we didn't take any protection sound on scenes like the chase. All that was filmed silently. I had to supply all the sound effect. I had to scrounge for whatever effects I could find—there were no libraries where you could get anything you wanted, as there are today. For the chase I went over to Columbia and paid Eddie Hahn a dollar a foot for what I needed. I didn't buy sound for the entire sequence; for 500 feet, it would have cost me 500 dollars. Too much. So I bought two ten-foot lengths of horses galloping. Then I looped them and I ran them over and over, one after the other.

Ford loved to underplay scenes. For the Indian charge I had put in a bunch of war whoops. "Take 'em out," he ordered. I did, and it was much better that way.

Dorothy Spencer, Editor

My goodness, that was a long time ago! But I do remember *Stagecoach* because it was one of the first good pictures I worked on. It was a joy to be on it, even though John Ford scared the dickens out of me. You never knew whether to take him seriously or not.

I cut the whole picture under the supervision of Otho Lovering. The Indian chase was the toughest sequence to do. There was a lot of footage on that one. Besides the location shooting in Arizona, Ford made a scene in the stagecoach with plates that Lovey had shot on second unit.

Ford was right; he cut in the camera. He got what he wanted on film, then left it to the cutter to put it together. Unlike most other directors, he never even went to the rushes.

He left you alone to do your work. But if you did something he didn't like, he'd let you know about it!

Stagecoach came out the same year as *Gone with the Wind,* so it didn't get much attention at the Academy. But it was a fine film. Too bad it was in black and white.

Andy Devine, Actor

The first time I worked for John Ford was in 1919, when he came to Arizona to make *Ace of the Saddle* with Harry Carey. I was working on a ranch then, wrangling cattle and horses, and he gave me a job in the picture. I didn't work for him again until *Dr. Bull,* with Will Rogers, in 1933.

Then he sent for me when he was doing *Stagecoach.* One day he got sore at me and said, "You big tub of lard. I don't know why the hell I'm using you in this picture."

I answered him right back: "Because Ward Bond can't drive six horses."

Ford didn't talk to me for six years. But I worked for him again, of course. Every time I did, he saw to it that I had a Mexican wife and nine kids.

Sometimes you'd like to kill the son of a bitch. But, God love him, he's a great man.

"Because Ward Bond can't drive six horses."

"I was horrified to see that her petticoat was exposed."

Walter Plunkett, Costume Designer
I had worked with Ford on *Mary of Scotland, The Informer* and *The Plough and the Stars*. I have a memory of *The Informer*. Jack insisted on more and more black shawls. They were eventually on every woman in the picture. I went to my office to sulk and muse that he was being willful and making the costume job ludicrous. A few years later I visited Dublin and was amazed to see every woman in the city wearing a black shawl over her head. I cabled my apologies to Mr. Ford.

Of course, my work on *Stagecoach* was done before shooting started, but I do have one precious memory from it. It occurred when the costumes were being tested. At that period in my life I had more than much to learn about costume designing. We made the test of Claire Trevor in her plaid dress, and I was horrified to see that her petticoat was hanging long and exposed below one side of her dress. I explained to Jack that it would be adjusted. He withered me, saying he was most disappointed, that he had thought it was a touch of genius—and now he found he had misplaced his admiration.

It was always remembered when my design tended to become unreal and too theatrical.

John Carradine, Actor
Ford always finds a patsy among the cast of his pictures and rides him with gentle sarcasm. Usually he chooses a stage actor, because he has a certain contempt for those who come from the "theatuh." On *The Hurricane* it was Raymond Massey. On *Grapes of Wrath* it was O. Z. Whitehead. On *Stagecoach* it was Tommy Mitchell.

Ford kept needling Tommy throughout the picture. The climax came when we had the scene at the bar when we were celebrating the birth of the baby. It was a difficult scene, because we were standing six feet apart, and all of us had dialogue. Ford sent away the stand-ins so we could work out the scene ourselves. All of us were engaging in badinage, and this annoyed Ford. He bawled out all of us, but mostly Tommy Mitchell. Tommy took it for a while and then replied, "That's all right, Mr. Ford. Just remember: I saw *Mary of Scotland*."

Ford left the set for 15 minutes. When he returned, not another word was said about the incident.

Stagecoach in 1939 and in Retrospect

"The self-sacrifice of a self-condemned aristocrat."

Andrew Sarris

*The fact is, I am quite happy in a movie, even a bad movie. Other people,
so I have read, treasure memorable moments in their lives—the time
one climbed the Parthenon at sunrise, the summer night one met a lonely girl
in Central Park and achieved with her a sweet and natural relationship,
as they say in books. I, too, once met a girl in Central Park, but
it is not much to remember. What I remember is the time John Wayne killed
three men with a carbine as he was falling to the dusty street in Stagecoach, and
the time the kitten found Orson Welles in the doorway in The Third Man.*

—Walker Percy, *The Moviegoer*

Among Hollywood historians 1939 has always been considered a big year for movies, particularly after the widely denigrated off-year of 1938. Indeed, most knowledgeable diagnosticians of the production pulse have always dipped the graph lines of artistic quality at 1929, 1934 and 1938; 1929 because of the awkwardness of the transition to sound, 1934 because of the resurgence of puerile censorship and 1938 because of a mysterious suspension of inspiration.

Be that what it may, 1939 was nothing if not ambitious. And not merely because it was the year of *Gone with the Wind,* that massive confection from the crowded kitchen and many cooks of David O. Selznick—two directors (George Cukor and Victor Fleming), a platoon of writers (all but Sidney Howard uncredited), a cast of thousands and a gross of millions. There were also Frank Capra's *Mr. Smith Goes to Washington,* Ernst Lubitsch's *Ninotchka,* Leo McCarey's *Love Affair,* George Cukor's *The Women,* Mitchell Leisen's *Midnight,* Michael Curtiz's *Four Wives* and King Vidor's *Northwest Passage.*

There were movies that seemed more significant at the time than they did later— William Wyler's *Wuthering Heights* (winner of the New York Film Critics Award over both Oscar-sweeping *Gone with the Wind* and *Mr. Smith Goes to Washington*), William Dieterle's *Juarez,* Anatole Litvak's *Confessions of a Nazi Spy,* and Sam Wood's *Goodbye, Mr. Chips.* There were movies also that seemed less interesting at the time than they would seem later—Howard Hawk's *Only Angels Have Wings,* Alfred Hitchcock's *Jamaica Inn,* Raoul Walsh's *The Roaring Twenties,* Cecil B. DeMille's *Union Pacific* and John Stahl's *When Tomorrow Comes.*

Then there were the kind of fun movies that are never taken seriously enough— George Stevens' *Gunga Din,* George Marshall's *Destry Rides Again,* Zoltan Korda's *Four Feathers,* Michael Powell's *The Spy in Black* and Busby Berkeley's *Babes in Arms.*

But yet, with all this lively competition, the one directorial reputation that shone more brightly than any other in 1939 was that of John Ford for his direction of *Stagecoach,* and this is one verdict that has stood the test of time.

What is most interesting about *Stagecoach* is that it does not seem to be about anything by 1939 standards. Nor is it derived from a Great Work of Literature, except possibly by osmosis. "I still like that picture," Ford tells Peter Bogdanovich in the book *John Ford* (University of California Press, 1968). "It was really *Boule-de-suif,* and I imagine the writer, Ernie Haycox, got his idea from there and turned it into a Western story which he called *Stage to Lordsburg.*"

Or, as I myself wrote in *The New York Times* of May 12, 1968: "Dudley Nichols' script has received almost as much credit for *Stagecoach* as John Ford's direction, but the literary ghost hovering over the entire project is de Maupassant."

Nonetheless, the plot line of *Stagecoach* is closer to such crisscrossing stranger-when-we-meet exercises as *Grand Hotel, Union Depot* and *Transatlantic* than to the bitter social ironies of *Boule-de-suif.* As Leslie Fiedler has observed, American folklore never even recognizes the feudal hangover of European class structures.

For de Maupassant, the social chasm between Boule-de-suif and her bourgeois traveling companions can never be bridged by sentimental plot devices. By contrast, Claire Trevor's Dallas is fully redeemed from her career as a Magdalene by her Madonna-like sweetness with the newborn babe of a respectable woman. And at the end of the film the two men who have despised her the most have had their comeuppance—John Carradine's gentleman gambler with an Apache bullet in his heart, and Berton Churchill's absconding banker by being publicly unmasked and hauled off to the hoosegow.

Thus, whereas de Maupassant's story evolves as a bitterly ironic investigation and indictment of bourgeois hypocrisy, *Stagecoach* emerges as a Christian-populist morality play with its heart on its sleeve. It might be noted in passing that the historical

"Berton Churchill's absconding banker being publicly unmasked."

heavies in the de Maupassant story are Bismarck's victorious Germans, and so the tone is cynically defeatist.

By contract, *Stagecoach* is the first of the Seventh Cavalry celebrations of the extermination of the American Indian, and Ford doesn't spare the horses in pounding out a dance of racial triumph and exultation. It must be remembered that audiences in 1939, particularly in the cities, were far from surfeited with the melodrama and mythology of the Indian savage on the warpath.

On the whole, the Western had not fared too well in the 1930s, and the epic Western least of all. *Cimarron,* in 1931, was less a celebration of Manifest Destiny than a liberal critique of materialistic values in old Oklahoma. After the land rush there was precious little spectacle, only turgid domestic discord and rhetorical flailing of underdog causes. *Billy the Kid, Law and Order* and *The Plainsman* tended to resolve their problems more with six-shooters at claustrophobically close range than with rifles at scenically long range.

Thus *Stagecoach* was more the beginning than the summing up of a tradition, and when we think of the Seventh Cavalry riding to the rescue of white womanhood, we are thinking no further back than *Stagecoach.* It is what has followed *Stagecoach* that makes *Stagecoach* seem traditional today, but in its own time, the Ford film was a stunning stylistic revelation.

Why?

First and foremost, it moved in the most obvious manner, and, hence, it was considered eminently cinematic. Today it is surprising to discover how much of *Stagecoach* is conventionally theatrical and expressionistic, and how little of it actually opens up to the great outdoors of Monument Valley, Ford's private preserve for the next quarter of a century. *Stagecoach* was the first movie shot in Monument Valley. As Ford explains the choice of locale to Peter Bogdanovich, "I knew about it. I had traveled up there once, driving through Arizona on my way to Santa Fe, New Mexico."

It is hard to realize today that moviegoers had never seen Monument Valley on the screen before *Stagecoach*. Anyone who has followed Ford's career with any consistency since *Stagecoach* must respond to the landscape of Monument Valley as to the New York skyline, that is, as to a fixed landmark of our visual imagination.

But with this difference: Monument Valley belongs to Ford and to Ford alone, and is thus not so much a locale or even a subject as a stylistic signature. And it belongs to Ford not merely because of *Stagecoach,* but because Ford has not hesitated to use Monument Valley afterward again and again and again to the occasional amusement and derision of his colleagues ever on the lookout for brand-new locations.

The point is that *Stagecoach* has been clarified and validated by what has followed. Its durability as a classic is attributable not so much to what people thought about it at the time as to what Ford himself has spun off from it in his subsequent career.

Indeed, there was a time in the late 1950s and early 1960s when New Critics in various countries tended to write off Ford and *Stagecoach* as the ultimate expressions of an outworn classicism. The very perfection of *Stagecoach* was held against it. Movies were supposed to slop off around the edges with intimations of personal obsession.

A particularly damaging attitude toward *Stagecoach* was contained in the end-of-an-era comments of the late, great, but nonetheless mistaken, André Bazin: "In seeing again today such films as *Jezebel* by William Wyler, *Stagecoach* by John Ford, or *Le Jour se lève* by Marcel Carné, one has the feeling that in them an art has found its perfect balance, its ideal form of expression, and reciprocally one admires them for dramatic and moral themes to which the cinema, while it may not have created them, has given a grandeur, an artistic effectiveness, that they would not otherwise have had. In short, here are all the characteristics of the ripeness of a classical art."

Bazin's importance as a critic—and he *is* one of the most important critics in the history of the cinema—lies in his persuasive challenge to the montage theories of Eisenstein and Pudovkin, theories which had reigned supreme not only among film aestheticians, but among producers who always believed that they could save anything in the cutting room.

Ironically, Bazin discovered new culture heroes in the Wyler of *The Little Foxes* and the Welles of *Citizen Kane* (both films photographed by the late Gregg Toland). I say ironically because Welles himself studied *Stagecoach* assiduously before undertaking *Citizen Kane*. Nonetheless, Bazin chose to consider Welles and Wyler more advanced than Ford. "The storytelling of Welles or Wyler is no less explicit than John Ford's but theirs has the advantage over his in that it does not sacrifice the specific effects that can be derived from unity or image in space and time."

Thus, from a certain point of view, *Stagecoach* is a triumph of classical editing in the 1930's manner, and nothing more. Given the Nichols-Haycox-de Maupassant material, any director of the 1930s might have come up with *Stagecoach,* or so Bazin expects us to believe.

However, with the benefit of 32 years of hindsight, it is more apparent than ever before that *Stagecoach* could not have been made by anyone but Ford. What seemed once like a functional mechanism of entertainment now reverberates with an impressive array of Fordian themes and motifs—the redemption of the harlot (Claire Trevor), the regeneration of the drunkard (Thomas Mitchell), the revenge of the bereaved brother (John Wayne), the self-sacrifice of a self-condemned aristocrat (John Carradine), and the submergence of the group in the symbolic conveyance of a cause (the stagecoach itself).

Above all, there is the sense of an assemblage of mythical archetypes outlined against the horizon of history, but not as the stiffly laundered statuary of Frank Lloyd's

Wells Fargo or the small-scale Leatherstockings of Cecil B. DeMille's *Union Pacific*. What makes Ford's characters unique in the Western Epic is their double image, alternating between close-ups of emotional intimacy and long shots of epical involvement, thus capturing both the twitches of life and the silhouettes of legend.

This, then, is the ultimate justification of Ford's classical editing, that it expresses as economically as possible the personal and social aspects of his characters. And it is this economy of expression that makes Ford one of the foremost poets of the screen.

I would argue that *Stagecoach*, even before *Citizen Kane*, anticipated the modern cinema's emphasis on personal style as an end in itself. And I would argue also that, though Ford's style is less visible than Welles', it is eminently more visual, as Welles himself would very generously admit.

—1970

VII.
Anatomy of a Chase:
The French Connection

That most venerable of film traditions, the chase, turns out to be not an American invention. Film historians indicate that the chase originated with inventive English moviemakers, who experimented with intercutting and switches in points of view. Among the first of the real chases was *Stop Thief!* in 1901. Ever since then, the good guys have been striving to stop thieves in a multitude of ways.

The first major use of a chase in an American film was *The Great Train Robbery*, directed by Edwin C. Porter in 1903. Porter's horse chase-gun battle set the pattern for decades to come. Since then it has been a standard feature of the Western film.

D. W. Griffith refined the art of the chase in *The Birth of a Nation* and *Intolerance*. Mack Sennett developed its comic possibilities. The gangster films of the 1930s gave it still a new form.

At times during film history it has appeared that the possibilities of the chase have all been realized. Then an inspired director puts new life in the old device: John Ford in *Stagecoach*, Peter Yates in *Bullitt*, Peter Bogdanovich in *What's Up, Doc?*

So it was with William Friedkin and *The French Connection*. He realized the challenge of attempting something new and different with the chase. In an article for ACTION, he told how he pulled it off.

The Chase

William Friedkin

*William Friedkin directed television films for Alfred Hitchcock
and David Wolper before turning to features with* Good Times *in 1966. His
other features include* The Night They Raided Minsky's, The Birthday Party *and*
The Boys in the Band.

About two and a half years ago Phil D'Antoni told me the story of *The French
Connection.* It was then a book he had just optioned, based on the true story of an
important narcotics investigation that took place in New York City between 1960
and 1962. I thought it was a terrific story filled with fascinating characters.

The narrative as set forth by Robin Moore contained all the raw material for an
exciting screenplay, except for a chase sequence. It was on this point that D'Antoni
and I were in full agreement: What we needed most of all was a powerful chase.
In fact, our thinking frankly followed formula lines: A guy gets killed in the first few
minutes; checkerboard the stories of the cop and the smuggler for approximately 20
minutes; bring the two antagonists together, and tighten the screws for another 10
minutes or so, then come in with a fantastic 10-minute chase. After this, it was a
question of keeping the pressure on for another 20 minutes or so, followed by a
slam-bang finish with a surprise twist.

D'Antoni, of course, had been the producer of *Bullitt,* which offered what was
probably the best car chase of the sound-film era. It was because of this that I felt
challenged to do another kind of chase, one which, while it might remind people of
Bullitt, would not be essentially similar. I felt that we shouldn't have one car chasing
another car. We had to come up with something different, something that not only
fulfilled the needs of the story, but that also defined the character of the man who
was going to be doing the chasing—Popeye Doyle, an obsessive, self-righteous, driving, driven man.

At this point, I should say that the chase sequence in *Bullitt* is perhaps the best
I've ever seen. When someone creates a sequence of such power, I don't feel it's
diminished if someone else comes along and is challenged by it to do better. The
chase in *Bullitt* works perfectly well in its own framework, and so, I feel, does the
one in *French Connection.* When a director puts a scene like that on film, it really
stands forever as a kind of yardstick to shoot at, one that will never really be topped.
That will always provide a challenge for other filmmakers.

Concept

After I had agreed to direct the film, D'Antoni and I spent the better part of a
year working on what turned out to be two unimaginative, unsuccessful screenplays.

The project was eventually dropped by National General Pictures, and lay dormant
for about ten months. During that time, D'Antoni and I continued to work on it. I had
been involved in production and postproduction work on *Boys in the Band,* so my
own involvement then was kind of sideline.

Every studio in the business turned the picture down, some twice. Occasionally,
we would get a glimmer of hope, and during one such glimmer, we contacted Ernest
Tidyman, who had been a criminal reporter for *The New York Times* and had written
a novel called *Shaft,* the galleys of which D'Antoni had read and passed on to me.

176

William Friedkin with actors Gene Hackman and Roy Scheider.

Tidyman had not written a screenplay before. But we felt, because of what we read of *Shaft,* that he had a good ear for the kind of New York street dialogue we wanted for *The French Connection.*

Tidyman agreed to work with us on an entirely new script. Up to this point we had a story line that was pretty solid, but we had nothing in the script that indicated the kind of chase we eventually wound up with. We had spent a year and gone through two screenplays without indicating what the chase scene would be—because we didn't really have one.

One day D'Antoni and I decided to force ourselves to spend an afternoon talking, with the hope that we could crack this whole idea of the chase wide open. We took a walk up Lexington Avenue in New York City. The walk lasted for about 50 blocks. Somewhere during the course of it, the inspiration began to strike us both, magically, at the same time. It's impossible for either one of us to recall who first sparked it, but the sparks were fast and unrelenting.

"What about a chase where a guy is in a car, running after a subway train?"

"Fantastic. Who's in the car?"

"Well, it would have to be Doyle."

"Who's he chasing?"

"Well, that would have to be Nicoli, Frog Number One's heavy-duty man."

"How does the thing start?"

"Listen, what would happen if Doyle is coming home after having been taken off the case and Nicoli is on top of Doyle's building and he tries to kill him?"

". . . and in running away, Nicoli can't get to his car."

"Doyle can't get to his."

"Nicoli jumps on board an elevated train and the only way Doyle can follow is by commandeering a car."

"Terrific."

And so on. During that walk D'Antoni and I ad-libbed the entire concept of the chase to one another, each building upon the other's thoughts and suggestions. The next afternoon we met with Tidyman and dictated to him our mutual concept. Tidyman took notes, then went off and put the thing in screenplay form. At this point the chase was all we needed to complete a new draft of the script.

The original draft of the chase ran about five or six pages of screenplay. It was very rough and hadn't the benefit of research to establish whether or not what we were proposing was possible.

The script in its new form was at that time submitted to 20th Century Fox, namely David Brown and Dick Zanuck, who decided to make the picture. It then fell to me to determine how we could go about shooting this sequence, which we always considered to be the most important element in the film. First, we had to contact the Metropolitan Transit Authority of New York City. This was done by our associate producer, Kenny Utt, together with production manager Paul Ganapoler. They had a series of meetings with Jules Garfield, the public-relations representative for the Transit Authority, who agreed in principle to our concept, but told us that there were numerous inaccuracies involved in what we were proposing. He said that everything having to do with the operation of the elevated train was inaccurate. We were suggesting that the runaway train crash into a stationary train that was just outside the station, but it was not possible for such a crash to occur because of safety precautions. He said that if we would agree to more accurate details, he would allow us to use the facilities of the Transit Authority.

Utt, Ganapoler and I met together with representatives of the Transit Authority Engineering, Safety and other departments, all of whom criticized the sequence as written. They indicated to us what would be more accurate. Happily, their suggestions were more exciting than what we had conceived.

178

For instance, I discovered that it was impossible for an elevated train to screech to a sudden halt. If the motorman, when threatened by a gunman, had a heart attack and took his hands off the forward mechanism, it would operate as a kind of safety brake, or deadman's brake, and would cause the train to come slowly to a stop.

I also learned of a device called a "trip lock," which is placed at intervals along the tracks. This is a small yellow hammer that lowers to allow the smooth passage of a train when the signal light is green. If the signal is red, the trip lock is in an up-raised position. If a train goes through a red light, the raised trip lock strikes the wheels and causes them to gradually slow down. This makes the train come to a gradual stop, rather than a sudden brake.

One thing the Transit Authority people were adamant about: There would be no crashing of the two trains. We agreed to this. We ultimately came up with a suggestion of a crash, not one that is graphically presented.

I worked with the TA people for several weeks. Then I went ahead and wrote a new sequence that was considerably longer than the first and more accurate in terms of what would actually happen, given the fictional circumstances that we devised. This sequence was approved by the Transit Authority and we had a go-ahead.

Execution

As everyone knows, most films are not shot in sequence. Our chase scene was shot entirely out of sequence, and over a period of about five weeks. It did not involve solid day-to-day shooting. One reason was that we were given permission to use only one particular Brooklyn line, the Stillwell Avenue, running from Coney Island into Manhattan. After numerous location-scouting trips with Utt and Ganapoler, we found a section of the Stillwell line that we thought would be ideal, stretching from Bay Fiftieth Street to Sixty-second Street.

It seemed right because the Marlboro housing project was located just two blocks from the entrance to the Bay Fiftieth Street station. The project was perfect for Doyle's apartment building, and it stood directly across the street from the Stillwell tracks.

Together with Utt, Ganapoler, my cameraman, Owen Roizman, and the first assistant director, Terry Donnelly, I proceeded to plan a shooting sequence. We knew that in shooting in the middle of winter we might run into a number of unforeseen problems. But no one could have guessed at some of the ones we were eventually hit with.

I decided to divide the shooting into two logical segments: the train and the car. They had to be shot separately, of course, but at times we had to have both for tie-in shots.

I had hoped for bad weather, because it would help the look and the excitement. But, of course, I also hoped for consistent light. We told ourselves that even if the light was not consistent, we had to shoot anyway; our schedule and our budget demanded it. I would try to accommodate the cameraman if the light was radically different from day to day. If we had a weather report saying the light was going to be different on one day from what it was on the preceding day, we would try to schedule something else. This occurred on a number of occasions. As it happened, the New York winter of 1970-71 was not a mild one. Although there was little snow or rain, there was a great deal of bright sunlight. It was painfully cold through most of December and January, when the chase was filmed. Very often it was so cold—sometimes five degrees above zero—that our camera equipment froze and couldn't start. One day the special-effects spark machine didn't work, again because of the cold. Once the equipment rental truck froze. We seldom had four good hours of shooting a day while inside the train.

One day, after having filmed for six consecutive days with bright sunlight, there was a time when we had to shoot a sequence with the car running underneath the

tracks. In the morning, after everyone had arrived at location, a massive snowstorm began. Needless to say, we didn't shoot any chase that day.

A part of our concept was that the pursuit should be happening during a normal day in Brooklyn. It was important that we tie in the day-to-day activity of people working, shopping, crossing the street, walking along, whatever. This meant that while the staging had to be exciting, we had to exercise great caution because we'd be involving innocent pedestrians.

The Transit Authority allowed us one section of express track on the Stillwell Avenue Line from Bay Fiftieth Street to Sixty-second Street, a total of eight local stops and about 26 blocks. But there was a catch. We could only shoot between the hours of ten in the morning and three in the afternoon! This was the time between rush hours. Quitting at three o'clock was a hardship, because it meant we would only have half a day to shoot with the train. Starting at ten was also a problem, because we had to break by one p.m. for a one-hour lunch. This meant, in effect, that we really had less than five good hours of shooting each day. It also meant that we would have to be so well planned that every actor, every stunt man and every member of the crew knew exactly what was expected of him. It meant that I would have to lay out a detailed shot-by-shot description of what was going to wind up on the screen before I had shot it.

The Best-Laid Plans

Some days we planned to film under a section of elevated track and arrived to find that section of track being repaired. So we had to change our schedule and try to shoot something else in the script.

Five specific stunts were planned within the framework of the chase. These were to occur along various points of the journey of the commandeered car. They were to be cross-cut with shots of Doyle driving fast and with the action that was going on in the train above.

A word about the commandeered car. It was a brown 1970 Pontiac four-door sedan, equipped with a four-speed gear shift. We had a duplicate of this car with the back seat removed so we could slip in camera mounts at will. The original car was not gutted, but remained intact so that it would be shot from exterior.

The entire chase was shot with an Arriflex camera, as was most of the picture. There was a front bumper mount, which usually had a 30- or 50-millimeter lens set close to the ground for point-of-view shots. Within the car there were two mounts. One was for an angle that would include Gene Hackman driving and shoot over his shoulder with focus given to the exterior. The other was for straight-ahead shots out the front window, exclusive of Hackman.

Whenever we made shots of Hackman at the wheel, all three mounted cameras were usually filming. When Hackman was not driving, I did not use the over-shoulder camera. For all of the exterior stunts I had three cameras going constantly. Because we were using real pedestrians and traffic at all times, it was impossible to undercrank, so everything was shot at normal speed. In most shots the car was going at speeds between 70 and 90 miles an hour. This included times when Hackman was driving, and I should point out that Hackman drove considerably more than half the shots that are used in the final cutting sequence.

While it was desirable to have Gene Hackman in the car as much as possible, we hired one of the best stunt drivers from Hollywood, Bill Hickman, to drive the five stunts. Consulting with Hickman, I determined what the five stunts would be, trying to take advantage of the particular topography of the neighborhood.

The Five Stunts

(1) Doyle's car driving under the tracks very fast. He looks up to check the prog-

ress of the train. A car shoots out of an intersection as he crosses it. Doyle's car narrowly misses this car, spins away and cuts across a service station to get back underneath the elevated tracks.

(2) From within Doyle's car, as he pulls up behind a truck we see a sign on the truck, "Drive Carefully." The truck makes a quick left turn without signaling, just as Doyle tries to pass him on the left, causing a collision and spin-off.

(3) Doyle approaches an intersection while looking up at the tracks. As he glances down, an enormous truck passes in front of him, obscuring his view of a metal fence. When the truck pulls away, the fence stands directly in his path. This particular fence was not part of the Stillwell Avenue route. It was something we discovered while location scouting beneath the Myrtle Avenue line, another elevated branch several miles away from Stillwell Avenue. I decided to switch locales because of this fence, which suddenly prevented a car from continuing beneath the tracks.

(4) Doyle speeds through an intersection against the light. As he does so, a woman with a baby buggy steps quickly off the curb and into his path. Doyle has to swerve and crash into a pile of garbage cans on a safety island.

(5) Doyle turns into a one-way street the wrong way to get back underneath the elevated tracks. Over his left shoulder we see the train running parallel to Doyle, a half-block away.

On the first day of shooting the chase we scheduled the first stunt, which was Doyle's car spinning off a car that had shot out of an intersection. I had four cameras operating. Two were in a gas station approximately 100 yards from where the spin-off would occur. One was on the roof of the station with a 500 mm lens, and another had a zoom lens on the ground, hidden behind a car. Two more cameras were on the street, directly parallel to the ones in the gas station, also about 100 yards from where the spin-off was to occur.

What we hoped would not happen, happened, causing this shot to be much more exciting than Hickman or I had planned. The stunt driver who was in the other car mistimed his approach to Doyle's car (with Hickman driving), and instead of a screeching to a halt several feet before it, miscued and rammed it broadside!

Both cars were accordions, and so on the first shot of the first day of shooting the chase, we rammed our chase car and virtually destroyed it on the driver's side.

Fortunately Bill Hickman wasn't hurt. The driver of the other car wasn't hurt. Each of them walked away shaken and mad, but safe and sound. And I was able to pick up the action after the crash and continue it with Doyle's car swerving off and continuing on its way.

Naturally, right after this spectacular crash occurred, all four cameramen chimed out, "Ready when you are, B.F."

We were forced to call our duplicate car into service on the first day of shooting, and on all subsequent days when we had to shoot events that would conceivably occur before the crash.

To achieve the effect of Hackman's car narrowly missing the woman with the baby, I had the car with the three mounted cameras drive toward the woman, who was a stunt girl. As she stepped off the curb, the car swerved away from her several yards before coming really close. But it was traveling approximately 50 miles per hour.

I used these angles, together with a shot that was made separately from a stationary camera on the ground, zooming fast into the girl's face as she sees Doyle's car and screams. This was cut with a close-up of Doyle as he first sees her, and these two shots were linked to the exterior shots of the car swerving into the safety island with the trash cans.

The only other special effect was the simulated crash of the trains. Since we couldn't get permission to actually stage a crash, we achieved the effect by mounting a camera inside the "approaching" train, which we positioned next to the train that

was waiting outside the station. We had the "approaching" train *pull* away and shot the scene in reverse, undercranking to 12 frames per second. Just after what seems to be the moment of impact, we included an enormous crashing sound on the sound track, completing the illusion.

For many of the shots with the car, the assistant directors, under Terry Donnelly's supervision, cleared traffic for approximately five blocks in each direction. I had members of the New York City tactical police force to help control traffic. But most of the control was achieved by the AD's with the help of off-duty members of the police department—many of whom were involved in the actual case.

Working with Donnelly were second assistants Peter Bogart and Ron Walsh, plus trainees Dwight Williams and Mike Rausch.

Needless to say, the cooperation of New York City officials was incredible. We were given permission literally to control the traffic signals on those streets where we ran the chase car. We rehearsed a shot in slow motion five or six times before I was satisfied that all safety conditions were met and that the coordination was there. Then we prayed a lot, and kept our fingers crossed.

For one particular shot we used no controls whatever. This was a shot with two cameras mounted, one inside and one outside the car. The inside camera was on a 50 mm lens, shooting through the front window; the outside camera was on a 25 mm mounted to the front bumper. I was in the car, Bill Hickman drove the entire distance of the chase run, approximately 26 blocks, at speeds between 70 and 90 miles an hour. With no control at all and only a siren on top of his car, we went through red lights and drove in the wrong lane! This was, of course, the wrap shot of the film. I made two takes and from these we got most of the point of view for the entire sequence.

Completion

The question I'm most asked in interviews about The French Connection is how the chase was filmed. As is obvious from the above notes, it was filmed one shot at a time, with a great deal of rehearsal, an enormous amount of advance planning and a good deal of luck.

But at least 50 percent of the effectiveness of the sequence comes from the sound and editing. The sound was done entirely after the fact. Several months after the completion of shooting and what looked like a good cut, I went back to New York City. With sound man Chris Newman, we made all the sounds for the elevated train. Then I returned to California and with Don Hall, the sound supervisor at 20th, made all the sound for the car on the Fox back lot.

We treated the recording of the individual effects with the same care and attention to detail as we did the photographing of the picture. The use of effective sound effects is, I feel, as important as the picture.

Individual frames or shots or still photographs from the chase are unimpressive. The manner in which all the elements are combined and how sound effects orchestrate the scene—that makes it effective.

I can't say too much about the importance of editing. When I looked at the first rough cut of the chase, it was terrible. It didn't play. It was formless, in spite of the fact that I had a very careful shooting plan which I followed in detail. It became a matter of removing a shot here or adding a shot there, or changing the sequence of shots, or dropping one frame, or adding one or two frames. And here's where I had enormous help from Jerry Greenberg, the editor.

As I look back on it, the shooting was easy. The cutting and the mixing were enormously difficult. It was all enormously rewarding.

—1972

VII.
The World of the
Assistant Director

Charles Washburn was twenty-seven years old and black. Part-time work in a Milwaukee television station had convinced him that the one thing he wanted to do was direct. His ambition seemed so impossible that his family and friends sought to discourage him.

Washburn was working for a Methodist film commission in Nashville in 1965 when he read a *New York Times* dispatch with the headline: "MOVIE DIRECTORS TRAINING NEW MEN." The article told of a new program set up by the Directors Guild of America and the Association of Motion Picture and Television Producers to train young persons for jobs as assistant directors.

Immediately Washburn sent off a letter to George Sidney, then president of the Directors Guild. The young man went to California for written examinations and interviews. He was accepted for the program, went through his training period and in 1968 became a second assistant director.

Washburn is one of the many young men and women who have qualified for the training program and have earned jobs in the film industry. The program began in Hollywood in 1964 and in New York in 1968.

The trainees have joined a unique and colorful profession. Since the earliest days of movies the assistant director has been stereotyped as a blustery fellow whose principal function is to yell, "Quiet on the set!" He does much more, as the articles in this section indicate.

Many assistant directors enjoy the challenge of their job and stay with it. Others become unit production managers. Over the years a notable number have graduated to director—Robert Aldrich, William Wellman, Howard Hawks, William Wyler, among others.

That remained the ambition of Charles Washburn: "I still want to direct more than anything in the world."

Portrait of an Assistant Director:
Pete Scoppa

Director Arthur Hiller behind Ali MacGraw; Pete Scoppa behind him to the left.

Norman Goldstein

On a typical day Peter Scoppa awoke at six A.M., drove from his Glen Cove, Long Island, housing development to the Manhasset station, and caught the 6:50 to New York, just like so many other suburban commuters. Scoppa looked much like any of the other victims of the whims and wheels of the Long Island Railroad, perhaps dressed a bit more casually, perhaps reading *Variety* rather than *The Wall Street Journal* or *The New York Times,* but otherwise "typical." Yet, while his commuter companions would go through their daily chores behind a desk or at board meetings, Peter Scoppa's colleagues for the day were likely to be Jack Lemmon or Sandy Dennis, Alan Arkin or Dustin Hoffman, Barbara Hershey or Ali MacGraw.

Peter Scoppa is a first assistant director, a dedicated one. He has been an assistant director for more than 20 years—and is still in love with his job.

Scoppa, a burly, blue-eyed man nearing fifty, shies from detailing the job of a New York-based freelance first assistant director—the movie groundwork, location scouting, rearranging schedules and scenes, overseeing actor calls, handling crowds, traffic, getting permits and police-department cooperation, exchanging ideas with the director—"Most of which he will not buy"—and generally serving as link between director, cast, crew and production manager, the technical magician who can help the creative director while keeping management happy about the budget.

But with his hands giving animation and emphasis to his words, Scoppa talked of the amorphous nature of his job:

"Let's face it: the job basically is just what it says—assisting the director. He's with the director all the time. It's the same regardless of what he's doing—a filmed TV show or a feature or commercials. It's to help the director do the best job he can; to make his job easier.

"*The Out-of-Towners* had a lot of special problems, for example. Crowd scenes at the airport, the train station. Somebody had to handle all the people. We had up to 500 extras for the scene at Logan Airport [Boston] . . . We had to make it look like a working airport."

That's Scoppa's job.

Marjory Adams, movie writer for *The Boston Globe,* happened to be coming through the airport at the time. She later wrote, in a rare bit of public recognition for an assistant director: "Assistant Director Peter Scoppa deserves credit too. I had a hard time persuading myself that all these people who looked exactly as if they were true average people traveling on TWA at the airport were working in a movie. I couldn't see any difference between them and the hundreds of spectators who pushed as close to the photographic area as they were allowed. It's all because of the system for making extras look real, devised by Director Hiller and Scoppa."

It was the third time Scoppa—"Call me Pete"—had worked on a feature with Arthur Hiller, this one between the earlier *Popi* and *Love Story.*

"Hiller and I are more than director and assistant. We're good friends; we respect each other. I hope to work with him again. He's a great guy. I'll tell you what kind of a guy he is. I'm sure he won't mind my telling this story. He tells it on himself. He was asked to do a quick TV interview in Boston for *Out-of-Towners.* The first question was how you handle the crowds in those airport and train station scenes. He answered: 'Quite simple: Get an AD by the name of Pete Scoppa and don't worry about anything else!' He had about four minutes on the air and he spent it talking about me," Scoppa laughed. "That's the kind of guy he is."

Then he pulled out one of his numerous photographic mementos. Shooting a scene for *Love Story* in the Bronx took them into Scoppa's old neighborhood. Hiller found out and had a big sign up over the front door of the house: "The Scoppas Lived Here."

Scoppa, indeed, is about as 100 percent New Yorker as the movie industry has in its midst. Born, schooled, married, living, working—all in New York, from the Bronx to Queens to Long Island. His father, Salvatore, was one of the founding members and business agent for IATSE Local 52, the film technicians' union in New York, so Pete grew up in the milieu, "migrated" to it, he says. During the war Pete worked not in any film-related service, but as a cryptographic clerk—"It had a Top Secret rating. G2 came around to check me out. I guess I was okay. I worked it from 1942 to 1946."

When he got out, through his father he got a job with RKO Pathé News on the news desk, assigning cameramen to stories. Then he worked on his first feature— *Portrait of Jennie*—in 1948 as a production clerk. Ultimately he became a member of IATSE, Local 61, the New York AD's union, later merged with the Directors Guild. His first feature as an AD was something called *The Tattooed Stranger,* of which he recalls very little.

He went over to RKO Pathé Productions, where he served as contact man—"Really another name for AD"—on their *This Is America* and *Sportscope* series and other documentaries. He stayed with Pathé for 10 years or so before getting into television with the well-known *Phil Silvers Show* (Sergeant Bilko).

"Yeah, that was fun, but it was really cut and dried when you came right down to it. We rehearsed two days, shot two days. We used the three-camera system."

Scoppa was on that for three years, then did *Deadline,* directed by Paul Stewart, for a year before joining Robert Lawrence in the filming of commercials.

"I did a lot of traveling on that, maybe four, five months of the year. . . . There's no real difference for an AD, whether he's working film TV or features or commercials. The problems are the same; the problems are relative. Maybe they're on a bigger scale with features. But it's not more difficult to do a feature. You have more help, more money."

Scoppa's other TV series credits include *Car 54, East Side West Side, Mr. Broadway, For the People, Trials of O'Brien, Hawk.*

His feature-film list: *A Lovely Way To Die, Stiletto, The Brotherhood, Paper Lion, Popi, The Out-of-Towners, The Pursuit of Happiness, Love Story, Little Murders,* and *Who Is Harry Kellerman and Why Is He Saying Those Terrible Things About Me?*

"I've been very lucky. I've been doing one feature after another for the past three, four years. It got to the point where I asked them to take me off the available list for a while—I wanted to spend some time with my family, too. This was the first time in three years the whole family [wife Lee and four children] was home for Thanksgiving."

Other directors he's assisted: David Lowell Rich, Martin Ritt, Robert Mulligan, Ulu Grosbard, Alan Arkin.

"I've been blessed with wonderful directors—and wonderful cinematographers. Either of these gents can make your life most difficult. But if they know what they want . . . don't change their minds 50 times . . .

"Generally, I have a week or two off between films. I relax at golf or we go out to dinner or I fix up the house. I can't sit; I'm like a hen on a hot griddle."

For wife Lee, the always-on-the-go characteristic often meant "there'd be times when he'd call and say 'pack my warm weather clothes,' come home, drop off one bag, pick up another and be off to location somewhere. It can be a real clothes problem, too. He needs a varied wardrobe."

Love Story was filmed outdoors in the Boston area in late November and December. The company spent three days shooting in Harvard's hockey arena, where the reputation of the "fastest ice in college hockey" means it was *cold* in there.

"I wore a heavy coat, boots, gloves, long johns, corduroy trousers, all that," Scoppa recalls. "But I was never warm enough."

At the other climatic extreme was Boca Raton, Florida, where Scoppa worked on *Paper Lion.* "That was a plum," Scoppa, a rabid football fan (New York Giants), said of the work with the Lions. "I could tell you stories about those guys."

That's the way it is with Pete Scoppa, as it is with so many of his AD colleagues: His work is his life.

"When I'm on a film, I'm on it completely. When I come home, after a 12- or 14-hour day, I don't hear what my wife is saying. I'm rehashing the day's work, thinking of tomorrow's. That goes on for two, three months at a time. Any AD should put that much concentration into the job; give it all or don't bother. There are so many things to remember in being a good AD. You have to give it 100 percent concentration and effort. I don't know—maybe that's why I keep getting calls. Would I like to direct my own? It's funny, everybody asks me that. I suppose it's a natural question. I didn't for a long time. I think now I might like to try it. But let's face it, you don't just say you want to direct a film.

"I'm not unhappy with what I do; I'm happy about it. Proud. But I'm beginning more and more to think, 'Could I do it?' Whether the chance will ever come, who knows? I'm not the kind to go knocking on doors. If my phone doesn't ring, I don't work.

"Production manager? I don't like it as much. I was a production manager on a second unit. But I like to be close to the director, on the set with the cast and crew. Don't minimize the importance of the production manager. He really makes things go smoother. It's just not my cup of tea.

Scoppa with Dustin Hoffman on the set of *Who Is Harry Kellerman and Why Is He Saying Those Terrible Things About Me?*

Scoppa observes star Elliott Gould and director Alan Arkin on the set of *Little Murders*.

"I wouldn't think of doing anything else; I don't know anything else. But, really, anything else would be dull."

It surely would, compared to some of Scoppa's chores:

—Running a six- or seven-car train, with some 300 extras, for *Out-of-Towners*. "It was like talking about toys, not real trains; it was like playing with toy trains."

—Getting stuck for an hour on a scaffold 30 stories up the General Motors building in New York for a scene for *Who Is Harry Kellerman . . . ?*

—Creating a traffic jam in New York's Wall Street area: 75 vehicles, 150 extras, cross-street barricades, timed traffic lights. "I felt like a general laying out a plan of attack. But it was the dog-gonedest traffic jam you ever saw!"

—Or, in the aptly titled *Pursuit of Happiness,* having to go out to pick up actress Barbara Hershey after her nude swim scene.

"The job has some rewards," observed Scoppa.

The test of a good assistant is what the director thinks of him. Arthur Hiller said: "It's not what Pete does that's so important. It's that he's so good at it."

Ulu Grosbard: "I have nothing but the highest regard for Pete. He's terrific. He knows his job very well; he is very much aware of production. More important, he cares—he is 'with' the director. He is so well acquainted with production he can anticipate problems. He's invaluable."

—1971

Assistant Director/Production Manager:
Chico Day

Chico Day and director Don Taylor study production board for *Escape from the Planet of the Apes.*

Bob Thomas

The face is youthful, yet deeply lined; the squint marks have been acquired from searching the sun for hopeful signs on film locations around the world. The eyes are clear, the mouth accented with a pencil-line mustache. His body is slender and he moves with the alertness of a professional boxer, which he once was. When he speaks, his speech is faintly accented with the soft tones of his native Mexico. The voice is warm and persuasive. It has been used to soothe hysterical actresses and to command the Egyptian Army.

He is Chico Day, long one of the ablest of Hollywood's assistant directors and now a valued unit production manager—the man who gets the film show on the road. He represents the quality of professionalism that has helped maintain Hollywood as the film capital, come boom or bust.

Chico's commitment to the industry is a personal one.

"I love the movie business," he says. "I am devoted to it, and I want to see it survive. Why else would I be in my office at five in the morning, calling the weather service to find out if we can shoot outside that day? Why else would I work 20 hours a day on the *Patton* locations in Spain? Because I love it."

The present headquarters of Chico Day are in a room behind the Production Office bungalow at 20th Century Fox Studio in Westwood. There he was plotting the production of yet another film—he has lost count of how many he has worked on. This one was *Escape from the Planet of the Apes*. When it started, Chico would be along on locations—"I like to be where the action is."

During a rare period of relaxation Chico reflected on his career and the state of the film industry, past and present.

He was born Francisco Alonso in Juarez, Mexico, the third son of a famed Spanish bullfighter. The boys' Spanish-born mother was also a fighter. With her husband off on the bullring circuit, she feared for her family in revolutionary Mexico. Pancho Villa was marauding the border, and he wouldn't allow Mexican nationals to leave the country.

Mrs. Alonso stalked into the headquarters of Villa and demanded safe passage to the United States for herself and sons Julio, Luis and Francisco. The astonished Villa granted her wish. From 1913 to 1918 the Alonso family lived in Texas; then the father decided to try his luck in California. The rest of the family followed.

After a semester at UCLA, Chico—as the youngest in the family, he was always called that—decided to follow his middle brother into the movie business. The brother had already made a name for himself in films, although the name wasn't his own. Luis had taken the last name of his idol, John Gilbert, and the last name of the serial star, Ruth Roland.

Gilbert Roland's kid brother started in Hollywood as technical advisor on the Sam Goldwyn picture *The Kid from Spain* in 1932. It was a bullfight movie, and Chico knew enough about his father's profession to lend advice. He also interpreted for the Spanish toreador who doubled for Eddie Cantor.

During the early 1930s Hollywood was making foreign-language films for distribution throughout the world, and Chico found many jobs as an actor in movies aimed at the Spanish market. But then Mexico and other Latin countries began making their own films, and Chico found jobs scarce. He applied for work as an assistant director at Paramount.

"You're too kind to people," he was told. "You'll never make the grade as an assistant."

Indeed, the calm, quiet-spoken Chico seemed unfit for the role of assistant director. In those days many assistants were men who could bawl for quiet and could maintain order on the set by sheer belligerence.

So Chico started in the Paramount mailroom at 18 dollars a week in 1937. His knowledge of Spanish won him a job as technical advisor on a film starring his brother, *Last Train from Madrid*. When the second assistant director, Holly Morse, was moved elsewhere to become a first assistant, Chico was called to take Morse's place.

"But I don't want Chico on the picture," said the first assistant, Rolly Asher. "He's got no experience." On the second day Asher said, "Forget about the substitute; I'll take Chico."

When Mitchell Leisen needed an interpreter for a film with a Spanish background, he chose Chico. Leisen made Chico second assistant director on all his films.

It was on *Hold Back the Dawn* that Chico proved his worth. Much of the action took place on the Mexican border, and Chico researched in Mexicali, Tijuana and other towns. A border street was constructed on Paramount's back lot, and Chico filled it with all the details he had observed in Mexico. When Leisen arrived for the master shot on the street, he surveyed the set with his usual keen sense of the pictorial. "You think you have everything, you smart Mexican," the director said to Chico. "Well, how about some horse manure?" Chico casually walked over to the mule shed and brought back a shovelful of what Leisen had suggested.

Toward the end of *Lady in the Dark* Chico left Paramount to enlist in the Seabees. He continued with the Seabees all the way to Okinawa, then returned to Hollywood after three years of service. During this period he acquired his name. An imposter had been passing bad checks and using the name of Francisco Alonso for credit; the FBI suggested Chico could avoid trouble by changing his name. So he adopted the family name of his wife, Day.

Returning to Paramount, Chico resumed with Mitch Leisen as second assistant, then was assigned to Cecil B. DeMille as first front-line assistant under Eddie Salven. Chico's duty: to stage the action behind the principals.

"Working with DeMille was a real experience," he recalls. "I had to stage action that would harmonize with what Mr. DeMille did with the principal actors; but I didn't know in advance what he was going to do. So I just had to guess."

Chico became a good guesser. One day on *Reap the Wild Wind* he tried to antic-ipate the Old Man by instructing each of 20 extras in separate pieces of pantomime. Then Chico waited for the reaction.

DeMille, who always looked through the camera three times—to view the fore-ground, background action and infinity—peeked in the second time and muttered, "That god-damn assistant hasn't given me a piece of individual business!"

Chico was learning what to expect from the autocratic DeMille.

For all his tyrannies, DeMille was an exciting director to work for. Among Chico's most vivid memories are the incidents on the Egyptian locations of *The Ten Com-mandments*. The logistics were enormous. One of the biggest scenes was the exit of the Pharaoh and his army from the walled city in pursuit of the fleeing Jews. On the night before the sequence, DeMille suffered a heart attack.

"We never expected him to appear," says Chico, "but the next morning a limou-sine drove up on the set and out stepped DeMille. He was amazing that day. He climbed all the way to the top of the temple to see a camera angle he wanted. Later he noticed that Yul Brynner was nervous about driving his chariot in front of the army.

" 'Don't worry—it's safe, Yul,' he said. 'Here, I'll show you.' And with that, DeMille got into the chariot, raced the horses in a circle and parked the chariot right on the spot where it was supposed to be."

Eddie Salven died after the company returned to Hollywood, and Chico was notified that he was being appointed first assistant. "I'll do it only if I can have an audience with Mr. DeMille first," he replied.

Promptly at nine the next morning Chico was admitted to DeMille's office and took his place in the "light chair," which the director spotlighted so he could scruti-nize visitors.

"Well, young man," DeMille began.

Chico interrupted him and walked around the desk to confront DeMille at close range. "I want you to know, Mr. DeMille," he said calmly, "that I'm not afraid of you. I worked the greatest under fire during the war. I'll do the same for you."

DeMille admired his spirit, but the director still tried some of his famed techniques of dealing with underlings. Chico responded with a technique of his own: he out-shouted the boss. When DeMille began yelling about a piece of action that was going wrong, Chico yelled back. DeMille, seated on the camera boom, was lowered to his assistant's level and the director demanded: "Young man"—he never called Chico anything else—"how long will it take you to fix that?"

"Ten minutes," Chico replied. He merely ran the procession through the scene once more, inserted a cart that DeMille had wanted, and the scene was ready. DeMille was impressed.

During production DeMille welcomed suggestions for pieces of business from his subordinates. One day Chico came up with a suggestion: During preparations for the Exodus, have a father handing down belongings from a second floor to his son —symbolic of the passing from one generation to another.

"I like it," DeMille said. "You direct it."

And so Chico Day directed the vignette for *The Ten Commandments*. The shot was complicated, involving flying pigeons and other pieces of business, and Chico ordered a third take.

"Isn't that like a new director?" DeMille muttered. "Not satisfied with the first take!"

Filming of the spectacle continued with amazing smoothness, thanks in large part to Chico's inspiration of assembling the DeMille entourage when he took over as first assistant.

"If you have any complaints, take them to the department head in charge, not the Old Man," he instructed. That eliminated a great number of DeMillean explosions that were characteristic of his previous productions.

The final scene of *The Ten Commandments* was a sandstorm while Moses (Charlton Heston) was crossing the desert. When the last take was completed, the crew began leaving the set, but DeMille remained in his customary pose, seated beside the camera on the boom. He spotted Chico and beckoned to him.

"Young man, come here," the director commanded.

Chico approached, and DeMille said, "I want you to know that this was the easiest, happiest picture I ever made. I'll never do another one without you." As it turned out, *The Ten Commandments* was DeMille's last picture.

Chico Day left Paramount to join Yul Brynner's production company and enter a new phase of his career. At the studio he had done second-unit direction of such films as *Whispering Smith* and *The Cowboy and the Redhead* and had substituted for ailing Jerry Hopper for a couple of days on *Pony Express*. Chico had even directed his own film—a two-reel featurette for Paramount. His career seemed headed toward being a director, but circumstance turned him toward production management.

"I still hate figures," he confesses. "But once I have accepted a job, I do it wholeheartedly and with the greatest enthusiasm. That's because I love the business."

Chico was to be in charge of production for the Brynner company, which had plans to film *The Gladiators* and *The Magnificent Seven*. But Kirk Douglas got into production first with *Spartacus*, the same story as *The Gladiators*. Then Brynner sold *The Magnificent Seven* to the Mirisch Company with himself as star. He suggested that Chico go along as unit manager and second-unit director.

After the Brynner company dissolved, Chico freelanced, then took a position in the production office of 20th Century Fox, where he has been ever since. Among his assignments as unit production manager have been *Hello, Dolly* (25 million dollars) and *Patton* (11.7 million dollars).

His philosophy: "I feel a certain contribution can be made by an enthusiastic person who loves the business and is willing to take a lot from people in the upper echelons, in order to keep the show going. The average individual wouldn't take it."

Chico is sometimes called upon to explain the nature of his work as unit production manager.

"I'm like the staff sergeant of a company in the service," he explains. "I enter the picture in the earliest days of planning. Sometimes I read a book that has been purchased and make an estimate of how many days it would take to shoot. The real work begins when the script is completed. I break down the script to show what is needed —actors, sets, animals, costumes, transportation, the whole works. I figure how many days' shooting will be required and estimate the budget. When the picture is scheduled, I make the production board, figuring what will be needed on each day of shooting.

"When production starts, I'm responsible for keeping it rolling. It's up to me to make sure that everybody and everything needed for the picture are on the set so that shooting can continue to flow.

"For the smoothest operation there must be complete accord between the assistant director and the unit production manager; if they work hand in hand, then you have a good combination. But in the end it is the director who is the key man. He's the one who can make or break a picture."

With the decline of production in Hollywood during recent years, many suggestions have been made concerning how to improve the situation. Chico Day has his own ideas:

"Honesty—that's what is needed. Those who take over the reins of a picture should make an honest effort to bring the production in as close to the schedule as possible. Too often a person gets his foot in the door and starts doing the direct opposite of what had been planned. Yes, I'm talking about directors. Too many times a director has come from television and he decides he is through with the television kind of shooting. He starts to go way over schedule. Let me tell you, there is nothing wrong with TV shooting. If a feature director prepares his work, there is no reason why he can't shoot in much the same manner as TV.

"You hear a lot about cutting down on crews. That's nonsense. The cost of a crew is a drop in the bucket compared to other costs. The better the crew and the more money paid to them, the more chance of coming in on schedule or under. The crew can make or break a picture.

"Above-the-line costs (scripts, actors, director, etc.) and overshooting—that's where the money goes.

"The idea of making pictures for a price is possible, but only if everyone will cooperate. It takes a team to make a picture. If everyone is enthusiastic and if all treat each other like human beings, then you stand a good chance of success."

Chico Day has another method for bringing pictures in on schedule: "I pray a great deal."

—1971

Travails of a Trainee

Jerry Ziesmer assisting on *The Wrath of God* location.

Jerry Ziesmer

Jerry Ziesmer, who graduated from Northwestern University as a Bachelor
of Science and won his Master's Degree from UCLA with a thesis
on Stan Laurel, left the security of a teaching job in the Santa Monica public
schools in 1967 to join the trainee program of the Directors Guild and
Producers Association. Under the program, which exists in both Hollywood and
New York, Ziesmer completed 400 working days as an apprentice on such
films as Hello, Dolly, The Boston Strangler, "tick . . . tick . . . tick"
and The Forbin Project. He then became a full-fledged second assistant
director, working on Fools' Parade for director Andrew McLaglen. Here he
writes of his reactions in applying for and serving in the trainee program.

An assistant director trainee is an ambitious young person between the ages of twenty-one and thirty, who has at least one college degree, has some film-industry experience, has scored in the top ten percent in an all-inclusive written examination, has successfully passed an oral examination given by union and guild leaders of the film industry, and finally, has resolved himself that he *can* live on the 120-dollar-a-week starting trainee salary.

Beginning in September applications are received by the Motion Picture Producers Association from the nearly 400 candidates for the 10 to 12 yearly positions in the DGA Training Program. About 300 applicants meet the minimum requirements of age and education, or industry experience, and are invited to take the written examination given on a Saturday in April at the University of Southern California.

With white shirt and tie, a sport coat only slightly soiled by chalk mistakenly erased from a blackboard in my classroom at John Adams Junior High School, and a packet of information supplied by the MPPA, I arrived at USC only to find a line of 300 other applicants in white shirt and tie and sport coat, with the same information packet.

Fortunately I was immediately told to enter the line in alphabetical order. I am still convinced that this first command was the primary reason I passed the written exam. With the name "Ziesmer," in one alphabetized line in grade school I did lose out when the chocolate milk ran out with "Woodward," but at SC on that April morning the long walk to the back of the line gave me time to regroup my thoughts and ego, and to review the competition.

Applicants for the trainee program come from every guild and craft within the film industry, from the mail departments and "production assistants" of every studio, from salesmen, students, teachers, research scientists, military and naval officers, would-be actors, and writers and directors, film-contest winners and losers—the Andy Warhol type, the IBM-junior-executive type, the suntanned from a university in Florida who flew first class to Los Angeles to take the exam, and the three from New York who drove a '57 Ford for six days.

I arrived at the back of the line convinced that I could better spend my time listening to a Dodger spring-training game than taking a test against this competition.

Just when I had firmly decided that I could not miss the Dodger game, I saw Charlie Ziarko walking toward the back of the line. At Northwestern University, every time I had to get into an alphabetized line, Charles Ziarko was always just in front of me; today was no exception. I was about to explain to Charlie about the biggest baseball game of the spring season when a voice from the front of the line told us to march in single file.

What I would do, I decided, was to tell my wife that I really didn't want to be an assistant director and . . .

"Sit down," the voice continued, "with two spaces between you and the person next to you."

Pencils and scratch paper were assigned ceremoniously to us by slyly smiling proctors; that all-knowing, superior smile, condescending to issue me two pencils and a piece of scratch paper just as they did at the College Board examination, the Graduate Record examination, the Army Induction examination, and now again—the Assistant Director Trainee examination. A testing booklet was silently passed out along with one of those IBM answer sheets where you make a vertical bar for the right answer and a machine does all the scoring.

"Begin. You have 60 seconds."

I opened the booklet, poised my pencil ready for a vertical stroke, read the question, read the five answers, and remembered how it seemed that the Dodgers always lost if I didn't listen to the game.

Vocabulary is not my strong suit, and I was quite sure the first word must be a fishing village near La Paz. Unfortunately, no fishing village was listed in the answers, so I marked number four with a vertical stroke, "Finnish Bath," and quickly went on.

"Time," the dean of proctors stated, and I dutifully stopped my random vertical strokes and wondered if all of the vocabulary words had been taken from the olde English edition of the *Canterbury Tales*.

More testing booklets were passed out, containing patterns that are mentally to be folded and refolded, then you select what the result would look like; the cubes that are turned and rotated; the spheres that are turned and rotated; reading paragraphs and selecting the correct meaning; reading the paragraph and selecting the best title; the ever-popular word problems where it seems you have two Israelis, two Arabs and a mad Turk all to get across a river in a boat, but, of course, you can't take or leave the Israelis and Arabs together and the mad Turk will cut off the right ear of whomever he's taken or left, and the boat leaks and sinks at a rate of one inch for every foot of river you have to cross, no one can swim, and piranhas are spawning, so how wide is the river?

You have 60 seconds.

After enough questions to keep a four-year-old satisfied until his twelfth birthday, the dean of proctors informed us we had 45 minutes for lunch.

I noticed the suntanned competition from Florida was a bit paler and the three who drove from New York now looked as though they had walked. (This was before the New York trainee program started.)

None of this buoyed my spirits or hopes, but as I ate my dried sandwich from one of those smiling sandwich-vending machines, similar to the machines that would grade this combination examination and endurance test, I heard more and more talk about the vital game the Dodgers were playing that we were all missing. Suddenly my machine-made sandwich began to taste better.

At exactly 5:45 P.M., or eight and one-half hours after beginning the exam, I completed the final set of testing booklets, dealing with ship speed in relation to ocean current and wind velocity; how to can peaches; what vocation would you prefer: *A* pipe welder, *B* saddle maker, *C* bead stringer at the Venice Pier, *D* house painter, or *E* member of the aristocracy of Lithuania.

And finally, 250 of the following: What would you rather be: *A* host at a party, *B* guest at a party, *C* drunk at a party, *D* not go to a party, *E* none of these, *F* more than one of these, *G* row across a river full of spawning piranhas with two Israelis, two Arabs and a mad Turk who is cutting off your ear.

I marched to the dean of proctors with my final answer booklet not unlike Alec Guinness in *Bridge on the River Kwai* leaving his three-by-five inhuman cage after 23 days and struggling across the parade field to the officers of the Japanese prison captain.

Just as the MPPA had promised, six weeks after taking the exam I received notification in the mail of the result. I had survived and was now invited to the oral examination, the final event. My wife carefully prepared my best suit, the one with the pants that did not look like I had rolled up the cuffs to walk through water; found a white shirt without the stains of teacher's marking pens in the pocket; insisted I polish my shoes with real polish, not the liquid stuff; and finally made an appointment to have my hair styled. My wife is a little 110-pound Irish wonder who knows nothing about sports save the name Sandy Koufax. Through six years of marriage I have learned that Sandy Koufax eats breakfast every morning, takes vitamin C, mows the lawn every other weekend and gets his hair styled.

There was no alphabetized line. The examinees sat around a couple of banquet-style tables. We didn't talk much, just nervous chit-chat to bolster our sagging egos.

The room was large with long conference tables in the shape of a U. Along each side sat unidentified men and the examinee sat at the head. Any introductions were meaningless; the men did have at least two pencils each and some scratch paper. I wondered if I might be a vertical mark.

I sat down and the first hypothetical question was asked me: "If you are in charge of a filming unit and are out in the countryside away from a phone and there is no fireman there and you know you have to have one and you are ready to film and everyone wants you to film but you know you must have a fireman and the grass is dry, what do you do?"

"You are riding along the freeway, and your best friend is driving, and he has an accident and it is his fault. Would you say it was his fault, but he asks you not to say it was his fault and he is your best friend and he will? What would you do?"

"You have three sets to film—Set No. 1, Set No. 2, Set No. 3. The producer has told you to film them in order, 1-2-3, but the director insists on filming them 1-3-2. It will cost a lot more money to film 1-3-2 and a lot more time. The director insists. What do you do?"

There were a few more questions and a little talk, the kind where everyone happily chuckles at no matter what anyone says, and then I was asked if there was anything I would like to say. I am convinced this is what God asked Moses as he was about to wade through the Red Sea to a drowning grave. I have a hunch Moses and I said the same kind of thing.

I was convinced that a thin envelope from the MPPA would mean I was not accepted; a thick envelope would contain forms and such, along with my acceptance. A medium-size envelope came on a Saturday from the MPPA and I read that I had been accepted as a trainee. I then realized for the first time in all of this testing and interviewing that now my life would be taking a direct turn away from teaching and toward exactly what I wasn't sure.

A trainee has a unique position on a motion-picture set; he has no position. He has no duties, no responsibilities, no authority, nothing unless a production manager, first assistant or second assistant director delegates duties, responsibilities and authority to him. The greatest problem a trainee has is simply that he has no problem. A trainee is not the person who is only on the set to answer the phone, to guard the door, to bring the coffee or lunches, to sit in a corner and do the production report and actors' time cards, to see that the actress got to the makeup department at 6:30 A.M., and then to spend the rest of his day calling people on the phone.

A trainee is, as the name implies, one to be trained, one to be schooled in the operation and production of a motion picture so that after his 400-day training program he may make his contribution to the motion-picture industry as a competent assistant director and a member of the Directors Guild.

As a trainee, one of the first areas of knowledge I was told to learn was the jobs of the various crew members and to gain a good rapport with the crew. I was on a film in Amherst, Massachusetts, for Universal, *Silent Night, Lonely Night*, with Daniel Petrie directing.

After two weeks of laughing and joking and being a general good fellow with the crew, I found myself carried out of the production office one evening and thrown into a snowdrift. At this time I learned a great deal about being an assistant director. An assistant director may be a good fellow, but he must be a good leader first; good leaders are not thrown into snowdrifts.

From the beginning of my training program I had been taught to stay near the camera at all times. One day on *The Boston Strangler*, with Richard Fleischer directing, I was following this axiom when I suddenly felt the crab dolly roll onto my foot. I have since expanded the concept to: always stand near the camera and pay attention.

I had more seasoned assistant directors tell me that the most important single thing to learn during my training program was simply "never assume." I could not grasp this simple lesson until late one night on location, when we had to revise the call sheet for the following day. I assumed all would want to know about the revised call sheet as soon as possible.

"Never assume."

A trainee is at the bottom of the totem pole. When things go wrong, the director turns to the first assistant director, who turns to the second, who turns to the trainee, who has nowhere to turn.

For example—and every trainee will bear me out—an actress is late because she says she was confused in her call. There are two basic ways an actress can get her call for the next day. She can read it on a call sheet, or she can be orally told her call. If the trainee gave her a call sheet, he is reprimanded for not phoning her and giving her the call orally. If he calls her and gives it orally, he is reprimanded for not giving her a call sheet. If he gives her a call sheet and then also phones to give her the call orally, he is reprimanded for not treating the actress as a professional.

Somewhere during the training program of each trainee he meets that production manager or that assistant director who is not afraid to give him responsibility, duties and the most important vehicles for learning—time and patience.

For each trainee it is a different person. For me it was Bill Gilmore, Jr. He took the time to explain to me the answers to questions that only experience could explain —theories that only experience could prove vital to an assistant director. Each trainee hopes to find such a person at least once during his training program. If he does, the rest is smooth sailing.

—1971

From Assistant to Director:
Wendell Franklin

Bob Thomas

At a Directors Guild awards dinner a few years ago assistant director Wendell Franklin was enjoying the euphoria of having worked on a big-budget movie in which he had great faith. The talk at the table naturally centered around awards, and Franklin commented to the director of the film: "Maybe next year at this time, the picture you just finished will be up for awards."

The director, who had received many honors, frowned. "Don't say that, Wendell," he remarked. "You don't make pictures for awards. You make them for people."

It was one of the many lessons Wendell James Franklin learned during his years as assistant director. He remembered it when the time came to direct his own feature.

The film: *The Bus Is Coming.* Franklin made it not for awards, nor for the critics (some found it amateurish, others did not—"taut economy, tingling crescendo and superb rounding of characterization . . . see this engrossing film"—Howard Thompson, *New York Times).* Wendell Franklin made *The Bus Is Coming* for people. Black people, and white, too. Audiences got the message. Filmed for 100,000 dollars, *The Bus Is Coming* grossed more than a million dollars in its first few weeks of release. The film's success opened a whole new world for Wendell Franklin. Now he is a film director, not an easy position for anyone to achieve. For a black man it seemed well nigh impossible.

Certainly it seemed an unattainable goal when Franklin was growing up in Los Angeles in the 1930s. His parents had come west from Little Rock, Arkansas, in 1890, and they operated a hotel in downtown Los Angeles. That was where Franklin got his first taste of show business. The Jacksons' hotel was a stopping place for entertainers who passed through town. Young Wendell was fascinated with them.

His parents had other ideas for him. After he graduated from Polytechnic High School, they persuaded him to enter the nondenominational Los Angeles Theological Seminary. But the religious life wasn't for him.

"I had already done some work in entertainment," he recalls. "In those days the Los Angeles black community was rather close-knit, and I staged events that had to do with black life. Things that involved stars like Benny Carter, Juanita Hall, Hattie McDaniel. Hattie was my guest at an affair in her honor on the night she won the Academy Award for *Gone with the Wind.*

"I met many wonderful people. Like Hall Johnson, who brought his choir to California to appear in *Lost Horizon.* I persuaded him to give a concert which I presented in the community. I was all of sixteen at the time.

"Fate is a funny thing. My direction was pointing toward show business. If my parents had had their way, I would have been a minister. But then, there are many ways of being a minister."

During World War II Franklin staged plays and organized glee clubs at a time when entertainment was badly needed for the morale of black troops. The Army sent him to Washington and Lee University, where a special course in staging had been set up.

Returning to Los Angeles after the war, Franklin found doors closed to him despite his experience. He danced in *Carmen Jones* in New York and on the road, then back to his home town to stage theatricals for black social clubs.

He learned that NBC had established a policy of hiring minorities, and he got a job with the network—in the parking lot. It was either that or start as a page. After four years, Franklin won a position as a stage manager. He became the second black to be hired as stage manager in television; Fred Lights had previously been employed in New York. The position made Franklin a member of the Radio and Television Directors Guild. With the merger with the Screen Directors Guild in 1960, he became a member of the Directors Guild of America.

"But then times got hard for live TV," he said, "and I was back in the parking lot."

One day in 1962 he received a telephone call from Joseph C. Youngerman, National Executive Secretary of the Directors Guild.

"Wendell," said Youngerman, "how would you like to be an assistant director in motion pictures?"

Franklin's reply was a happy affirmative. His first job was with George Stevens on *The Greatest Story Ever Told.* As assistant director he proved his competence on other films such as *The War Lord, Kitten with a Whip, Strange Bedfellows, Madame X, The Model Shop, Enter Laughing, Funny Girl, Gaily Gaily, Medium Cool* and *Three on a Couch,* and on such television series as *The Name of the Game, The Monroes, Racket Squad, Peyton Place* and *The Bill Cosby Show.* He served on the Assistant Directors-Unit Managers Council of the Directors Guild.

It wasn't easy always for a black man to make his way in a predominantly white world.

"I had a hard time when I walked on some lots," he admitted. "I got the treatment now and then—from actors, from crew, from production men. They gave me a rough time, but hell, I didn't expect it was going to be easy. I don't harbor any hurts or grudges. But I don't hide anything, either. I have a blunt tongue; I tell it like it is."

In 1963 Franklin became acquainted with a remarkable man named Horace Jackson. A combination of dreamer and realist, Jackson had somehow managed to put together a film about the black experience, *Living Between Two Worlds*. Franklin saw a rough cut and was moved by the film. He arranged for a showing at the Directors Guild theater before leaders of the industry. They praised the earnestness of *Living Between Two Worlds*, but nothing happened.

"That night at the Guild we made history, as far as the black world is concerned," Franklin recalled. "But the time wasn't ready. Horace couldn't get distribution—that's still the big problem with filmmakers. He carried the film himself to Chicago and packed 'em in. The premiere in Los Angeles was a big success in the black community. But Hollywood didn't notice."

Franklin and Jackson discussed their mutual dream of making films, but there was no way of achieving that dream. Franklin continued his work as assistant director. Jackson resumed his education and went to work as a grammar-school teacher.

Late in 1968 Franklin received a telephone call.

"Baby, are you ready?" asked Horace Jackson.

"What are you talking about?" said Wendell Franklin.

"I mean, I got a script."

The script was *The Bus Is Coming*. It was the story of a black soldier who returns from Vietnam to find that his brother, a nonviolent civil-rights leader, has been murdered. The returnee is caught between seeking a peaceful settlement to the racial tension in his home town and joining the militants in violence.

Jackson had taken a job at Paramount, bicycling film between editing rooms. He had talked to some of the studio workers about his project but, according to Franklin, had evoked "a lot of laughs—people said, 'Here we go, Amos 'n' Andy all over again.' "

But Jackson did locate some sympathetic listeners. He found several who would support his project and soon he moved into offices at Producers' Studio. Then Jackson realized that he could not achieve his dream on a studio lot. He decided to move the project to Compton—"The best thing we did," said Wendell Franklin.

Compton is a few miles south of central Los Angeles, 85 percent black, and one of the ten model cities of the United States. The filmmakers presented their plan before the mayor, city council and police chief, and they received complete cooperation.

When it came to union matters, both Jackson and Franklin agreed, "We will go the way the rest of the boys go." In other words, union. They sought and received permission from the Directors Guild, Screen Actors Guild and IATSE to operate on a deferment basis. Franklin's assistant directors on the film were Ralph Sariego and Reuben Watt, both Directors Guild members. They are white and black, respectively, and that was the nature of the whole company—mixed.

"We had nothing but the greatest cooperation from everyone," said Franklin. "Glen Glenn gave us as good sound as you would get on a ten-million-dollar production. Morgan Rents, Mark Armstead (camera rentals) and Bob Kramer at DeLuxe General Film—all of them were terrific. When we needed cars for the picture, Horace called up Chrysler, and the cars came through. In everything we looked like MGM."

Even with such cooperation, bank money ran out. Shooting which was scheduled for eight A.M. sometimes did not begin until three, merely because there was no film

Wendell Franklin instructs young actors in *The Bus Is Coming*. In background: producer Horace Jackson.

for the camera. Sometimes a sympathetic friend such as Marvin Mirisch came through with the stock.

The Bus Is Coming was scheduled for five and one-half weeks, but required nine weeks to complete. The reason, Franklin stated simply: "Bread." Not the easiest of situations for a director to make his debut.

Beyond the physical difficulties, Franklin was collaborating with a dedicated producer-writer, Horace Jackson. The director admitted that they often clashed.

"But never in front of the company," Franklin said. "We always came to my apartment and had it out—sometimes with great acrimony. But we were soul brothers, and I say that despite the cliché that it has become. We fought it out, but always for the good of the picture. Sometimes he won, sometimes I won. One time he came on the set when I was shooting a scene with the militant blacks. I had them dressed up with dark glasses and gloves. 'Hold the cameras! Hold every damn thing!' Horace said. He argued with me: 'You're doing it just the way Mr. Charlie wants it.' On this occasion he was right. I was shooting the militants from a white viewpoint. After all, a militant doesn't have to wear dark glasses and gloves. He can look like anybody."

The directorial experience was a revelation to Wendell Franklin.

"A director is like a surgeon," he observed. "He can diagnose a case one way. But when he makes an incision, he may find an entirely different situation. Well, a director is just like that. When he gets on a set with the actors, everything may seem entirely different from how he planned it. The trouble with our business is that a lot of directors don't have the freedom to make the change. They are stuck with photographing 20 pages a day, no matter what happens. That's tough on them. They can't be the directors that are inside of them."

Wendell Franklin intends to pursue his directorial career. He is associated with Jackson and Thurston Frazier and DeForest Kovan in K-Calb (read it backwards) Productions, and they have plans for the future.

"We are now in the nice position of having top writers submit scripts to us and having top producers ask us to make pictures for them," he said. "I believe there will be a surge of black films. Distributors are realizing that 33 percent of the motion-picture audience in the cities is black—partly because the white city people have moved to the suburbs and left the cities to the blacks.

"There will, of course, be a whole slew of black detective stories and Westerns, and all will be copying each other. We hope to find the unusual. There are thousands of minority stories that have never been touched."

—1972

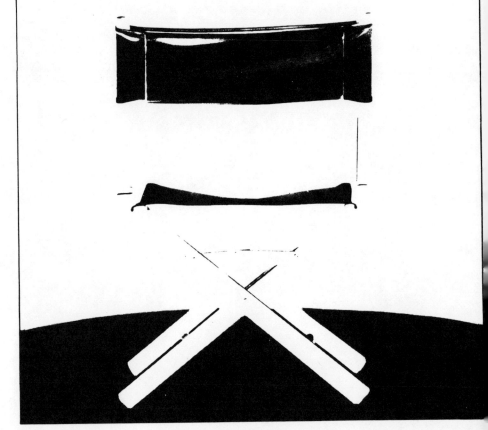

1ST FEATURE

VIII.
The First Feature

Most directors remember their initial film with the bittersweet fondness of a first love. Frank Gilroy, author of *The Subject Was Roses* and other plays and films, made his debut as a director with *Desperate Characters*, starring Shirley MacLaine. He described his feelings in an ACTION article:

"I'd heard it took a lot of energy to direct, but I underestimated how much. You're asked to make a hundred decisions a day, most of them final and irrevocable. Judgment—mine at least—flows directly from energy. The shooting period is remembered as one long, sweet fever. I'm sure I had the flu, but there was no time to acknowledge it."

The "long, sweet fever" is described in this section by other first-time directors. Recognizing the infusion of new talent into the art of filmmaking, ACTION has devoted special issues and regular articles to the making of the first feature. The directors who speak here about that unique experience emerged from a wide variety of backgrounds. Former students Paul Williams and Bill Norton, scriptwriter James Bridges, and writer-producer Cy Howard all wrote their first films. Hal Ashby was a film editor; Lawrence Turman a movie producer; Gilbert Cates a theatrical producer; Dick Richards a commercial photographer. Michael Ritchie and Richard Colla emigrated from television. Their accounts vary, but they all agree on one thing: they want to continue making movies.

Paul Williams: *Out of It*

Jon Voight, Paul Williams (in foreground).

In college I did still photography and made three short films, and wrote dozens of earnest film reviews for the school newspaper. The next year I went to England and met Edward Pressman, a young producer and philosopher. We made a short together which eventually won a Golden Eagle, which gave us the unjustified confidence to embark on our first feature film. I wrote it, Ed titled it: *The Man Who Killed Men*. Budgeted at five million dollars, *TMWKM* (as it became known) interested United Artists, but since we insisted on my directing and would not consider selling the property, United Artists explained that they couldn't have a twenty-one-year-old direct a picture of that size. I think it was Chris Mankiewicz who suggested, "Try something smaller, first."

Since we didn't want to waste potential production money on a script, we decided that I should write an original. I think I wrote a simple but honest semiautobiographical script about a sensitive kid in high school who never got laid. We called the movie *Out of It* and it took us seven months to find out that no major or minor or schlock company would finance a first feature film (a) based on a "plotless" original script about kids; (b) which called for and would use no stars; (c) to be directed by a young virgin, so to speak. "Strike three!" said Sid Kiwitt, then of Seven Arts.

Ed Pressman, a prince, to put it mildly, then privately raised 100,000 dollars which is more easily written about than done (this was before the American Film Institute, a wonderful thing, existed). In fact, it took Ed long enough to raise the bread for me to almost finish studying advanced acting and directing with Herbert Berghof and elementary techniques with Elizabeth Dillon (it was Ed's idea, based on casual observation of my short films, that I study acting).

During the summer of 1967, when I was twenty-three and Ed was twenty-four, we made *Out of It,* starring, as the ads read now, Barry Gordon and Jon Voight. (I was knocked out when I first met Jon, told him so and have stayed that way since.) *Out of It* ended up costing 350,000 dollars with deferrals (everybody) and took seven weeks to shoot and ten months to edit. When David Picker of United Artists saw it, he said to Ed, "I like it. What do you want to do next?"

Now to answer some of the more particular questions.

My background covered important areas—still photography, shorts, writing. But the most exciting area for me was acting. Being able to start to look at a dramatic problem using an actor's cognition was a tremendous help to me. Most of my insights previously were visual and intellectual; studying the actor's craft got me thinking— and much more constructively—about character, rhythm, pace and structure.

My background handicapped me primarily in its lack of depth. I could have used more of everything. When I finished making *Out of It* I had found out what I was going to have to learn. (When I finished *The Revolutionary* I knew enough to quiet my panic, temporarily.)

It is difficult to talk about preparation on *Out of It.* I wrote the screenplay based on my own experience. This can be a substitute for some aspects of a director's craft. I went to school with the people in the script and therefore could get better performances than my sheer technical ability could justify. As far as camera was concerned, I had taken so many still photographs in the years before that I didn't worry too much about setups or moves until on the set, I still don't. That is not to say that I don't care—it is just that I spend more of my time *worrying* about acting and about what Lindsay Anderson calls the "musical qualities" of telling a story.

The camera, on the other hand, is fun. I like to do things simply and keep trying to figure out how to do things within a shot (or a series of a few shots) in a fluid, visually elegant, rhythmic way. I remember many setups and choreography from many movies.

As I've indicated, I was deeply involved with the script. In addition, I had to be ridiculously involved with the budget and production preparations. I cut characters because we couldn't afford them (even at SAG minimums) and shot in a severely "classical" style so, among other reasons, we would not have to rent tracks for the camera.

Did I meet with any surprises? During the summer of 1967 on Long Island it rained 23 out of 41 days on this all-location film. That's the only surprise I haven't managed to repress. After that, I decided that my next film was going to be a variation on *The Exterminating Angel,* about a man who would not or could not leave a sound stage.

It's hard for me to write with any confidence about the actor's reactions to me. As the writer, I was concerned about stepping on my own toes as a director. I had to alter the constructions I had of each character and let the persona of each actor affect and change the character I had written. In some cases the changes were substantial.

But my first requirement for myself was to make a truthful film about kids—and that meant true performances; so the characters as I had directed them were different organisms from the characters I had originally written. Of course, this is not news to any experienced director, but it was a fairly basic insight for me at the time. I had decided that most first features by young, inexperienced directors suffered from poor acting and overexcited visualization and so I concentrated on performance and shooting simply. (Of course, we didn't really have the time or money to shoot any other way if performances weren't going to be sacrificed—so this is also a case, clearly, of overdetermined behavior.)

As far as how I reacted to the cast, I was most amazed at how different each one was, professionally and personally. I didn't realize it at the time, but one of my strengths as a director seems to be intuiting the personal sensibility and professional attack of each actor and responding to him in his own framework. I functioned essentially as an aid to the performer as he discovered the character in a form which would work for the film and me. Some of the actors benefited most from very technical suggestions; others, a more intellectually structured attack. Of course, the differences are accounted for as much by the fact that some actors were doing difficult character work while others were working closer to themselves. The problem for a director, naturally, is to somehow give an ensemble feeling, stylistically. I don't think I was as successful in this area as I would have liked.

I am not supposed to talk about my crew to the "industry" because they were only young people who loved filmmaking. The cameraman, John G. Avildsen, has since directed *Joe*. Some of the other guys are still trying to break in. It is very hard and very unfair. I think the AFI's apprentice program is a great idea. Every director should take one or more.

Editing—Ed Orshan and I learned a lot. It was his first featuring editing job. We both talked too much and [producer-director-editor] Carl Lerner came over biweekly to tighten up dialogue scenes (four frames here, eight frames there—great to watch him "ride" the moviola) and offer suggestions: "Why don't you make scene four scene thirty-six, huh?"

Making decisions daily, based so tangibly on time, heightened my awareness of categories I hadn't thought adequately about before shooting. I think AFI apprentices should be required to stay in the editing room, too, as long as they don't tell anybody about what happens in there.

I had complete freedom, except for the basic economic limitations. Ed Pressman and I have had an unusual and happy professional relationship on both *Out of It* and *The Revolutionary*. I am responsible for artistic decisions once certain perimeters are set.

On both films I had final cut and final responsibility for casting, but Ed and I were constantly consulting and didn't have any arguments about control or responsibility. It's hard to think of him as my producer—"partner" sounds better to me, anyway. Of course, people ask about the distributor. United Artists didn't touch a frame after they bought *Out of It*. They also gave me complete freedom on *The Revolutionary*. They are a marvelous company in that department.

Knowing what I know now, I realize how lucky we were the film wasn't a disaster. If you have a story to tell and want to tell it when you're so inexperienced, you have to work with plenty of ungrounded faith. Who knows where it comes from?

There are several other ideas that I would like to share with Directors Guild members and really ambitious film students (who are the real readership of ACTION):

214

1. It has been my experience that getting a first film is ridiculously complicated in the sense that it is necessary (though hopefully not sufficient) to be a hustler. You have to make your opportunity happen and such skills have little to do with any artistic vision. And, almost by definition, American directors must be hustlers, even the great ones like Kubrick. This insight must be lived with.

2. When you get your chance to do your first feature, it may well be the last—especially since the budget, and hence time, will be insufficient to use even the minimal craft you may have learned. Later, when you know what you're doing, you'll have money, time, technicians and cast to make things less tense, but only if you've done well enough the first time out to keep people interested. The first one is the most difficult and dangerous.

3. When you get on your first set, it is a very easy thing to think that nothing happening on the planet is as crucial as your film and each decision you make every ten seconds. Unfortunately, this may be a pragmatic truth for you, but the big problem of this disorientation is readjusting to the world afterwards. If one doesn't, one's vision becomes tunnel-like. That is a major occupational hazard, as far as I can see.

4. Of course, on reflection, moviemaking beats working.

I'd like to say, finally, that when I look back at how I got to make feature films, it seems personal and idiosyncratic. It had nothing to do with the Hollywood system. I've talked to other young directors and they say the same thing of their own experience. It seems to me that if one is too close to the business, it is difficult to break into feature directing; if one is too far from it, uninterested and ignorant of the ways of money and the picture business, it is impossible to learn how to hustle—to achieve the insight, vocabulary and tactics which are essential in our system.

—1970

Paul Williams' third feature was Dealing: or the Berkeley-to-Boston 40-Brick Lost-Bag Blues.

Bill Norton: *Cisco Pike*

Norton discussing scene with singer-actor Kris Kristofferson.

Q: What was your background before directing *Cisco Pike*?

Norton: I was a film freak and UCLA motion-picture department student. As a director, I had done very little. I directed a couple of TV commercials, some rock and roll shorts, and a couple of short films at UCLA. The most successful of my UCLA films was called *Coming Soon*. It won me an investigation by the FBI.

Q: How did that happen?

Norton: Well, the film was a satire on the Vietnam War, made in 1966. The final scene involved a soldier, in full battle gear, running through a field of tombstones at the veterans' cemetery while "Stars and Stripes Forever" played. It was a great scene and it really supplied the proper satiric touch for the end of the film. It worked so well, in fact, that I thought I would be very clever and paint the end credits on the tombstones. I wrote "Directed by Bill L. Norton" on the back of some poor dead soldier's tombstone. Unfortunately, the paint that I thought was removable wouldn't remove. I guess the graveyard folks discovered it, because about a month later I got a call to come down to visit the FBI at their offices in the Lawrence Welk bank building in Santa Monica. Of course, I didn't have a location permit and I could have been hanged, but they were pretty nice about it and it ended up that they only charged me a 25-dollar cleaning fee for the tombstone.

Q: How did you manage to become a director while so young?

Norton: It was always my goal to become a director. My problem on getting out of film school was finding *the way*. I worked at almost every craft. At various times

I've been a grip, a cameraman, editor, and writer of commercials. It didn't take long to discover that working your way up through the crafts was probably the hardest way to do it. My father, William W. Norton, who is a writer, convinced me that I should try writing and, hopefully, find someone who would allow me to direct my own script. So I tried it. I started three scripts and finally completed the fourth. It was then called *Dealer*. It was loosely based on my experiences and the experiences of a friend of mine who made his living as a marijuana dealer. He was also a film student, by the way.

I took *Dealer* to Alan Howard, who was then assistant to Gerry Ayres, who was a vice-president at Columbia. Alan liked it and gave it to Gerry. Two weeks passed, then Gerry finally read it. He phoned Alan up at two in the morning and said that he wanted to produce it. It couldn't have happened at a better time, because I was living on unemployment.

When Gerry and I met, I really didn't expect to be able to direct it, but I thought I would ask anyway. He thought about it and came up with a very clever and brave scheme. He personally financed a short test which I would direct. The idea was that if the test was successful—if I passed—he would submit it to Columbia as proof that I could direct. We made the test. I passed, and Gerry, the original silver-tongued devil, saved me probably ten years of banging on doors, trying to convince people that I could direct. It goes without saying that I am very grateful to him.

Q: As a writer-director, do you subscribe to the theory that film is a director's medium?

Norton: Not really. I think the *auteur* theory has tended to discount the role of the writer. We forget that some of the great directors also used great writers. You can't make a good movie without a good screenplay. It just can't be done. I believe in structure. That may sound strange coming from me, because I tend to allow actors to improvise a lot. But I've found that improvisation only works well when you have a well-structured, well-written scene to fall back on. When you have a good scene to start with, all you can do is improve on it. I'd say that film is equally a writer's and director's medium.

Q: Do you plan to write all your pictures?

Norton: No. I want to take a hand in the writing, of course, but there are so many good writers I'd like to work with.

Q: How much preparation did you have before shooting?

Norton: Not as much as I would have liked to have had. But I guess that's true on almost every picture made. We had a tremendous lot of locations in the picture and, unfortunately, they weren't all chosen beforehand. I preplanned all my camera stuff, but of course, I ended up changing much of that.

Q: What were your reactions to the first day of shooting?

Norton: I was scared to death. I had never worked with a big crew of actors like Gene Hackman. I didn't know what to expect.

The first morning I went out to the location when it was still dark. It was a nursery school. I wanted to walk everything through to make sure that I knew exactly what I wanted and how to explain it to the crew. It was about an hour before the call, so nobody was there to open the gate to the nursery school where we were shooting. I did what came naturally and started climbing the fence. When I got to the top, I heard a voice behind me. I looked around and it was a motorcycle cop. About a gallon of adrenalin shot through my system. I thought, Here I am, in the dark at five o'clock in the morning, with long hair, and seedy appearance, climbing a fence and entering private property. I thought for sure I would be shot or, at best, get arrested and miss the first day's shooting. I raised my hands over my head and went to talk to that guy. It turned out that he was the motorcycle cop hired for the production, Jerry Ray—a nice guy.

217

Kristofferson, Norton and Karen Black.

Otherwise the first day was hectic. I was nervous and I suppose it reflected in the acting, because the day's work was eventually cut.

Q: What did you learn about directing?

Norton: More than I could tell you here. It seemed that each day my knowledge would increase geometrically, particularly in areas of production, the budgeting of time and the ways of handling scenes economically, quickly. I was fortunate in having as production manager and co-producer Herb Wallerstein, who is a very smart fellow and was a great help to me. He was the first person whom I would go to for advice. And it is largely due to him that the film came in on time and within the budget.

Q: What was your reaction to working with a large Hollywood cast and crew?

Norton: It wasn't like dealing with a small student crew. That's for sure. But both have their advantages. When you're making a film with a small group of friends, you have their enthusiasm to feed on. That's important. Also, you have their technical ineptness. And that can work both ways. Sometimes it forces you to experiment and things happen that just don't happen with professionals. The biggest advantage of a student film crew, however, is cost. Nothing costs. There are no salaries, and time is not money.

On the other hand, a big Hollywood crew gets the job done. Their technical competence is much greater. Contrary to what I had been told to expect, the crew I had was faster than any other crews that I had worked on or seen working. Our crew was small by Los Angeles standards, approximately 35 people, but even at that, it was too many. One advantage of a film-school background is that you learn how very simple making movies can be. For most situations you really don't need more crew and equipment than you can fit in two station wagons. That's it. I can't help feeling that as an industry we are strangling ourselves with too many people, too much equipment and luxury. Even with our small crew, much of the time the actors and I felt claustrophobic, like we were tap-dancing in an elevator. On the last day of shooting we did a close-up of Kris Kristofferson while he was driving. The camera was mounted on the hood, preset, without an operator. I rode along in the passenger seat so that I could see what he was doing. We rode across the desert until we were a couple of miles away from the rest of the crew. I looked at Kris and realized that this was the only time in the entire production when Kris, a camera and I were alone together.

Q: Did you have any disappointments?

Norton: The film doesn't play on the screen like it played in my mind. But I suppose that it's rare when a director can get a one-to-one relationship with what he hopes for and what he gets. Myth has it that Hitchcock and some of the greats know exactly what they are going to get and get it. I wonder. It seems to me that it is an art of compromise. An actor shows up in the wrong costume. It is cloudy when it should be sunny. You have an hour to do something that should take four hours. I think the art comes in finding the best compromises.

Q: What was your reaction when shooting ended?

Norton: I slept.

Q: What's next?

Norton: I'm writing a screenplay that Larry Turman will direct. After that, I'll write an original and try to get it made.

—1972

James Bridges: *The Baby Maker*

[*James Bridges interviewed himself.*]

Q: What made you decide you wanted to become a motion-picture director?

A: It just seemed logical. I had been writing so much and seeing it realized by someone else—never what I envisioned—sometimes better, but mainly worse. A kind of instinctive drive some people might call "ambition." But you want it the way you want it, you know? And the mystique of it. I think the mystique of it and all that that implies had a lot to do with my wanting to direct.

Q: Would you elaborate?

A: No.

Q: How did it happen?

A: A lot of hard work. I started directing in the theater in 1966. Would go back to New York and do a show off-off-Broadway in a loft. Directed at the Mark Taper. For the Actors Studio at UCLA. Friends of mine in audition scenes, etc. All the time writing films and keeping my eyes and ears open, spending as much time as possible on the sets, in the cutting rooms, and bought myself a 16 mm camera and began shooting some stuff and fooling around splicing it together. Seeing movies a second time to see how they're made. The first time I'm still audience. Thank God. Then when I felt that I was ready I wrote a script that I knew was commercial, that I wanted to do, that was relatively personal to me (I knew the real people), and told my agents that under no circumstances could anyone else direct it. Richard Roth (then agent, now

producer) took it to Max Lamb at Robert Wise Productions and in less than a week I had a super meeting with Wise and he took an option.

Q: How long did it take to set up?

A: From May to August, something like that. I wasn't around during that time so I don't really know much about what all went on. I enrolled at USC and directed a play at the Edinburgh Festival. I felt it important to get out of town. One very cold, rainy August day in Scotland a telegram arrived saying, "Come back—we have a deal."

Q: You must have been excited.

A: Smugly stunned. Scared witless.

Q: What happened when you came back?

A: There were a lot of meetings while I still had jet-lag. It's kind of blurred, but Richard Goldstone, the producer, and I got together, met with National General, Dan Polier and Al Yeager. It snowballed. No need to bore anyone with the tiresome details of polishing the script, getting a budget and a shooting schedule, from 50 days ("And that's really pushing it") to 35 ("Take it or leave it"), several postponements, but finally the green light.

Q: And you began to cast . . .

A: The pieces of the puzzle fell out of the box. I don't remember the exact order of my good luck in putting it all together, but through a series of fortunate timings Charles Rosher, Jr., became my cameraman; Howard Koch, Jr., my first assistant;

Winki Harris, my right hand, closer to associate producer than secretary, but try to get a credit without a contract; Larry Jost on sound and all the other terrific people. Casting (crew and/or actors) is completely intuitive with me. That's all I knew to trust. And I'm very stubborn. It took some doing, but when Barbara Hershey, Collin Wilcox-Horne, Sam Groom and Scott Glenn all faced each other for the first time it felt good, it felt right.

Q: And then?

A: Blurred preproduction, some sketching, a firing and hiring of art directors, beautiful Mort Rabinowitz! Joining the Guild, reading every interview with a director I could get my hands on, talking with directors, etc. Then two weeks of rehearsal with Chuck and Walter Thompson, the editor of the film.

Q: You insisted on that?

A: Couldn't have made the film without it. Not on that schedule.

Q: And your first day?

A: Suddenly there are all these people walking behind you. You look at something. They all look. All waiting to see if you know what you're doing. I was prepared. A little cocky. I cut in the camera. Stayed on schedule. The next day at the dailies we discovered we had had a camera jiggle, but I didn't care. I had the wrong lens on one of the shots and was delighted to get to reshoot it. But the steady stuff was very good and I had already shot the second day and the show was on the road. And it had a life of its own. From then on I didn't have time to be nervous, there was too much work to do. And I was having too much fun.

Q: There's a lot of rain in the film.

A: I agreed to shoot no matter what kind of weather. I liked it. I thought Howie did a good job in that department. The sense of seasons is nice in the picture, particularly since it is structured in time. The nine months, right? We kept a board with what kind of flowers would be growing in each month, what the weather would be like normally, etc.

Q: There must have been some bad days.

A: The worst day I can imagine on any film shooting out of sequence is the day in the middle when you shoot the end.

Q: The last scene?

A: Right. The best day is the day when you see the footage and the end works.

Q: Were there any surprises?

A: Couple of times I got spatially surprised when I didn't look in the camera, but by a couple of times, I mean only two. But big surprises? No.

Q: What about your relationship to yourself as writer?

A: I made a lot of jokes about the manacled writer in the cellar, but it didn't really feel like a two-hat experience. I never felt divided, but only extended.

Q: You say you had a lot of fun making the picture?

A: I sure as hell did.

Q: Cutting? Dubbing?

A: Yeah.

Q: Scoring?

A: Yeah.

Q: No problems?

A: Yeah. But nothing really bad. The picture is close to 90-95 percent what I intended. That's a pretty good percentage for a first film. I owe that to Robert Wise, Richard Goldstone and Walter Thompson. I had a lot of protection. In the creative areas. Plus the Denver preview audience. I owe a lot to that audience. They laughed where I said they would laugh and responded to certain scenes that I had to fight tooth and nail to keep in that cut. For example, the demonstration scene with Jeannie Berlin in front of the toy shop.

Q: And the selling?

A: Big but wrong

Q: And your plans?

A: I have a new script. It's called *Soap*. I hope it's next.

—1971

Cy Howard:
Lovers and Other Strangers

Cy Howard directing nun extras.

When I was asked to write this article I was told, "Keep it light, Cy." I said it would be, because I had been around films. How long? For personal reasons I don't like to answer that question or think about it. However, there must be those who remember when *My Friend Irma* became a motion picture; when Martin and Lewis were in films, still a team and talked to each other; when Hal Wallis was at Paramount; and Betty Hutton was Paramount's biggest star.

But I never had directed a film. I was basically a writer and then a producer. I had cut films; I had quarreled with directors; I had anxiously watched my watch as directors worked; I had cast—but I was unprepared for the shock on September 22, last year, in New York when Andy Lazlo, a fine gentleman, calmly and politely asked me in his best Hungarian accent eight fatal words:

"WHERE DO YOU WANT THE CAMERA, MR. HOWARD?"

I looked around—the entire crew was waiting; the extras were waiting; the actors were waiting; the executives from ABC were waiting—nervously—and the producer,

David Susskind, was closing his eyes trying to remember Freddie Fields' telephone number so he could call for my replacement. Andy's question was a normal and professional one, but if you've never actually been the director of a film, it's a rough one. I don't know how other directors responded to that question on their first directorial jobs, but I can tell you how I did—I answered back with something very unclever like, "What did you say, Andy?" Professionally he repeated, "WHERE DO YOU WANT THE CAMERA, MR. HOWARD?"

By now I'd like to lie and say that, because of the reviews I've received (as director of *Lovers and Other Strangers*), I did something very brilliant—like taking my finder out and then very rapidly saying, "Put in this lens. Let's mount this thing on a crane. We'll start from this position and on the third movement I'll push in. The shot will take seven moves."

Then I feel I should have turned to the script girl and said, "My coverage will be two over-the-shoulders, two close-ups . . ." etc., etc. But I don't feel that my first act as a new member of a very esteemed guild—The Directors Guild of America—should be to lie. I also don't think anybody'd believe it.

What I did say was, "Why don't we move the camera from side to side? They're starting to stare at us."

And that, ladies and gentlemen, was the first thing I said as a director. Not a very brilliant remark, I assure you, but it was an honest one and later I found out that if I had said anything less honest, the cameraman and the crew would not have given me the tremendous amount of help that they did.

Since *Lovers* was my first picture, and I am only now starting my second (incidentally, with the same cameraman), I really don't feel I'm in a position to instruct anyone on my particular technique of direction, but some of my experiences might prove interesting.

The task of staging a scene for comedy did not bother me, because I've worked with comedy and comedians for over 25 years. Outside of Gig Young, Annie Jackson and Harry Guardino, who are great pros, the rest of the cast was composed of relative newcomers and some brand-new people who were making their film debuts. The old pros were very helpful, and the new ones were very eager, because we all wanted to make a good picture.

Since the crew realized that it was my first picture, I cannot say enough about the help my cameraman, my assistant director, Lou Stroller, my script girl, Barbara Robinson, and the rest of the crew gave me. I don't think this was due particularly to my personality. I think it was because they were professionals and I had declared myself at the beginning—that I wanted and needed their help and they were eager to give it. They told me later that if I had taken another tack and tried to bluff my way through the technical parts of the film, they might have had a different attitude. But we all pitched in and started shooting and made it on schedule.

Because it was my first picture, I was not hung up by any old-fashioned ways of shooting. I'd block out the scene, rehearse it and turn to the cameraman, tell him what shot I wanted and he would get it. I was very pleased to find that this technique is used by a great number of fine directors. On a lunch break during the second day of shooting, when I was feeling very low, I was reading an article by Antonioni, the great Italian director. When they asked him, "What is your technique?," he said very simply, "When I figure out a scene, I tell the cameraman. If he can't get the shot, I fire him."

I did, however, have funny experiences that happened to me. Like, I took many low shots at the Italian wedding while they're dancing the tarantella. I was not aware while I was filming this sequence that the publicist on the picture had brought out a young, intense film buff from one of New York's leading newspapers to interview me. After I took four or five of those low shots he tapped me on the shoulder and said, "Mr. Howard, you seem to shoot from low angles. That interests me. Is there any particular reason for that type of technique?"

I said, "Yes—I'm not used to getting up at five in the morning and at my age. Once I start low I have to stay low for a while—it's hard to get up!" I thought he'd laugh at that because I said it for that reason, but instead he went home and wrote a wonderful article about my new technique-type of low shooting. Naturally the next time I was asked about my low shooting, I quoted this man extensively.

As for how it feels to direct your first film, I think everyone must have one similar experience—that is, the average amount of anxiety which even old-timers tell me they have, and the everyday just plain hard work of directing.

I had never realized that directing was such a monastic, lonely business. I thought writing—to quote the old cliche—was a lonely business, but I found directing even lonelier because of the power that the director has. So many people depend on you and you are the final one to make the decisions. When you say, "Print it," it's final. That responsibility can only make one feel lonely. It did me.

The only rule that I set for myself when I started to direct *Lovers and Other Strangers* was one of doing comedy honestly. I've heard throughout my entire professional life, "We want an honest, gentle comedy with real people—some tears, but with a lot of yoks!" That, of course, is the jackpot if one can do it. I'm sure everyone starts out trying to do that.

I decided that I would shoot honestly. If something were funny, just put the camera on and record it. I was not worried too much about the marks because I never saw marks get a laugh in the theater. I was not too interested in how the cameraman was lighting the scene or what lens he had on the camera, because Andy Lazlo knew far more than I did about that. I did, however, know that comedy is best played in a two-shot so that one can get reactions.

In *Lovers and Other Strangers* I made no compromises in casting whatsoever. Names were not a factor. In fact, I replaced two members of the cast (who shall be nameless)—one on the first day of rehearsal and one on the first day of shooting. They were mistakes and I must say "bravo" to management for backing me up. Because, at that time, I must tell you I had very little professional "muscle," and even though I would like to believe it for ego's sake, I was not the first director offered this play.

But then it wasn't because of faulty judgment on the part of my fellow director that he had turned it down. The original *Lovers and Other Strangers* was a series of three sketches done as a play which failed on Broadway. It was talky and did not lend itself at all visually to the screen. I, too, might have turned it down had I not been given the following unique deal.

I was not originally hired as a director of the film, but was hired to work with the original writers of the play (Renee Taylor and Joseph Bologna) to fashion it into a screenplay. If I could accomplish this, the bait was that I would be allowed to direct my first film. So I was really first hired as a writer and then later as a director.

Working on the script took about four months, in which time the original writers were let go because of artistic differences and a new writer, David Z. Goodman, was brought in. He finished the picture with me.

The entire picture was shot in New York, of which about 90 percent was done on location. We took over the Hilton Hotel in Tarrytown, New York, and I shot the wedding sequences, the ballroom and the reception and the rooms in the actual places where the Hilton accommodates these occasions. It never occurred to me that this would be difficult because at that time I didn't know what a wild wall was, anyway (but I do now).

226

I had a definite conception of what I wanted to do with the picture based on my previous experiences as a comedy writer. The conception was merely added to and made visually as a director.

I allowed myself certain psychological revenge on pet hates, such as: Don't let the makeup people touch up the actors just before a take so that they come out looking like plastic people; ruffle up the bed so it looks as if people slept in it; use the props as though they were functional; don't let the prop man clean up the ashtrays; in the eating scenes eat real food and make the actors talk while they're eating—for realism.

And I tried for as many visual jokes as possible. I only had one rule that I never varied from. I listened to everybody and then decided to fail or succeed on my own instincts because all of the Guild members I have respected over the years gave me my best advice. They said: If a picture is a hit, everybody takes bows—but if it's a flop, the director is responsible for it.

Lovers and Other Strangers, they say, is a hit—but there still isn't a shot in the picture that I wouldn't want to redo.

—1970

Cy Howard has since directed Every Little Crook and Nanny.

Hal Ashby: *The Landlord*

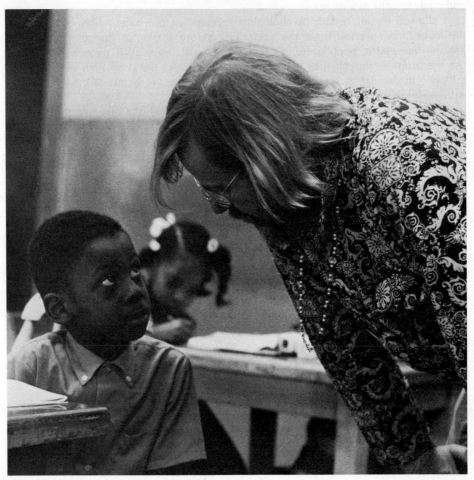

Ashby coaching a young actor in schoolroom scenes.

I was born in Ogden, Utah. Never a Mormon. Hated school. The last of four children. Mom and Dad divorced when I was five or six. Dad killed himself when I was twelve. I struggled toward growing up, like most others, totally confused. I joined the dropouts in my senior high year. Didn't get along with my family. Married and divorced twice before I made it to twenty-one. Hitchhiked to Los Angeles when I was seventeen. Started smoking grass at eighteen. Had about 50 or 60 jobs since I was ten, up to the time I was working as a multilith operator at good old Republic Studios.

One day, while running off 90 or so copies on some now-forgotten page 14, I flashed on the idea of becoming a film director. That was about 15 years ago. With the hope of achieving my directorial dream, I plied my multilith trade and asked advice from those I met.

"The best school for a director is in the cutting room," was the reply I heard most often. So I looked, looked some more, and finally found a friend who would hire me as an apprentice editor. Then came the union. I applied; luckily the timing was right and I was accepted, or at least allowed to go to work.

It was good advice. When film comes into a cutting room, it holds all the work and efforts of everyone involved up to that point, the staging, writing, acting, photography, sets, lighting, and sound. It is all there to be studied again and again and again, until you really know why it's good or why it isn't. This doesn't tell you what is going on inside a director or how he manages to get it from head to film, but it sure is a good way to observe the results, and the knowledge gained is invaluable.

But the life of a fledgling editor is far from ideal, and getting through it was a trip and a half. The union has an eight-year rule, which demands you work that length of time as an apprentice, or assistant, before you are eligible to edit film. It's a bad rule, which tends to debilitate those who might have any creative juices going for them at all. It can become a full-out struggle just to hang on during those eight long years, and some good talent has gone down the tubes in the process.

Desire and sheer luck were responsible for my keeping it together. First, desire made me a hard worker and kept me at it here and there for a couple of years. Then came the luck. I went to work on *The Big Country*. I was about the fourth assistant in a super-large crew, headed by the chief editor, Robert Swink, but the experience was something that turned me on to film as the wildest, most exciting medium of all.

Mind-blower number one came rushing at me the first day. One of the editors had cut his way to the end of a reel, and we all—I mean the whole crew—marched up to the projection room to look at it. Before we ran the film, somebody remembered I was the newcomer, so Bob Swink or William Wyler—I'm not sure which—laid a little speech on me.

"If you have any ideas, any—no matter how wild they might seem—get them out. I, or we, might argue with you and tell you it's a dumb idea and you are a dumb son of a bitch, but that doesn't matter because the heat of our anger comes only from the desire to make a good film. You must understand how we all *feel* about this film, or any film, and know in your heart that the words said in anger have nothing to do with anything personal. It will sound that way because we are driven by those strong feelings, and we don't take the time to be polite, but personal it isn't. So get those ideas out into the open and remember, the only thing any of us wants out of all this is to make a good film."

Needless to say, there was a lot of yelling, hollering and swearing that went on down in those cutting rooms, but there were also about 18 tons of love floating around there, too. It was, indeed, a beautiful year.

Some more good time was spent. Bob Swink took me with him from film to film. *The Diary of Anne Frank, The Young Doctors, The Children's Hour, The Best Man* and a couple of others. When I was lucky enough to be working with Bob, he hit me with everything from the technical aspects to the philosophy of film.

"Once the film is in hand," he would say, "forget about the script, throw away all of the so-called rules, and don't try to second-guess the director. Just look at the film and let it guide you. It will turn you on all by itself, and you'll have more ideas on ways to cut it than you would ever dream possible. And use your instincts! Don't be afraid of them! Rely on them! After all, with the exception of a little knowledge, instincts are all we've got. Also, don't be afraid of the film. You can cut it together 26 different ways, and if none of those works, you can always put it back into daily form, and start over."

As I watched and absorbed, Bob proved editing to be a truly creative force, and it really turned me around. I almost, but not quite, forgot about wanting to be a director.

Finally, my eight years were up. Bob got me on *The Greatest Story Ever Told* as a fourth editor. After a few months I left and went over to *The Loved One* as chief editor. The George Stevens people were mad at me—I hope they still aren't.

I did the first cut on *The Loved One*, but that was it. Tony Richardson had a commitment in London, so he took the film with him to finish it there, and left me here. It was a bad time. Depression and paranoia ran rampant. In short, I was on the superbummer of the year.

Then some more good luck came my way, via John Calley, who produced *The Loved One*. John knew Norman Jewison was looking for an editor, so he set up an introduction. It must have been a good meeting, because Norman took a chance, and I ended up cutting *The Cincinnati Kid*. I also got my head together at the same time. I was feelin' good, and from there on, things really happened.

I worked with Norman on *The Russians Are Coming, The Russians Are Coming, In the Heat of the Night* and *The Thomas Crown Affair*. It was the most productive relationship imaginable. From in front, Norman always gave me good film. Then, to top it off, he trusted me and my instincts. He never stood behind me in the cutting room. He let me select and cut his film as I felt it. It was an editor's dream and, in the end, it brought me two Academy nominations and one Oscar.

As time marched on, Norman boosted me up to the position of associate producer, and I was able to gain some of the much needed experience in the areas of preproduction and production. Norman had me involved in everything from scouting locations to being used as a sounding board for new ideas on script, casting and new projects. It was the total trip, and I really felt as if I were giving as much to the film as possible, without actually being the director. What more could I ask?

What's really wild is the fact that I didn't even have to ask! One day, while we were working on *Thomas Crown*, Norman looked at me, smiled and then asked, "What do you want to do?"

It really blew my mind. In all the time I had known Norman, we never once touched upon the subject, and here this beautiful, sensitive dude was standing there asking me about my dream.

"Well, I want to make films," I said. Christ, I couldn't even get the damn word out of my mouth.

Another long moment while Norman just stood there with his impish grin. Finally it came out.

"I want to direct. That's where it's at, isn't it?" I said.

"Right!" Norman replied. "So let's find something for you." And he did!

Of course, it didn't happen just like that, but happen it did. We were still shooting *Gaily, Gaily*, when Bill Gunn sent the first 82 pages of his first draft of *The Landlord*. Norman and I read it and were both very up on Bill's screenplay and anxious to receive the 40 or so pages still due. Then, in the simplest manner possible, Norman said, "Why don't you direct *Landlord*?" I jumped up and did a fast dance around the office.

Landlord was initially set as a project for Norman, but he had a couple of time-schedule problems still unsolved, so he laid it on me.

I immediately took the pages we had to my dear and close friend, Beau Bridges. Beau read the pages and said yes. I was home free. One whole day as a director. One major decision made. And no rejections.

In the meantime, Norman had set things in motion to gain approval from the brothers Mirisch and United Artists. Not an easy task, I'm sure, to ask for two million dollars so some unknown factor of a director can make his first film. Nobody ever made mention of it to me—at least I don't recollect having ever talked about it to Norman—but it certainly crossed my mind, as it must have crossed some others. They probably even talked of it in some circles. It being what I call "deductive knowledge."

Mainly: "If Ashby falls on his ass, Jewison can take over and we'll be covered."

I honestly don't know if anyone ever had such a thought, but I do know Norman was my producer, and for that I am truly thankful.

So I had the financing, a script, a star, a producer, me and the absolute need to fulfill about 1,080 unmade decisions, all of them to be resolved before the first day of shooting. And once you get there, as I later discovered, the pace jumps up to about 1,080 fast decisions per day.

I was really learning the difference between being a sounding board and using a sounding board. I couldn't just sit around the office and rap with Norman about the script or the casting anymore. Now I found myself with the responsibility of making decisions. Final decisions. It was nervous time.

We were into the casting, and I really do believe it was the toughest time on the film. Maybe that was so because it was the first time I had been forced to make such a definite commitment. Not words on paper. Or film to be cut, then changed later.

This time, when the decision was made, that was it. Not to be changed. Of course, as I look back, I'm sure the major fear I had about my being a director was taking its toll. The fear of not being able to communicate my thoughts to the actors.

I felt fairly secure in all other areas, such as the visual aspects, and I never doubted for a moment the abilities of the actors I chose to play the parts. No, the knowledge I had gained as an editor would serve its purpose well, but it had nothing to do with telling an actor what I wanted.

Beau was a friend, so the fear subsided somewhat when it came to him, but how was it going to go with Lee Grant, Diana Sands, Lou Gossett or Pearl Bailey? I had no way of knowing. Time, as they say, would tell—but that didn't help at all. By that time it could be too late.

The snowball was rolling, and some super-good people were around to help it grow. As production manager, Pat Palmer was the greatest. But his talents went much, much beyond that, and he took on the chores of associate producer, too. The gigantic talents of Bob Boyle were being used to do the best damn job ever as the production designer and art director. I didn't know Terry Nelson, who was going to be my first assistant director, but my instincts told me, "Yes!" the moment we met. As time went on, they were proved right.

The time had indeed come! This was it! We had a week or so of rehearsals in New York and everybody got to know each other. I had hopes this would ease some of the fears I held about the communication-with-actors thing, but it seems luck was definitely with me.

The first day of directing my first film, and I couldn't breathe. The damn fear had actually managed to make me sick. The doctor came to the location, checked me over, and said I had walking pneumonia. I would have to go to bed. I said, "Hell, no!" and told him to pump everything he had into my arm, rear or foot, if necessary. He did just that and three days later I was a well man with three days of directing my first film forever behind me.

Within a week I had completely rid myself of that old communication fear, and we were on our way. Norman, as usual, was doing everything right. To stress his point that it was my film, he stayed away from New York. He didn't want to run the risk of intimidating me by standing around in the background, getting nervous and maybe suggesting a shot now and then.

Pressures there were. The first thing the Mirisch Company came down on was the photography. It was too dark. They couldn't see the actors' eyes. I explained how I wanted the look of the ghetto footage to have the etched feeling it did so we would have a contrast to the so-called blown-out, billowy, white-on-white sequences which we would be shooting in a few weeks.

"But this is a comedy," Walter Mirisch said, "and you've just got to see their eyes."

Then I would get into how I could see their eyes, and how nice it would be if they would just have a little faith in me and trust me. It went on and on, with neither

Ashby rehearsing Beau Bridges and Pearl Bailey.

side giving in, until we got to the so-called white footage. Then I guess they saw what I meant, and the pressure of that issue eased off.

But there were other things to get them up-tight, too. I had fallen behind schedule and on top of that I was shooting a tremendous amount of film, much more than normal. As to the schedule, what the hell could I say? I wasn't any happier about it than they were.

We did run into 14 days of rain while shooting out on Long Island, but the main reason for being behind was me. I set the pace, and that was that. Actually, it wasn't a slow pace at all. We were running our tails off, and the idea of being behind really ate away at me.

After we were six weeks into the shooting, Pat Palmer rescheduled the picture. He wanted to ease my anxiety, and enough time had elapsed for him to study and gauge my tempo so he could come up with a more realistic schedule to fit me.

As usual, Pat hit it right on the nose. Then we were right on, and I, for one, felt much, much better. I'm not sure if the complaints were fewer, or if I just ignored them, but I didn't notice them as much.

And then it was over. It took 66 days and 2,400,000 dollars—about 400,000 over the budget—to do it, but we did it, and the shooting was finished.

A goodly portion of the overage was spent on postproduction. I really did shoot a lot of film, a lot more than I realized. In one sense, it was okay; I believe the more film you have, the more latitude you have, but I was floored when I saw what a load I had placed on Bill Sawyer, the editor. Bill had been in L.A. during the shooting, and I, the ex-editor, didn't have any idea of just how much film we had. To help Bill out, I jumped in and took a couple of sequences to cut, and we put another editor, Ed Watschika, to work as well.

Did I encounter any surprises? Yes, one very pleasant and nice surprise. I believe one of the best things a director can do for his film is to get as many others as possible to become a part of the film. Get their creative juices turned on, and most people will give and give and give. To gain this end, I submerged my ego so it wouldn't be out there getting in the way of someone else who might be able to get it on, given half a chance, and really contribute something special.

As I honestly practiced such a policy, it really blew my mind when I sat there looking at the dailies and saw so much of me coming out on that screen. For some reason, I hadn't expected any such thing, but I must say my ego was most pleased to see it happen. It was indeed a most wonderful surprise.

Will I do anything different next time? Yes, I will try to apply even more concentration. I had a tendency to try and get away from the film for a few hours each evening, hoping for a fresher outlook the next day. I don't think that is where it's at anymore, so I will try, on the next one, to give it 24 hours of concentration each day, during the entire shooting.

Students often ask me how they can become directors. The only thing I can tell them is this: Don't follow my example. The cutting room is an excellent place to learn much about directing, but that eight-year rule is ridiculous. So forget that whole scene, and go out and make a film. Any kind of film. Do a short 10- or 20-minute film on a shoestring, or borrow 40,000 dollars and make a feature. If it's good, it will be seen. Above all else, put as much honesty as you can into everything. That's what comes across on the screen: Honesty.

—1970

Hal Ashby *followed* The Landlord *with* Harold and Maude.

Lawrence Turman:
The Marriage of a Young Stockbroker

Richard Benjamin and Larry Turman.

[Before his directorial debut Lawrence Turman produced films, among them *The Flim-Flam Man, The Graduate, Pretty Poison* and *The Great White Hope.*]

Q: When did you first realize you wanted to direct?

Turman: I swear I don't know. It didn't come to me in a single moment. I had incepted film projects in their entirety, taking part in script preparation, casting, pre-production, postproduction, etc. I guess I figured if I was doing all that, I might as well go ahead and make the total commitment.

Q: Did you have an early experience directing in another medium?

Turman: Absolutely none.

Q: Then did you have any trepidations about directing a film—did it seem forbidding and mysterious to you?

Turman: Forbidding, yes. Mysterious, yes. Trepidations—some.

Q: What directors did you particularly admire?

Turman: Stevens, Wyler, Kazan, Nichols, Kubrick—ad infinitum. Fellini, Truffaut—all kinds of people. Bergman, Polanski, Penn, many more. Before I started to direct, I ran movies of all of these men, hoping to learn something from them. All I learned was that in each case this was a very talented man. I learned nothing specific at all.

After the first couple of reels, I would be pulled into the story, and I simply enjoyed it. They all made it seem too simple. But I know it wasn't simple. It's simple to make a bad picture.

234

And, oh, yes—Ford! I can't forget Ford.

Q: How did you make the decision to direct?

Turman: It's something like marriage. You fall in love and then you decide you just must be married to the girl. Well, I had been very happy as a producer. I found it very fulfilling to take part in all phases in production and implement my taste in every way. All the films I have done, I've loved. Yet with each of them I also had a sense of disappointment. They never came out as I had envisioned them. That was the biggest comedown: to work on a picture for a year and envision it one way, only to have the director do it differently. Maybe his vision was better than mine. But still, that didn't satisfy me. I had to get married—to direct a picture myself.

Q: How did you select the material?

Turman: Webb showed me the first half of the manuscript for the novel. I liked it and I bought it. I must say, I would have preferred my first job as a director not to be Webb material. I'm a bit paranoid about the possibility of people saying, "So he's going back to the same source as his biggest hit [*The Graduate*]!"

Q: Obviously you see something in Webb's work that strikes a note with you.

Turman: I'm sure. Webb's characters have qualities that are close to me. A kind of funny-sad surrealness with underlying sexual tension, a resistance to involvement, yet an inability to avoid being caught up in the life that is swirling about.

Q: How did you set up the deal to direct?

Turman: Very simple. I told Dick Zanuck I wanted to direct this one, and he said, "Okay." He's very good at making decisions like that. Not that he makes snap judgments; he's a good executive. He knew my past record, and he knew the studio would have certain controls if I goofed up. He was willing to take a chance. He did the same on *Pretty Poison*. I said I'd like to have it done by the kids who made the short *Skater Dater*. Dick said okay, knowing that I would be there to keep an eye on things.

Q: What preparation did you have for *The Marriage of a Young Stockbroker*?

Turman: Not as much as I would have liked. I am a great believer in preparation, and I wanted plenty on my first picture as a director; I guess I had a certain insecurity.

I was still in postproduction work on *The Great White Hope* a month before I had to start shooting. I wanted to start in the spring [of 1971], but the studio wanted me to start in the fall [of 1970]. I said to myself: If they're eager to have the picture made in the fall, I'd better not dally; next spring they might change their minds.

Q: Did you have enough time to prepare the script?

Turman: By my lights, the script was prepared to my satisfaction. I had worked closely with Lorenzo Semple, Jr. When I started shooting I felt satisfied with it. But, of course, later you see where you weren't so smart, where you might have done a better job with more time.

Q: What were your reactions on the first day of shooting?

Turman: Exhilaration. Self-consciousness. A modicum of apprehension. Actually, I went through three cycles while shooting: (1) fear; (2) euphoria; (3) settling down to struggling with the entire process of directing.

Q: What was the reaction of the cast and crew to a first-time director?

Turman: That's interesting. In life we're all insulated from getting a candid feedback from those you're associated with. All in all, I felt a good reaction. Many people tell me the picture was the most exhilarating experience they had known on a film. That's not necessarily the truth, but I must say that the feedback was terrific. Making a film requires a lot of pressures and compromises, but all helped make it as smooth as possible. I believe a film should be a participatory democracy as filtered through a benevolent autocrat. I always encouraged suggestions and often I heeded them. But in the end, I had to do what I wanted to do.

Q: What did you learn about directing?

Turman (left) directing Benjamin and Elizabeth Ashley.

Turman: I told my wife, "You know, it's easy and it's hard to direct." Anybody can direct a movie—going through the motions is easy. But to direct a movie well, that's hard.

Q: Did you have any trouble with the mechanics?

Turman: Some. I found myself saying to the cameraman that I wanted to pick up a single on Dick Benjamin and he would say, "Where?" Then I had to decide. Did I want to cut Benjamin off at the chin or go a foot lower at the middle of his chest? Did I want to shoot him straight-on or a three-quarter shot? Did I want the camera higher than his face or lower? These were not major decisions, but I kept wondering how Stevens or Ford or Capra would know how to make the right choice.

Q: Did you have any surprises?

Turman: Yes—that directing was so exhausting physically as well as mentally.

Another thing, I had thought if I directed my own picture, it would come out the way I envisioned it. Not true. I could plan a scene exactly as I saw it in my mind. But when I saw it on the screen, it could be something entirely different.

Q: Any disappointments?

Turman: That I am not Fellini, Kubrick and Lean rolled into one. And that I can't do the whole thing all over again.

Q: Any problems during production?

Turman: Not really. The studio was sniping at my heels, but I expected that. I gave them no real cause for alarm. We went over budget, but no more than one percent. And that was largely because we were weathered out a day and a half.

Q: What was your reaction when shooting ended?

Turman: "Hey—I did it!"

Q: Did you learn anything in the postproduction period?

Turman: Not really. I had always been so heavily involved in postproduction in previous films that I had the feeling of "I've been there." Yet there was one surprise. Even though I'd "been there," I discovered something about myself. I had always prided myself on great objectivity. I could come in and see a scene that everybody loved. Yet it had to be sacrificed for the good of the picture, and I would say, "Okay, take it out immediately." I couldn't be that way with *The Marriage of a Young Stockbroker.* I found myself saying "Gee, that's a good scene; maybe I should leave it in."

Q: What about the future?

Turman: I'd like to keep on directing my movies. I wouldn't say that I would never consider a film that I couldn't direct. It's foolish to say "never" in this business, and if no one lets me direct, I'll certainly produce. But as of now, I want to go on directing.

—1971

Gilbert Cates:
I Never Sang for My Father

Most films have unusual production histories. At least they do to the men who make them. But even in a business filled with unusual beginnings, *I Never Sang for My Father* had a most different background.

It all began in 1962 when Robert Anderson wrote an original screenplay he called *The Tiger*. It was the story of an eighty-year-old man and his grown son. Fred Zinnemann, a good friend of Robert Anderson, read the script and liked it. Zinnemann said he would do it if Spencer Tracy played the old man. Tracy decided not to play the part because it was too demanding.

Another good friend of the author, Elia Kazan, read the script. Kazan thought *The Tiger* was Anderson's best piece of work and asked whether Bob would consider turning it into a play for the Lincoln Center.

Later, John Frankenheimer read the script and sent it to Fredric March. March loved the script and it seemed that Frankenheimer, March and his wife, Florence Eldridge, would make the film. After a period of time Frankenheimer got involved with *The Train* and suggested that Bob try to encourage another production. Also, during this period Kazan and Robert Whitehead had formed their Lincoln Center Company and told Bob they did not have an actor to play the old man.

Well, friends, that is only the beginning, but hold on—it gets more interesting as it develops.

Robert Anderson, representing the best in tenacity and an intuitive understanding of our business, finally turned it into a play. When it was finished he named it *I Never Sang for My Father* because Murray Schisgal had a play produced called *The Tiger*.

I read *I Never Sang for My Father* about the same time I read Bob's other play, *You Know I Can't Hear You When the Water's Running*. I loved them both. Jack Farren and I produced *You Know I Can't Hear You* and it was a big success. After that, I immediately began work on the Broadway production of *Father*.

It was to be an impressive physical production. Jo Mielziner designed the sets, which included two massive turntables. Alan Schneider directed, and Hal Holbrook, Alan Webb, Teresa Wright (Mrs. Robert Anderson) and Lillian Gish starred in the play, which opened at the Longacre Theater on January 25, 1968.

It was staged beautifully with an effortless style that was rooted to its earlier cinematic form. The more I saw of the play, the more I thought of its potential as a film. I began visualizing scenes which were not on stage and missing scenes which were cut out of the play version.

The single biggest problem in getting the play on was finding an actor to play the old man.

I was spending a month with my family in Cape Cod in a little town called Wellfleet during the summer of 1967. At the end of each day I would report to a mosquito-filled telephone booth near the highway on Route 6 and telephone actor after actor.

Edward G. Robinson received a few of those citronella-laden calls. He was interested in playing the part but . . . Ah, the *But*. Anyway, he finally said no. So did Fredric March, Ralph Richardson, Melvyn Douglas and Alfred Lunt, to name a few. I think Alfred Lunt said no because the father's part was bigger than the mother's, which I offered to Lynn Fontanne, who is Mrs. Alfred Lunt.

Melvyn Douglas provided the most interesting, if disappointing, rejection for me. We were to meet for the first time for a drink at the Plaza. This lengthened into a three-hour discussion followed by a brisk walk, continued through an impromptu dinner at Sea Fare of the Aegean and another more leisurely walk. All in all, over six hours—but to no avail.

He thought it was a great part but the character of the father was one he did not want to play night after night. He told me that he would probably "die with his boots on" and viewed every role accordingly. I remembered that conversation well because when we next met, almost two years later, to discuss his playing the father in the film, my major point was that he would not have to go on playing the role as was necessary on Broadway. Once the film was shot he would be finished with it. He agreed.

The question most often asked is why I didn't use the same four actors who played the parts on Broadway in the movie. They all received excellent reviews and were truly marvelous. The reasons in this case were simple. Alan Webb is an English actor of exceptional quality, but since this was an American film story, I naturally wanted an American actor.

Unlike the play, which could generalize the location through the use of stylized sets, we would see in great detail the color of the surroundings and the specific qualities of the other characters. While the theme is universal, the specifics are Westchester County and New York City.

Lillian Gish was unavailable for the part of the mother. She was busy touring the country with her one-woman show. Dorothy Stickney agreed to play the mother.

Columbia Pictures suggested Gene Hackman and Estelle Parsons for the brother and sister. After much thought and rescreening of some of their films, I agreed. These four new choices proved superb.

That is one of the problems of producing or directing a film of a play which you have produced. All the good actors who appear in the play have a perfect right to feel they should get to do the film. I am glad we had a totally new cast for the film. That way, their attitudes were fresh and we could all start at the beginning together.

In putting the elements of the film together I began as the producer. The first person that I told of my desire to direct was Audrey Wood, Bob Anderson's agent. She did not respond badly. Audrey was familiar with my background as a television director and actually was quite encouraging.

Then I told Bob. He was also encouraging. We knew each other quite well and his agreement was not surprising. Bob had agreed to write the new screenplay and his approval was important. I thought it would be impressive to Columbia Pictures if a first-rate author like Bob approved me as director.

The next step was to discuss it with Stanley Schneider, then executive vice president, now president, of Columbia Pictures. He too agreed. I think his agreement was based on several factors. First, he knew me quite well. I had made a small circus film for Columbia four years earlier called *Rings Around the World*. The film came in on a tight budget and the studio was pleased with it. Second, the fact that I was so closely involved with the play was another mark in my favor. Third, and most important I think, was his instinct. Stanley Schneider knew how much I felt for this material. It had indeed become a part of me.

The next problem was to determine how the actors would respond to this new director. Melvyn Douglas, who has worked with the great directors in the history of film, was surprisingly agreeable. We talked briefly about the part. He said I would probably do quite well, and that was it.

I don't know how much of a consideration my directing the film was to Gene Hackman, Estelle Parsons or Dorothy Stickney, because none of them voiced any concern, at least to me. Whatever questions they might have had were discussed with their agents and counsellors in private.

The package was now assembled. All the other actors and personnel were hired. The preparation for the film seemed very much like preparations I had made in the past for theatrical productions and television shows. The details are different, but the intent is the same: "Prepare Everything—Avoid Surprises."

One thing felt familiar: the preparation time did not seem long enough. I scouted all our locations with my associate, Everett Rosenthall, and our art director, Hank Aldrich. We spent weeks trying to find the right suburban house for the Garrison family. Some of the action in the film is autobiographical in nature and therefore I was eager to see the house that Bob Anderson was brought up in. It is located in New Rochelle, a suburb of New York City. Bob and I went to see it. It was available, but it was not right.

Curious, isn't it? The house that the author had in mind when he wrote the script was not right.

Finally we found the house. It was vacant and was owned by the mayor of White Plains, New York. I considered that a good omen because the father in the film was once the mayor of the town in which he lived.

The first day of shooting quickly arrived. It was the opening sequence in the film at Kennedy Airport. This was a rather ambitious sequence to begin with, but I felt it important to begin shooting the film at the beginning of the story, where Gene meets his mother and father. The commotion of shooting at Northeast Airlines with hundreds of passersby, crew, extras, etc., seemed reassuringly familiar to me from my television days as director of remote shows.

After three days at Kennedy we moved into the Biograph Studio in the Bronx. Biograph is in an ancient building with an impressive history of service dating back to the silent screen. We had had a week of rehearsals prior to Kennedy, but the real excitement started when we began shooting in the studio. Those weeks were filled with discovery and hard work.

As all of us know, each actor has a different method of working. Frequently these

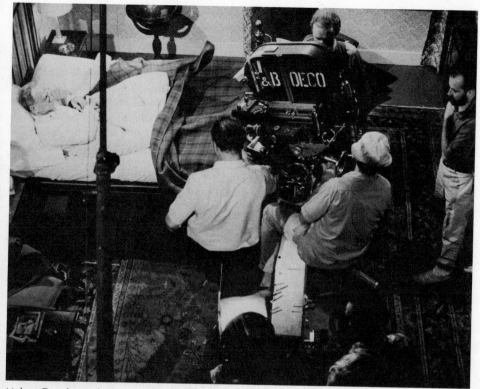

Melvyn Douglas (in bed) being directed by Gilbert Cates (extreme right).

differences are small ones. But as there is a variety of personalities, backgrounds, experiences and attitudes involved, it is only natural that these variations should be reflected in work. The relative speed with which it is necessary to make adjustments in working technique surprised me. In the theater this seems less of a problem, because the rehearsal period is such a relatively long one, averaging four weeks.

The problem resembles the pacing of a long-distance runner. In making a film, at least mine, rehearsal for a scene seldom took longer than a few hours (with the exception of the last big scene). Therefore the correlation between performances based on different methods of preparation required constant supervision.

All the actors responded magnificently. Melvyn Douglas was a tower of strength. He was the most experienced film man on the set. He was also the most courteous. He listened carefully to everyone he was involved with and he took direction beautifully. Nothing is so precious to him or so important that it won't bear honest scrutiny.

Melvyn set a standard for performance and attitude that the rest of us could only marvel at. When it came time for those difficult scenes he had, requiring great energy and concentration, he insisted on doing them again and again until perfect. When I would suggest that perhaps we take a break or pick up the following day to allow him to relax a bit, he would insist that we try once more.

Part of me was always prepared for the day Melvyn might say, "That's not the way Lubitsch would do it."

It never happened. Not because he didn't have cause, but because Melvyn Douglas only draws from the past; he does not live in it.

There are many controls that a film studio has on a production and Columbia availed themselves of most of them. Because our budget was carefully drawn, we managed to avoid costly surprises and, as a result, there was no conflict between us and

Columbia. At tight as their surveillance was on our spending, that was how free and relaxed they were with me artistically. Once the screenplay and major cast were approved, we literally were left alone to make the film.

They screened rushes. But that I believe was more to determine that the work was getting done rather than to make a qualitative evaluation of the artistic elements. This reflected a basic new awareness of filmmaking in the 1970s.

In order for a filmmaker to deliver a film at "a price," once the budget and major elements have been agreed on, he must be left artistically alone to make the film. Naturally, if anything wild happens or if the film begins to get out of control, then the studio must step in. The difficulty for the studio is in making the initial decision. After that, there is little they can do except hope that their decision was correct.

Our relations with Columbia were first rate. At a time when many filmmakers are complaining about studios and the difficulties of dealing with them, it is a delight to be able to report this.

A most exciting time for me was in the finishing of the film. To me, the editing involved in a taped television show is primitive compared to film. My own experience with the most complicated and up-to-date video editing systems seemed elementary compared to the endless possibilities afforded by film.

Of course, you are still limited to the footage shot, but I seemed to have greater freedom of choice. Also, the intimate relationship you have with just the film editor and moviola is much more manageable than with the complicated tape machines and various pieces of electronic equipment necessary for TV tape editing.

Later I found myself deeply involved with the preparations for opening. Perhaps that is a hangover from producing on the stage, where you are involved with advertising, promotion and booking. In any event, my first major experience as a filmmaker was both a great challenge and thrill. I can't wait to do it again.

—1970

Gilbert Cates has since directed The Killing Zone.

Dick Richards:
The Culpepper Cattle Co.

Dick Richards and cast.

I know it's a cliché, but I have always thought—and have always operated under the belief—that one picture (photograph) really does speak 10,000 words. I started my career as a still man for advertising and magazine photography, and I never really knew which one of my photos would be used or how it would be used in the final print. So I tried to concentrate every thought, nuance and "message" into each photograph just in case it had to stand alone—on its own—to deliver the intended message. To this end, I've always been a nut for detail, and I have a mania for perfection. Clothes, backgrounds and props, the right light and the right colors have to be just—well, right—before I can know I have something to shoot. Other than my own personal foibles, I feel this regimen is an absolute necessity for every form of effort, in order to get the intended message across. It has always been my policy to hedge all bets all the time by making the physical atmosphere and background totally proper and conducive to the right feel to get the look we want across.

By the time I had graduated—and it is, I think, a natural progression—from still to motion photography via television commercials, I had the above philosophy totally ingrained into my psyche. We had the luxury of more than one photo—more than one frame—to tell our story and create our mood, but I still believed in going for broke, of treating each frame as if it had to stand on its own.

By the time I had made my first film, *The Culpepper Cattle Co.*, I had carried the look of the movie around in my head for almost five years, and I know I must have directed my movie hundreds of times before I ever set foot on a sound stage. I first got the idea of doing a Western film—above and beyond the fact that I've been a Western buff all my life as only a Manhattan-bred moviegoer can be—after I directed a television commercial for the Heinz Soup Company. I had to create a couple of scenes around a cattle-drive campfire—with a can of soup ever so prominent—and by the time I scoured around New York for the right clothes and the right props and chose a location in West Texas, I had the technical beginnings and inventory for my film.

While shooting another commercial, in Oklahoma, I met an old man in the lobby of a hotel one day—he was ninety-five years old—and he told me he had started herding cattle and working around cattle drives when he was fourteen years old. His story plus my Heinz soup commercial, started my creative juices flowing.

I wrote a 35-page outline and showed it to Greg Prentiss, who was teaching at NYU. He took what I had and put it into a first-draft screenplay. I then took it to a Hollywood-based movie writer, Eric Bercovici, who made it into a shooting script. I kept developing his script—kept going back, redoing it, and finally I took it to Paul Helmick, a veteran production executive, who then took it to Fox—and before we knew it, we had a deal to make it.

It was going to be made at a price and we stuck to the price pretty well, despite our tremendous logistical problems. For example, the script called for at least 800 to 1,000 head of cattle. We found a Mexican who lived in Sonora, Mexico, and he made a deal with us to deliver so many head of cattle, for so many days, for so much money, and did it! He had never been involved in a film before. He was a cattleman, but he also was a film buff, and he decided to take a crack at the film business with us.

I had spent three years in research—everything from clothes to wagons, to learning about how my characters spoke, walked, talked, the food they ate in that period of time. I interviewed old cowboys and heard old cowboy stories. Most of the stories that are told in the picture are true stories of that era. I went out of my way to interview people who were actually there. I traveled through the Southwest to interview everybody. Every bit of clothing, every extra's outfit, every gun, every wagon, every horse, everything was picked with history in the background. I had a great assistant—I even picked the people who were going to pick the clothes carefully. I chose them basically for their knowledge, secondly for their personalities.

This passion for authenticity extended to the style of the film. I didn't want the audience to be aware of the camera in any way. I just wanted the audience to experience what the people of that period went through at that time. I used the quality of light that I felt would bring out the rich feeling of the West. I tried to create Russell paintings on the screen in every one of my scenes. There was a whole feeling in the Charles Russell paintings and the Remington paintings—soft, always late day and long shadows, an early-morning feeling. I tried to match those feelings. I tried to marry all the feelings of early John Ford, Remington, Russell, Hawks—all the classics, all the people who had created the Western mystique.

I think the people of the world will always think of the West as having a big look and that's what I borrowed from my masters. I tried to accomplish that feeling. I had the help of Ralph Woolsey and Larry Williams, two very fine cinematographers in their own right, who understood what I was striving for and helped me get it.

I picked a Western for my first film because this is a part of our American culture, something we had that no one else did. We don't date back to the Romans, we don't date back to anything much. Our history and our being, I feel, really started with the opening of the West, and I felt that this culture should be told as it really was. All my people and all my characters, I think, portray or give a feeling of that era, and I have kept them as honest as I could make them. I had my actors live as I felt the people lived during that time. I chose to shoot the movie during the hot summer so there would be more hardship for the actors.

We had a good crew. It was a mixture of the new—people I had worked with in my commercial filming days, who knew my methods, needs, moods and idiosyncracies —with the best of the traditional, skilled Hollywood craftsmen. My associate producer was an ad-agency television-commercial producer; my stunt coordinator was a veteran of more than 50 motion pictures.

I think it's very important for a director to pick a crew as carefully as he picks his cast; he must pick them for their personalities as well as their knowledgeability. A bad crew is one from which you have to send 18 people home. We didn't do that. We were a family. I didn't agree with a lot of the things some of the people griped about, but I gave them the right to gripe about it, and I'd hear their gripes.

We got some of the crew out of Mexico City. We found a wrangler—Pepe Cueto— who was an unbelievable guy. He took out cattle and had them on location for us, on time, every day. His wife was our caterer.

A warm feeling arose among the company because we were all living under the same horrible conditions. Since a movie had never before been made in the locale we used, our accommodations weren't very good. We all had to live and eat as a family fighting for survival, instead as a movie company on a spree. Our company wasn't anything like some of the location companies I've read about.

I came to my movie job the first day having properly done my homework; that is, having created and worked out a formula for still and motion photography after nearly 15 years as a veteran of the New York magazine and TV-commercial experience. My background had taught me economy, improvisation, knowing my strong—and weak—points (I floundered the first time I tried to direct an off-Broadway show within the confines of a small, naked stage), and knowing how to prepare myself for almost any eventuality.

I must admit there was a certain freedom I felt directing my first movie I'd never experienced before. I guess it was because I didn't have an advertising agency commercial producer whispering, "Are you sure you have enough light on the product?" And making my first movie was completely different from any experiences I've ever had making commercials. I found myself totally alone, having to say "yes" or "no" and living with my commitments.

When doing commercials, I would produce my own. In other words, if I didn't come in on budget, I wouldn't make money. Although The Culpepper Cattle Co. was completely financed by 20th Century Fox, I still had the feeling of doing it with my own money. It was a big film for the money we spent and we think, according to Hollywood standards, this movie should have cost four to five million dollars. We did it for just a little over a million.

Making commercials is usually a two- or three-day affair. You prepare for these days and go out and give them your all. Your first take is the one you've done your homework for. The next two are usually variations, and from there on, you do the "agency producer" takes: the clients pool their thoughts for at least two versions; and some bright, well-built girl from the ad agency usually suggests at least one other.

On the first week of my feature I found myself shooting a ratio of about six to one. By the second week my shooting ratio went down to four to one. I was now feeling secure. Once in a while I would turn around and expect to see a client or a friendly agency producer, but all I found was my crew—sometimes interested in what was going on, sometimes bored.

In filming commercials you still can go home, leisurely look at what you've done the next day, think about it, talk about it, run it—it's usually a few days out of your life. When you make a motion picture and you're out there for weeks on end and there's no relief—Sundays are spent looking at dailies or looking for locations, talking about what you've done, what you've got to do—there's just no relief!

Commercials are much easier. You put in a tough day or two, shoot, and you manage time to recoup. In films you just don't do that. You just go out there and you plug away like your life was at stake. And sometimes it is.

—1972

Michael Ritchie:
Downhill Racer

Michael Ritchie fighting Eurovision for camera tower position to film the Olympics.

If anyone had told me two years ago that my first feature would be about competitive skiing, I would have laughed. After all, I'd never been on skis in my life, never had witnessed a ski race, and the only ski films I remembered were the ski jumps in the old newsreels.

When they reached me with the offer for *Downhill Racer*, I was in southern France. All I could hear over the bad connection was: "Robert Redford, Paramount. Lotsa European locations." I can't remember whether skiing was ever mentioned.

After reading the first draft, there was no doubt it was about skiing. The writer, James Salter, knew skiing very well. So, obviously, did Redford. I agreed to do the picture and planned on a crash course in the hours available between script conferences.

A strong plus in the project, as far as I was concerned, was Redford himself. I had followed his career from his earliest parts on Broadway and knew him to be what Charles Champlin finally declared after the release of *Downhill Racer*—"the finest young American actor around."

Style: From my experience in *cinéma vérité* documentaries with the Maysles Brothers, I had been developing a semidocumentary style for dramatic TV films. *Downhill Racer's* script provided an opportunity to develop these concepts for a feature film. I wanted the picture to look accidental. I did not want the audience to feel that a director was "designing" what they were seeing. Frequently setups were chosen to give a minimum amount of information (the backs of Hackman and Redford at a critical moment). Background noises built in, and there was frequent use of overlapping conversations.

There is nothing new about any of these techniques. After all, Orson Welles' use of them in *Citizen Kane* makes him the daddy of us all. However, the "cool," low-key performances, the fragmented nature of the scenes, the lack of convenient connective devices between scenes, the controlled use of color (for instance, the opening white-on-white sequence in which color becomes gradually apparent), all these contributed to a screen naturalism that hopefully made audiences feel they were seeing the real thing.

Of course, to this day I have ski buffs complain to me about a certain scene with a loose ski binding, or a character who's wearing a green goggle on a cloudy day or our blending of Megeve and Kitzbuhel in one race bothered them. Since those are the complaints, I guess our premises for naturalism must have worked.

Working with a star: Redford's involvement in the early stages of the film was an enormous advantage. By the time we began shooting we had discussed every aspect of every scene. We were in agreement about what we wanted. There couldn't have been any long delays on the set while star and director argued about concept. The only disagreements with Redford I can remember during shooting were about in which scenes he would chew gum.

In fact, it was the running battle over gum that inspired Bob to one of the great ad libs in the picture. It's after he's laid the hometown girl in the back of his dad's Chevy. She asks him about his aspirations. He replies, "Do you have any more of that gum?"

The only major discussions we had during shooting were about how much of a heel we should make our hero. His most obnoxious actions—throwing the Ovaltine into the crowd, insufferable pride with the girl, rejecting his teammates' congratulations—all occur during his moments of victory. It was important to show the audience that the character would be unable to handle a championship if he got it.

Casting: Once the script could be scheduled, I generally had a free hand in the

248

casting. Redford was busy finishing *Butch Cassidy and the Sundance Kid* and producer Richard Gregson had to be in Europe to line up support of the ski associations.

Several in my cast had never acted professionally before—examples: Walt Stroud as Redford's father and Kenneth Kirk as his roommate; others had never done film work. To fit in with the semidocumentary concept of the film, I wanted as many unknown faces as possible.

The coach was a different matter. Here was a part that was half-formed in the script. It needed an extraordinary actor to bring it to life. Everybody kept saying we were looking for "somebody like Gene Hackman." I did the obvious. I visited Hackman on the set of *Marooned* to talk him into it.

The script was never really finished. For key scenes we were up all night right to the end of production. This was a condition nobody liked, especially Paramount, but our start date was immovable—linked to the beginning of the European ski races.

Start date: For budget reasons a British crew was selected. I had admired Ken Loach's first film, *Poor Cow,* and selected his cinematographer, Brian Probyn, and his sound crew. It was an important setup in getting that documentary texture.

We were all set to go when the axe fell. The picture was canceled! Paramount's budget department in London had finally come up with what they thought the picture would cost. They said it had to be over three million dollars. Since neither the producer, Redford, nor myself had met with them, we hoped that they would allow us to convince them of our ability to make it for 1.8 million dollars.

And so it was that I found myself up late on a December night in a compartment of the Orient Express from Paris to Munich, making up my own production board from a new version of the script. I stepped off the train the next morning, a bit bleary-eyed as I handed the completed board and day-out-of-days to the Paramount accountant.

We won the day. It meant a lot of sacrifices. Throughout the picture, for instance, there was never a folding chair for the director or star to sit down. I was happy that every one of those 1.8 million dollars found it's way up onto the screen.

Surprises: Many of the experiences I faced would have been unique even for a feature-film veteran. Others are probably being faced by first-timers even now.

In television I'd never had more than 80 extras in a single day. And there I was in Austria with 750 a day for two weeks, none of whom spoke English and none of whom had any experience in pictures. It was exasperating on the set and often humiliating in the dailies.

Speaking of dailies, we were shipping our negative to Technicolor in London and the return shipments would bunch up in strange ways. Some days after working on the slopes from dawn to dusk, we'd have to sit down and look at three hours of film.

I'd been pampered with a five-day shooting week in most of my television. Because of an early spring thaw, we were shooting a *seven*-day week in March and April. I don't know how the cast and crew avoided exhaustion. It must have been the "tea breaks."

Any American director is aware of the "tea breaks" when he contemplates a British production. On the sound stage or a small interior location it's nothing to worry about. But when you've got 800 people lining a hillside filled with Olympic banners, and somebody calls the tea break, you can cash in your chips for the rest of the afternoon. Down the hill they scramble for tea and coffee, not to mention knackwurst, strudel, sacher torte, etc., etc.

Shooting was on a 70-day schedule with an added 25 days of second unit, which, because it involved Redford in scripted scenes, was really "first unit." All my previous experience had been in television. The longest schedule I had ever been given was

Ritchie confers with Gene Hackman and Robert Redford.

23 days to do the *Outsider* pilot as a two-hour movie for NBC. Ninety-five **days** seemed like heaven!

On the contrary, at times the pressure was much greater. Either because of weather, or melting snow, or lack of mobility, everyone was often in a panic. Setting up the BNC in the snow meant getting the shot in 25 minutes or breaking for 20 more minutes to fix the camera, which had sunk two feet in the snow. The words "Cut," "Print" and "Over here" were never used. Any change of setup involving more than a dozen feet meant breaking down the BNC and loading it onto a Snow Cat **and then** setting it all up again.

A weather change at noon could easily put us a half-day behind. The snowstorm race in the film was an accident forced by a series of stormy days the first **week** of shooting when we didn't have adequate cover sets.

To get the feeling that a ski racer experiences at 70 mph we trained one of our former ace racers, Joe Jay Jalbert, to ski while holding a camera. We started him off with an Eyemo, just for practice, so that he could get used to the balance of skiing with a camera. His first footage was pretty horrible. Next, we gave him an Arriflex and, for some reason (either because of the additional weight or the fact that the Arri looks like a big-time movie camera), this suddenly brought out the best in him. We ran his footage over and over with him, almost the way a coach does with a football team after the game—and he improved very rapidly.

Our skiing cameraman did not use harnesses, simply because we knew that these limited flexibility. We wanted him to be able to get raked camera angles as he rounded the curves—or to swing out to the side going past the flags. He used 9.8 mm or 14 mm lenses, which often include the ski tips in the frame, because we wanted the audience to feel that he was actually on skis and not riding in a Sno-Mobile or helicopter. We were not after a pretty picture, but rather to get that hard, gutsy type of footage that emphasizes the dangers of speed.

In *Downhill Racer* there is quite a bit of hand-held camera work, but I feel that it was warranted by the type of action we were shooting. I believe that's the key to it. To use a hand-held camera for a sit-down dramatic scene in a restaurant could be disastrous because the camera calls attention to itself. The filmmaker is saying: "Look how clever I am. I'm using a hand-held camera." The whole point of a documentary film is to make the audience feel part of it—as if they are witness to something that is actually happening. Whenever the audience steps back and says, "Boy, is that a clever shot!," they are not participating in it.

The final stages of shaping the film in the editing rooms were as arduous as the four months of photography. Because Paramount had set an early release date for *Downhill Racer*, the preview cut (which was mine) became to all intents the final cut. Until the happy day when the Guild can secure preview-cut rights for every feature director, I hope that other first directors can be as lucky as I was.

Looking back on it a year later, I see that I was very lucky in every respect—lucky to have built into the film from the beginning one of our best actors, lucky to have a script by James Salter written in lean documentary style that was in keeping with the kind of film I wanted to make, lucky to have a free hand in the casting, lucky to have a lengthy schedule, lucky to have the freedom I needed in the editing room.

I hope I'm as lucky on number two.

—1970

Number two was Prime Cut, *starring Lee Marvin and Gene Hackman, followed by* The Candidate *with Robert Redford.*

Richard Colla: *Zig Zag*

Richard Colla (right) shooting from water level.

I, of course, wanted *False Witness* (that's what it was called before MGM changed the title to *Zig Zag* in order to make the picture more contemporary), to knock everybody's eye out, to win overwhelming acclaim and admiration while the box-office grosses grew to such astronomical heights that it would drive my career to the plane of total freedom in my next project and financial security for the rest of my life. For one's first theatrical feature, could that be asking too much?

I first met Herb Solow when at an arranged lunch he asked me to do some TV episodes of an MGM series. I thought, "The lead is a fine actor whom I respect, the concept is good, and it would be fun to be that far from a studio to do some really free work."

"Thanks, anyway," I said, playing the game, "but if you come up with a feature, I'd be glad to."

Well, can I tell you how surprised I was to have him call me a couple of months later about *False Witness!*

Now you know something's up, because "they" are looking at some of your film; and you haven't seen a decent feature script yet that was worth anything; you're dying to get out of television (even for a little while, but you don't look at that then). And you don't want to read it before they make an offer (you'll take it, whatever the offer, if it's a good piece), because you're afraid it will be good and they won't make an offer.

Fifty thousand dollars. I think that's what it was. I'm not quite sure, since Universal rented me out to MGM for the picture, but that's a magic number, 50,000 dollars. It's a number you've heard of, like 100,000 dollars and one million dollars; or the price of a doughnut and two cups of coffee—those are magic numbers, too, no matter from which side of the line you look at it. But somebody's going to trust you to direct a motion picture, by God! You've got the lowest grades in drama school for six years. Yale asked you to leave because they thought you were crazy. But they're going to give you a motion picture to direct, and all you can give them is your guts. Now, that's easy. You do that on every project. But have you got the talent? That's where it gets tougher. If the problem was only to dedicate all your passions 24 hours a day for the duration . . . But can you make an appreciable contribution to the film? That's the real question, and that can only be answered by the audience after you're committed. And I was.

I first met John T. Kelley when I was still back working as film editor for a small company, and John had graduated from the same company. He was a Giant.* They called him in to criticize a piece of my work. "Do it your own way," he said, looking at the film. "When I worked here they always called in some Giant to tell me how to do it."

I liked John, and the picture was important to him, too. You can tell if something's important to somebody—they want to help you solve your problems, flat out. If it's just an ego trip, all they do is tell you you're wrong.

John was beautiful!

By the time we began shooting, we had a script that we all thought would work. Now, nobody believed that we had the Sistine Chapel or the statue of David, but we figured we had a pretty good puzzle picture if we could stay one step ahead of the audience all the way without losing them.

If I could tread a very thin line, I figured I could complement the story with night shooting—fragmented imagery—pieces of the world around the lead, George Kennedy, revealed moment by moment to the eye as the story was unfolded to the mind. A dangerous style that could become obvious instead of revealing, and an open invitation to get slammed against a critical wall as pretentious rather than incisive. But if part of a director's job is to function as an audience of one, then it was basic at least to attempt to bring a unique point of view to the execution.

Every new assignment fills me with trepidation, because you're always working in the unknown. If you are certain how to do it, it's only because you've done it before or copied someone else. Either way, it's a repeat and there's no magic in it then.

There was a director of a TV episode I observed who gave me something that he had learned. I had an assignment coming up on an *Ironside*. Ray Burr trusted me after I wasn't able to get a job for a year and a half. I'd made a mistake on another series—*Gunsmoke*. I didn't shoot a *Matt Dillon Starring Gunsmoke!* I shot a picture. That's where my attention was—in making a well-balanced film with certain emphasis on character and structure as I truly believed it, without regard to a title or a star.

*Making A Living At It.

The company hated it, of course, and didn't ask me back. That, being my second major studio show, didn't help my career and the next 18 months were long ones. I thought I'd learned something from that—Rule No. 15-A in my personal rule book: Keep your eye on the power people and don't simply believe that they have the same vision of the film that you do, because they may be more insecure than you are. That must be a nonworking rule for me, because I recently made the same mistake again, but this time it wasn't so bad, because I knew that I had done the right thing, and it was they who were making the mistake. Funny thing, some of them even knew it.

Anyway, Charlie Dubin told me something when I watched him work: "Never copy anybody else's film because everyone has the same fears that you do and what good would it do to reproduce somebody else's doubts? Besides, all you have to sell is yourself. If anyone buys you, your particular viewpoint is what they're buying, so you have nothing but knowledge and security to gain by exposing your own talent."

I've always been grateful for that moment with Charlie, because I run that conversation through my head every time I get scared. And facing my first 110 minutes of Panavision, I was running it like a continual loop.

We had been putting together a fine cast of actors and George Kennedy was a joy to work with—a prepared, contributing actor with the strength of his own personal convictions about me, which allowed us to work together toward his delivering an exciting performance.

Sometimes when you stop and look around, a director seems to be carrying so many people's hopes and dreams. This was an important piece for George as well. As far as he was concerned, he would have worked any hours, and he never refused to try something I suggested. If it worked, we'd keep it. If it didn't work, we'd try something else. I made a personal vow to myself that, in return for that trust, I would make sure that no one would be able to fault George's performance. I would make suggestions, protect him from making any inconsistent choices, but the performance and characterization would be his and not mine.

I have worked on the other side of the partnership and I know that an actor can only be free when he is completely subjective in the part, having worked out ahead of time all the beats and units—the mechanics—and has the faith to rely on his director for the objective observation. George granted me that, trusting that I knew where the focus of the audience should be, even when the character was in the background and never covered a close-up. See what I mean? With trust like that, you could never let him down.

Every open relationship that a director has with his cast is demanding of that reciprocal respect and responsibility. Sometimes it demands that you just hang tough together—like one day on location when an actor didn't show up for the first day of his part. Well, I began shooting around him as much as I could. Meanwhile, I'm on the phone to Bob Enders, MGM Casting, the actor's agent, my agent. His agent tells me he hasn't been able to notify the actor for the last two days to tell him he got the part in the first place; he didn't bother to tell me this before, because he thought it necessary to protect his client. However, he did have another client who could play the . . .

I hung up as fast as I could, called for help, gave the crew a setup, broke for lunch and got back on the phone. An hour later the crew was back on. They lit the setup and we waited.

I had never met Walter Brooke before that hot August afternoon when he stepped out of the elevator into the plush penthouse (complete with swimming pool) that we were using for an office set.

"Mr. Brooke, my name is Dick Colla. I'm very glad to meet you. Has anyone given you a script? They haven't; I see. Well, sir, we have this setup that you are in. You play a company lawyer and there's only one line in this cut; it's not the introduction or the climax of your character. That will give us time to talk before the next setup. I'm sorry to seem so rushed, but the building is sold and we have to be out tomorrow and, as you know, we're a little behind now. I truly am sorry. We aren't using any makeup and, by the way, that's a very good-looking suit."

In some remarkable way, after that kind of introduction, Walter and I managed to generate a good relationship during the picture. He still speaks kindly about me and even talks to me when me meet.

The image of the director is, of course, the man with the answers. God forbid he doesn't come up with them when it comes right down to the wire and nobody else has the answers, because ultimately a picture only works if there is one point of view. Since the balance of moods, schedules, pacing, performance and structure of the unfinished picture exists only in the mind of the director, he had better come up with the answer or the whole project is in trouble. He had better be able to get the company to follow him or the picture is in trouble whether he's right or wrong.

So sometimes it's tough to have been working on a scene and setup the whole afternoon in the cramped kitchen of a location house and it's still not coming together and your mind is dry as dust and as creative as a blob of strawberry preserves. You stand up behind the camera and say, "You know, I haven't the least idea how to make this damn scene work, so if anybody has any ideas, please tell me."

The stunned silence that follows seems to indicate a selection of blown minds. I mean, you don't say things like that. But after a few moments, the afternoon tension drained out of the room and one of the grips said, "If you really want a suggestion, how about . . ." And somebody else thought, "How about . . ." Pretty soon all the juices were going again and everyone was involved in making it happen. It was beautiful.

I must say Herb Solow and Bob Enders gave me a great deal of freedom and faith. In taking out a picture that had been scheduled and budgeted for the sound stages (especially from the studio's standpoint, with all those stages standing empty), or accepting my word that after four days' shooting, being three and a half days behind schedule, I would be out of the location at the end of five days. We were, but that's "Fair, Baby."

Or even the end of the film. We had started the project with the character of Cameron (Kennedy) extricating himself from the dilemma into which he had got himself in the first place. But I could never figure out how to make the end of the picture exciting, just walking away into the sunset. Then Bob suggested it was because the end was wrong; by all rights, he should be shot and killed. It would be much more unexpected. It was the right answer, of course, but what I needed was a "blow-off." We're going to be driving to an end and we'd better be able to make it pay off or we'd have a dud. There wasn't any scene to play. Cameron had to be given the answer he had been seeking to save himself and be killed in the next moment. That was it. There was nothing else to be said.

Eight years earlier, my same cameraman (we always said we'd do my first feature together)—Jimmy Crabe—and I sat in the sand at Oxnard Beach with a 16 mm 800 fps Photo Sonics rotating-prism camera, preparing to shoot Billy Shatner's ultra slow-motion killing in a short called *The Soldier*. We couldn't think of anybody who had photographed death by a bullet at that speed before and weren't sure what it would look like, but we figured it's gotta be at least interesting. I was on the first piece of film where I was able to call myself the director, and it scared the hell out of me. We couldn't do that same thing again or we would have been copying ourselves. Besides, even if we did want to cheat a little, it had been done and done and done. Sam Peckinpah wiped me out from using it for the next 20 years. Yet we knew it was in there somewhere. Somehow we had to capture that moment-to-moment slowdown when the adrenalin slams your system into survival gear and you separate yourself out and watch time come apart.

We set George up on a beach at night, a police helicopter arc light driving a cone of daylight through the rotor-whipped sand around him and we photographed a shotgun blow-out in his chest from two angles with two nonsync cameras.

In picture continuity the killer (Walter Brooke) on the run shoots Kennedy in the leg. We edited in four different angles of George's reaction, repeating that moment to distort time before the second shotgun blast hits Cameron in the chest. We took the two angles of his death, bipacked them together and printed each frame eight times. The images were stony as we watched the frames "pop" by, each with a distinct and different moment of awareness of this man having his body torn apart by bits of steel. You can watch the consciousness change and fade as the two images overlayed each other. They begin to move in sync, then begin to lose sync and separate out in time, more and more as the figures fall to the ground.

Nobody seemed too encouraged by the idea until it began to come together on the optical printer. Even I wasn't dead sure. But I knew, for all our sakes, that it had to work, that I could make it happen.

I spent a couple of days on a moviola off by myself, running different takes trying to make it happen—strange bits of mag spliced together to indicate the sound and music tracks, chopping in clear and black leader slugs. All the time I was looking for the right feeling and timing. The editor, Ferris Webster, would come over from time to time and I'd say, "What do you think?"

"Well," he'd nod, "maybe it'll work. There sure won't be much of an end if we cut it together straight."

"Yeah," I'd grumble at him, tearing another splice as I went back to work on it some more. I sent it through for an optical pass, recut it and sent it through again. Finally, I knew it was going to work and be somehow unique. Not because of the "gimmick," but because that moment of death that we've seen so often in film was extended in time. Frame by frame we would get into George and be forced, or permitted to walk around in those last few moments of life in a dying man. But ultimately it was George who made it happen. All I could do was try to create a point of view that was at least slightly different from what anyone had seen before.

I suppose I've played with lenses and speeds and optical printers and film stocks as much as most directors, but all of those craft tools can only create an attitude, a mood and setting. A viewer needs someone to relate to, to empathize with—someone to react for them to the world in any reality where we find the actor.

The beauty of what we do is this: we create awareness; we make people feel, and perhaps reflect, on what they have felt. In that way, hopefully, we make each individual we affect more of a whole—more of an aware human being. It doesn't matter what tools we use or what techniques we develop. If it works, use it as long as it is toward that end.

—1970

Richard Colla's second feature was Fuzz.

Notable First Features

The Great McGinty 1940 Preston Sturges

Citizen Kane 1941 Orson Welles

The Maltese Falcon 1941 John Huston

The Major and the Minor 1942 Billy Wilder

Cabin in the Sky 1943 Vincente Minnelli

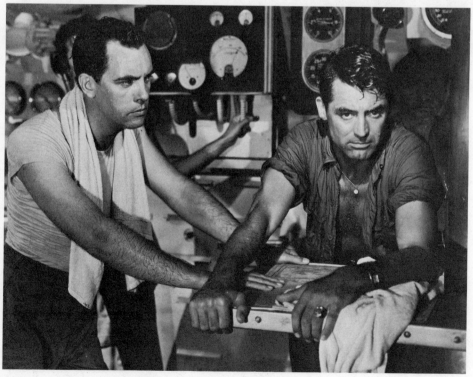

Destination Tokyo 1943 Delmer Daves

The Curse of the Cat People 1944 Robert Wise

Johnny O'Clock 1946 Robert Rossen

Good News 1947 Charles Walters

The Boy with Green Hair 1948 Joseph Losey

Marty 1955 Delbert Mann

Picnic 1955 Joshua Logan

Not as a Stranger 1955 Stanley Kramer

Fear Strikes Out 1957 Robert Mulligan

The Left-Handed Gun 1958 Arthur Penn

David and Lisa 1963 Frank Perry

The Stripper 1963 Franklin Schaffner

Who's Afraid of Virginia Woolf? 1966 Mike Nichols.

Directors Guild of America Award Winners for Theatrical Direction:

1948. A Letter to Three Wives
JOSEPH MANKIEWICZ
Gaston Glass, *Asst. Dir.*

1949. All the King's Men
ROBERT ROSSEN
Sam Nelson, *Asst. Dir.*

1950. All About Eve
JOSEPH MANKIEWICZ
Gaston Glass, *Asst. Dir.*

1951. A Place in the Sun
GEORGE STEVENS
C. C. Coleman, *Asst. Dir.*

1952. The Quiet Man
JOHN FORD
Wingate Smith, *Asst. Dir.*

1953. From Here to Eternity
FRED ZINNEMANN
Earl Bellamy, *Asst. Dir.*

1954. On the Waterfront
ELIA KAZAN
Charles Maguire, *Asst. Dir.*

1955. Marty
DELBERT MANN
Paul Helmick, *Asst. Dir.*

1956. Giant
GEORGE STEVENS
Joe Rickards, *Asst. Dir.*

1957. Bridge on the River Kwai
DAVID LEAN
Gus Agosti and Ted Sturgis,
Asst. Dir.

1958. Gigi
VINCENTE MINNELLI
William McGarry and
William Sturgis, *Asst. Dir.*

1959. Ben-Hur
WILLIAM WYLER
Gus Agosti and
Alberto Cardone, *Asst. Dir.*

1960. The Apartment
BILLY WILDER
Hal Polaire, *Asst. Dir.*

1961. West Side Story
ROBERT WISE and
JEROME ROBBINS
Robert Relyea, *Asst. Dir.*

1962. Lawrence of Arabia
DAVID LEAN
Roy Stevens, *Asst. Dir.*

1963. Tom Jones
TONY RICHARDSON
Gerry O'Hara, *Asst. Dir.*

1964. My Fair Lady
GEORGE CUKOR
David Hall, *Asst. Dir.*

1965. The Sound of Music
ROBERT WISE
Ridgeway Callow, *Asst. Dir.*

1966. A Man for All Seasons
FRED ZINNEMANN
Peter Bolton, *Asst. Dir.*

1967. **The Graduate**
MIKE NICHOLS
Don Kranze, *Asst. Dir.*

1968. **The Lion in Winter**
ANTHONY HARVEY
Kip Gowans, *Asst. Dir.*

1969. **Midnight Cowboy**
JOHN SCHLESINGER
Burtt Harris, *Asst. Dir.*

1970. **Patton**
FRANKLIN SCHAFFNER
Eli Dunn and Jose Lopez Rodero,
Asst. Dir.

1971. **The French Connection**
WILLIAM FRIEDKIN
William C. Gerrity and
Terry Donnelly, *Asst. Dir.*

1972. **The Godfather**
FRANCIS FORD COPPOLA
Fred Gallo, *Asst. Dir.*

Recipients of the D. W. Griffith Award

1953. CECIL B. DEMILLE
1954. JOHN FORD
1956. HENRY KING
1957. KING VIDOR
1959. FRANK CAPRA
1960. GEORGE STEVENS
1961. FRANK BORZAGE
1965. WILLIAM WYLER
1968. ALFRED HITCHCOCK
1970. FRED ZINNEMANN
1973. WILLIAM WELLMAN

Directors Guild of America
Award Winners
for Television Direction:

1953. **The Last Voyage**
ROBERT FLOREY
Bruce Fowler, *Asst. Dir.*

1954. **The Answer**
ROY KELLINO
Jack Sonntag, *Asst. Dir.*

1955. **The Little Guy**
DON WEIS
Jack Corrick, *Asst. Dir.*

1956. **The Road That Led Afar**
HERSCHEL DAUGHERTY
Richard Birnie, *Asst. Dir.*

1957. **The Lonely Wizard**
DON WEIS
Willard Sheldon, *Asst. Dir.*

1958. **All Our Yesterdays**
RICHARD BARE
Claude Binyon, Jr., *Asst. Dir.*

1959. **The Untouchables**
PHIL KARLSON
Vincent McEveety, *Asst. Dir.*

1960. **Macbeth**
GEORGE SCHAEFER
Adrienne Luraschi, *Assoc. Dir.*

1961. **A Study in Silence**
ERNIE KOVACS and JOSEPH BEHAR
Ken Herman, *Assoc. Dir.*

1962. **The Price of Tomatoes**
DAVID FRIEDKIN
Edward Denault, *Asst. Dir.*

1963. **Pygmalion**
GEORGE SCHAEFER
Adrienne Luraschi, *Assoc. Dir.*

1964. **Oscar Underwood Story**
LAMONT JOHNSON
Mickey McCardle, *Asst. Dir.*

1965. **My Name is Barbra**
DWIGHT HEMION
Earl Dawson, *Assoc. Dir.*

1966. **Death of a Salesman**
ALEX SEGAL
James H. Clark, *Assoc. Dir.*

1967. **Do Not Go Gentle
Into That Good Night**
GEORGE SCHAEFER
Adrienne Luraschi and
Rowland Vance, *Assoc. Dir.*

1968. **My Father and My Mother**
GEORGE SCHAEFER
Rowland Vance and
Adrienne Luraschi, *Assoc. Dir.*

1969. **Teacher, Teacher**
FIELDER COOK
Steve Barnett, *Asst. Dir.*

1970. **My Sweet Charlie**
LAMONT JOHNSON
Ralph Ferrin, *Asst. Dir.*

1971. **All in the Family**
JOHN RICH
Bob Lahendro, *Assoc. Dir.*
Harry Rogue, *Stage Manager*

1972. **That Certain Summer**
LAMONT JOHNSON
Warren Smith, *Asst. Dir.*

Notes on Contributors

Russell AuWerter is a freelance author who writes on film subjects for many publications.

Judith Crist is film critic of *New York* magazine and the *Today* show on NBC television.

Digby Diehl is Sunday Book Section editor and columnist for *The Los Angeles Times,* former editor of *Show* and freelance author.

Norman Goldstein writes on film matters for the Associated Press in New York.

William Hall is film columnist of *The London Evening News.*

Franklin Heller is a veteran television director and co-chairman of the Publications Committee of the Directors Guild of America.

Arthur Knight teaches cinema at the University of Southern California, criticizes films for *Saturday Review* and has written books on movie matters.

Leonard Maltin edits *Film Fan Monthly* and has written several books on films.

Maurice Rapf, Director of Film Studies at Dartmouth College, is a documentary filmmaker and a member of the Directors Guild of America.

Joel Reisner and **Bruce Kane** have written many articles on film topics.

Andrew Sarris, film reviewer for *The Village Voice* and author of *Confessions of a Cultist* and other books, teaches cinema at Columbia University.

Philip K. Scheuer was motion-picture editor of *The Los Angeles Times* until his retirement.

Bob Thomas, who has covered film matters for the Associated Press since 1944, is the author of biographies of Harry Cohn, Irving Thalberg, David O. Selznick, Walt Disney and others.

Photo Credits

PHOTOGRAPHS of *Citizen Kane, Alice Adams, The Curse of the Cat People, The Boy with Green Hair,* courtesy of RKO; of Stanley Kubrick, *The Learning Tree, Rachel, Rachel, Rio Bravo, The Wild Bunch, The Maltese Falcon, Destination Tokyo, The Left-Handed Gun, Who's Afraid of Virginia Woolf?,* courtesy of Warner Bros.; of *2001: A Space Odyssey, North by Northwest, Far from the Madding Crowd, Brewster McCloud, Shaft, Cimarron, Zig Zag, Cabin in the Sky, Good News,* courtesy of M-G-M; of *Psycho, Shane, True Grit, Love Story, Downhill Racer, Fear Strikes Out,* courtesy of Paramount; of Roger Corman, *The Pit and the Pendulum, The Wild Angels,* courtesy of American-International; of *Play Misty for Me, Two Mules for Sister Sara, The Beguiled, Lonely Are the Brave, The War Wagon, The Great McGinty, The Major and the Minor,* courtesy of Universal; of John Frankenheimer, *I Walk the Line, Husbands, The Comic, Major Dundee, Cisco Pike, I Never Sang for My Father, Johnny O'Clock, Picnic,* courtesy of Columbia Pictures; of *A Kind of Loving,* courtesy of Governor Films; of *Billy Liar, David and Lisa,* courtesy of Continental Distributing; of *Darling, The Producers,* courtesy of Avco Embassy; of John Schlesinger, *Midnight Cowboy, Sunday, Bloody Sunday, A Funny Thing Happened on the Way to the Forum, High Noon, Red River, Out of It, The Landlord, Marty, Not as a Stranger,* courtesy of United Artists; of *The Twelve Chairs,* courtesy of U.M.C. Productions; of *Kotch,* courtesy of Jalem Productions; of *Bracken's World, Butch Cassidy and the Sundance Kid, The Gunfighter, The Ox Bow Incident, The French Connection, Little Murders, Escape from the Planet of the Apes, The Marriage of a Young Stockbroker, The Culpepper Cattle Co., The Stripper,* courtesy of 20th Century-Fox; of *Who Is Harry Kellerman and Why Is He Saying Those Terrible Things About Me?,* courtesy of Cinema Center Films; of *The Wrath of God,* courtesy of Rainbow Productions; of *Stagecoach,* courtesy of Martin Rackin Productions; of James Bridges and *The Baby Maker,* courtesy of National General Picture Corp.; of *Lovers and Other Strangers,* courtesy of Cinema Releasing Corp.

Photograph of Sam Peckinpah by Wendell Hamick. The photographs in "The Story of *Stagecoach*" were taken directly from the film by Joan Loque of the American Film Institute. The photograph of John Ford in "John Ford on *Stagecoach*" is by Bruce Bixenz. The sketch in the "World of the Assistant Director" section is by Lee Mishkin. Al Fortune did the art for the "First Feature" section.

Photographs of *Citizen Kane* were obtained from Leonard Maltin, Richard Wilson, and the Museum of Modern Art Film Stills Archive; of *2001: A Space Odyssey* from M-G-M and the Museum of Modern Art; of Stanley Kubrick, *North by Northwest, Darling, Rio Bravo, High Noon, Red River,* and *Shane* from the Museum of Modern Art.

Index

Films, Plays, Television Shows

Index of Names and Subjects